NO Kidding About BULLYING

126 Ready-to-Use Activities to Help Kids Manage Anger, Resolve Conflicts, Build Empathy, and Get Along

Grades 3–6
Updated Edition

Naomi Drew, M.A.

free spirit
PUBLISHING®

Library of Congress Cataloging-in-Publication Data
Names: Drew, Naomi, author
Title: No kidding about bullying : 126 ready-to-use activities to help kids manage anger, resolve conflicts, build empathy, and get along / Naomi Drew.
Description: Updated edition. | Minneapolis, MN : Free Spirit Publishing, 2017. | Includes bibliographical references and index.
Identifiers: LCCN 2017010510 (print) | LCCN 2017027367 (ebook) | ISBN 9781631981814 (Web PDF) | ISBN 9781631981821 (ePub) | ISBN 9781631981807 (paperback) | ISBN 1631981803 (paperback)
Subjects: LCSH: Bullying in schools—Prevention. | School violence—Prevention. | School children—Conduct of life. | BISAC: EDUCATION / Teaching Methods & Materials / General.
Classification: LCC LB3013.3 (ebook) | LCC LB3013.3 .D74 2017 (print) | DDC 371.5/8—dc23
LC record available at https://lccn.loc.gov/2017010510

Cover design: Steven Hauge and Shannon Pourciau
Interior design: Michelle Lee Lagerroos and Shannon Pourciau
Illustrations: Marty Harris
Cover photo: Jupiterimages

10 9 8 7 6 5 4 3 2 1
Printed in the United States of America

Free Spirit Publishing Inc.
6325 Sandburg Road, Suite 100
Minneapolis, MN 55427-3674
(612) 338-2068
help4kids@freespirit.com

Dedication

This book is dedicated to educators everywhere. You create the future every single day. May this book help you foster a generation of upstanders who collectively become the solution to bullying.

Acknowledgments

No book is ever written alone. This book was created and brought to life with the help and input of so many talented, caring people. My deepest, most heartfelt thanks go to:

My wonderful publisher, Free Spirit. I'm deeply grateful for Free Spirit's flexibility and for all the work, time, and care that went into the book, including coordinating our national survey and enabling the many unheard voices of children to be included and heard. Very special thanks go to Judy Galbraith, whose vision makes Free Spirit Publishing an exceptional house of the highest integrity. Special thanks also go to the Free Spirit editorial and creative team whose work and talents contributed to this book in so many ways: Brianna DeVore, Darsi Dreyer, Douglas Fehlen, Steven Hauge, Heidi Hogg, Michelle Lee, Marjorie Lisovskis, and Charlie Mahoney. Many thanks to my wonderful editor Alison Behnke for her keen eye and skilled hand in the revised edition of this book, and to designer Shannon Pourciau for this fresh update.

The many teachers and counselors who participated in our survey. We couldn't have done it without you!

The 2,171 kids who filled out the survey and shared their real-life stories. Your words and experiences form the core of this book.

The many schools I've worked with, talking to teachers and kids, conducting interviews, and being in classrooms. Special thanks to Cathy Brettman for going the extra mile in setting up student interviews.

The wonderful teachers at Berkeley Elementary School who sent in pictures and stories of peacemaking in action.

Librarians Laura Gruninger of the Lawrence Library and Pat Brown of Lawrence Intermediate School who provided excellent resource recommendations.

All of my family and friends who gave so much moral support in the years of hard work that went into the development, research, and writing of this book. Thanks for being there! Special thanks to my daughter in-law, Emy Drew, for the idea of "10-Minute Time Crunchers."

The folks at City Market in Lambertville, New Jersey, for the many hours I spent writing and drinking coffee at your sunny window.

Contents

Additional Material in Digital Format

Eight Enrichment Activities You Can Use at Any Time

    1. Prepare a Public Service Announcement (PSA)

    2. Write and Perform a Song

    3. Create a Book

    4. Perform a Puppet Show

    5. Connect with Another Classroom Online

    6. Meet with the School Administrator

    7. Contact the Press and Public Officials

    8. Create a Podcast

Schoolwide Bullying Response Protocols

Student Reporting of Bullying Form

Informational Handouts for Parents

    Four Steps to a More Peaceful Home

    Using Active and Reflective Listening

    10 Ways to Help Kids Stop Fighting

    Mediating Kids' Conflicts with the Win/Win Guidelines

    Helping Children Deal with Bullying

    Promoting Tolerance at Home

Poem

    You Belong

List of Reproducible Pages

Foreword by Stan Davis

In your hands, you hold an important book. In recent decades, we've seen a proliferation of resources about bullying and bullying prevention. Yet now more than ever, there is an urgent need to teach students the critical understandings you will find in *No Kidding About Bullying*.

One element that sets this book apart is its focus on increasing kind and inclusive behavior. The longer I work with young people, the more I am convinced that fostering positive actions by students is a crucial element of our work to reduce bullying and to reduce the harm that cruelty can do. My research with Dr. Charisse Nixon at Penn State University, Erie, for the Youth Voice Project reveals the importance of this focus. We found that bullied young people who reported that they felt they belonged at their schools, or that they felt valued and respected at their schools, were significantly less likely to report negative outcomes from the bullying they experienced than those young people who described themselves as not belonging or not feeling valued at school.

The students we surveyed also told us that the most helpful things adults did after bullying incidents were listening and giving emotional support, while the most helpful things peers did were including and encouraging the targeted students. Inclusion by peers led to significantly better outcomes for bullied students than any other intervention by peers. (For more details about our research and what we learned, please visit youthvoiceproject.com.) Dr. Abraham Maslow wrote that belonging is a fundamental human need, and that when we experience belonging, we are better able to learn, grow, and become our true selves. When we build belonging, we also foster resiliency and empower young people to overcome negative life events. This book contains many activities and practices that will increase students' sense of belonging, and will help them strengthen that sense in each other.

Skill building and practice make up another powerful focus of this book. We all need practical, useful skills—and teaching strategies that build students' applications of these skills. I learned many years ago from Dr. Steven Danish to make a distinction between teaching knowledge and teaching skills. Knowledge, he taught me, can be gained by reading or listening. Skills, on the other hand, need to be practiced over time, and with feedback, in order to be mastered. When we focus on increasing kind, inclusive behavior and reducing hurtful actions, we do best when we teach specific skills over time.

That's what this book will help you do. Within its pages, you will find practical activities to teach skills that lead to kind actions, inclusion, self-calming, and positive conflict resolution. You will find activities to help your students develop skills in anger management and to strengthen their ability to make positive choices in difficult situations. And of the book's many activities, you can choose the ones that meet your needs and the needs of your students. These activities are built on a foundation of showing and modeling respect for students. This foundation is crucial, because, as James Baldwin wrote, "Children have never been very good at listening to their elders, but they have never failed to imitate them."

I thank Naomi Drew for her continuing work to improve children's lives, and I am confident that you will find *No Kidding About Bullying* a valuable addition to the work you do with young people every day.

Stan Davis *has worked as a child and family therapist in residential treatment, community mental health, and private practice. Stan trains educators, parents, and students in effective bullying prevention. He is a certified Olweus bullying prevention consultant and a founding member of the International Bullying Prevention Association. Stan is the author of* Schools Where Everyone Belongs: Practical Strategies for Reducing Bullying *and* Empowering Bystanders in Bullying Prevention, *and he maintains stopbullyingnow.com, an informative website for parents and educators.*

Introduction

Guiding students to navigate an increasingly complex and interconnected world is one of our most critical jobs as educators. It's more important now than ever before that we teach and model respect, acceptance, empathy, and other traits that can help kids interact peacefully and work out differences. Bullying, aggressive conflict, and other cruel behaviors can be prevented when we address them at their roots.

In this new edition of *No Kidding About Bullying,* you'll find updated research and data showing how educators can best prevent bullying, confront cruelty, and build compassion. The purpose of the book is, as it has always been, to help teachers and kids by providing concrete ways to stop cruel behavior and strengthen prosocial attitudes and skills. And while the book's primary goal is to counteract bullying, its approach to doing so is broad. When we work to encourage kindness and respect, we plant the seeds of positive and lasting change.

We have many reasons to continue focusing on this important work. Past decreases in bullying have shown us that our efforts to promote acceptance, empathy, conflict resolution, and other bullying prevention strategies are paying off, but we still have much more work to do. Consider the words of students and teachers who were surveyed and interviewed for this book:

"They called me names because of the color of my skin."
—5th-grade girl

"This kid and his friends told me to go back to where I came from." —6th-grade boy

"Even though I knew what he said wasn't true, it killed me inside." —4th-grade boy

"Anger and bullying are among the major issues I see as a teacher." —4th-grade teacher

"How do you end the name-calling? This is a BIG problem. I have tried many things, and I have not found a way that really works." —3rd-grade teacher

Many students and teachers shared similar stories, questions, and concerns in the survey and face-to-face interviews my publisher and I conducted for the original edition of this book. The survey was administered to 2,171 third through sixth graders and 59 teachers across the United States and Canada and confirmed a truth that we know continues to persist: Bullying is one of the greatest challenges kids face. Educators consistently reported being troubled by bullying, name-calling, and meanness among their students. Seventy-three percent of kids we surveyed said other kids are somewhat to very mean to each other. Forty-four percent said bullying happens often, every day, or all the time, and over forty percent said they see conflicts happening often or every day. Students also expressed, sometimes longingly and often poignantly, that they don't want to be hurt by bullying. Sixty-three percent of kids said they wanted to learn how to stay out of physical fights. Eighty percent said they wanted to learn ways to stop the bullying, avoid fighting, get along better with peers, and work out conflicts.

And while educators and others have made significant gains in their work to reduce and prevent bullying and cruelty, data shows that in 2015 and 2016, U.S. schools and communities experienced a sharp increase in the use of hate speech and in hate crimes against immigrants, people of color, LGBTQ people, non-Christians, and other marginalized groups.[1] The U.S. Department of Justice (DOJ) defines hate crime as "the violence of intolerance and bigotry, intended to hurt and intimidate someone because of their race, ethnicity, national origin, religion, sexual orientation, or disability."[2] The DOJ also states, "Hate crimes have a devastating effect beyond the harm inflicted on any one victim. They reverberate through families, communities, and the entire nation, as others fear that they too could be threatened, attacked, or forced from their homes, because of what they look like, who they are, where they worship, whom they love, or whether they have a disability."[3]

In response to the spike in hate crimes, in 2016 the Southern Poverty Law Center (SPLC) conducted an online survey of over 10,000 educators across the United States. Ninety percent reported that school climate had been negatively affected by hate speech, racist remarks, and negative actions, including many incidents specifically targeting immigrant children. Eighty percent described "heightened anxiety and concern" in their students. Respondents to the survey also reported seeing an increase in "verbal harassment, the use of slurs and derogatory language, and disturbing incidents involving swastikas, Nazi salutes, and Confederate flags." Additionally, four out of ten educators said they didn't believe their schools had action plans for dealing with incidents of hate and bias.

The SPLC urges all schools to seriously confront any actions that target or marginalize an individual or group and cautions that incidents of this nature tend to have "long-lasting impacts" and require long-term solutions.[4] Such solutions are exactly what this book provides. A new lesson in this edition addresses, head-on, the importance of combating hateful actions and words, including those that stem from prejudice and bias. Yet hate can't be stamped out by a single lesson or discussion. Disentangling its roots requires steady attention, focus, and understanding. And every minute you invest will be worth your time.

Over my decades working with teachers and students across the United States and beyond, I have witnessed firsthand the self-efficacy and pride students gain when they learn how to stop and think before acting, and when they learn to handle disagreements respectfully by using deep breathing, self-calming, respectful listening, and conflict resolution skills. I have also seen the remarkable changes that occur when kids experience the power of compassion—both in giving and receiving it. Navigating the world in a decent, humane way requires understanding that respect is a fundamental human right. It requires remembering that inside every person is a heart that beats and a mind that feels pain when cruel words are spoken. It requires that we accept people and groups we perceive as different from ourselves, and that we choose to do the right thing even when no one is looking. These are the concepts and behaviors kids need to absorb in order to eliminate hatred and bullying and, ultimately, to lead healthy, rewarding lives. And when we teach these skills and concepts as part of every student's daily routine, classrooms and schools transform. Instilling these attitudes and practices in your students is just as important as teaching academic skills, and by doing so, you can establish a peaceful classroom environment while giving kids the tools they need to have positive, respectful relationships throughout their lives.

Research on Bullying and Its Impact on Children's Lives

Bullying: deliberate, aggressive behavior intended to harm another person. It frequently involves an imbalance of power, is often repetitive, and can be done face to face or through electronic media.

According to the 2015 "Indicators of School Crime and Safety" report from the U.S. Bureau of Justice Statistics, 15.7 percent of public schools reported that bullying took place among students once a week or more.[5] Additionally, the report stated that roughly one-third of students who said they were bullied at school reported being bullied "at least once or twice a month during the school year." Among students who said they were cyberbullied, about

27 percent reported that the cyberbullying took place at least once or twice a month. Other research shows that, when it comes to cyberbullying, kids who are bullied at school are also bullied online, and kids who bully at school also bully online.[6] Additionally, the Massachusetts Aggression Reduction Center surveyed over 11,000 kids in third through fifth grade and found that cyberbullying and in-person bullying both increased steadily between third and fifth grade.[7]

More data comes from the 2014 "Bullying in U.S. Schools" status report, which summarized surveys of students in grades three through twelve and found:[8]

- An average of 14 percent of students reported being bullied, and 5 percent reported bullying others.
- Bullying behavior was most common among third-grade students, with about one-quarter of kids reporting that they bullied, were bullied, or both.
- When students who are being bullied reach out to others about it, they are least likely to tell their teachers or other adults at school.
- Among boys in grades three through five, 25 percent didn't tell anyone about being bullied. (Among boys in sixth through eighth grade, this number increases to 34 percent.) While girls are more likely to speak up than boys are, they are also less likely to confide in others about bullying as they get older.
- Regardless of grade level, girls are more likely to try to help a fellow student who is being bullied than boys are.

Gay and transgender students are particularly at risk for being bullied. According to the "2015 National School Climate Survey" of students by GLSEN (the Gay, Lesbian & Straight Education Network), more than 50 percent of LGBTQ students said they heard homophobic language "often or frequently in their schools." Additionally, "nearly three quarters of students reported being verbally harassed at school because of their sexual orientation; more than half were verbally harassed because of their gender expression." Physical bullying is also problematic, as more than 25 percent of LGBTQ students said they'd been "physically harassed at school because of their sexual orientation; one in five were physically harassed because of their gender expression."[9] Although this survey was conducted with students in grades six through twelve, younger students you're teaching may well have had similar experiences. GLSEN also commissioned a study of students in grades three through six in more than 1,000 elementary schools across the United States, which revealed the following:[10]

- "Students who do not conform to traditional gender norms are twice as likely as other students to say that other kids at school have spread mean rumors or lies about them . . . and three times as likely to report that another kid at school has used the internet to call them names, make fun of them, or post mean things about them."

- "Students who do not conform to traditional gender norms are less likely than other students to feel very safe at school . . . and are more likely than others to agree that they sometimes do not want to go to school because they feel unsafe or afraid there."
- Only 24 percent of teachers surveyed said that their schools' anti-bullying policies made specific mention of sexual orientation and gender identity or expression. However, other studies (conducted in secondary schools) have shown that comprehensive anti-bullying policies that specify protections based on these and other personal characteristics are associated with "a lower incidence of name-calling, bullying, and harassment."

Among all students, bullying and cruelty can create an undercurrent of fear and mistrust. They can also affect learning, development, and even a child's future mental health. Whether bullying takes place in person or online, and whether it is verbal, relational, or physical, it takes a steep toll on kids and can contribute to problems ranging from depression to disengagement in school and, in rare cases, suicidal ideation. According to the Centers for Disease Control and Prevention (CDC), "victimized youth are at increased risk for depression, anxiety, sleep difficulties, and poor school adjustment." Similarly, another study found that students victimized by their peers were 2.4 times more likely to report suicidal ideation than youth who reported not being bullied and 3.3 times more likely to report a suicide attempt.[11] And the risks are true not only for those who are targeted, but for those who target others as well. Kids who bully others are at an elevated risk for "substance abuse, academic problems, and violence later in adolescence and adulthood."[12]

The negative impact of bullying goes beyond students who are bullied or who bully others, affecting those who see it take place as well. The CDC reports that kids who have observed bullying "report significantly more feelings of helplessness and less sense of connectedness and support from responsible adults" than those who haven't been witnesses. Similarly, according to the American Psychological Association, research suggests that "students who watch as their peers endure the verbal or physical abuses of another student could become as psychologically distressed, if not more so, by the events than the victims themselves."[13]

The children who suffer most are those who both bully and are bullied. They are at greater risk for mental and behavioral problems than students who only bully, or who are only bullied.[14] The CDC notes, "Youth who report both being bullied and bullying others . . . have the highest rates of negative mental health outcomes, including depression, anxiety, and thinking about suicide."[15]

And despite the severity of bullying's impact, a survey conducted by the National Center for Educational Statistics found that 20 to 30 percent of kids who were bullied didn't tell an adult what was going on.[16] This has to change, since telling an adult is one of the most effective tools kids have against bullying. Through the understandings in this book, we hope kids will feel safer approaching teachers and more able to help each other. Too many kids are struggling, often in silence. We all have the capacity—and the responsibility—to help.

The Need to Foster Respect for Diversity

Day by day the world is becoming visibly more diverse. People from different cultures interact in schools, communities, workplaces, and online more than ever before. Schools strive to meet the needs of diverse students, including dual-language learners, students with learning differences and disorders, students with disabilities or behavioral challenges, students who identify as gender variant, and students whose families have recently immigrated.

"It is not our differences that divide us. It is our inability to recognize, accept, and celebrate those differences."
—Audre Lorde

An essential component of confronting bullying and building compassion is to weave the threads of kindness, respect, and acceptance into every interaction that takes place in our schools and classrooms, and to consistently and gently remind students—and ourselves—that our differences are our strengths. Our world's vast diversity has helped shape musicians, artists, writers, doctors, scientists, teachers, builders, problem-solvers, and the many others who improve and sustain communities and societies. By embracing each other in all our variety, we support and nurture every one of us.

Yet the challenges are many. Racism, sexism, classism, homophobia, ableism, and other forms of bias and bigotry impact students on a daily basis. People who are not part of a society's dominant group (or groups) may be subject to unfair treatment, restrictions on their rights, physical attacks, bias-motivated crimes, and more. And a study published in the *American Journal of Public Health* about the negative impact of bullying on kids concludes that "bias-based harassment is more strongly associated with compromised health than harassment."[17]

Helping kids develop respect and appreciation for diversity decreases their likelihood of harming others due to perceived differences. Therefore, teaching students to respect and value differences—and modeling these attitudes for them—is a critical part of bullying prevention.

What Works in Preventing and Addressing Bullying?

A first step in preventing, reducing, and responding to bullying is to instill in students the understanding that everyone's actions matter. A National Institutes of Health (NIH) study shows a direct link between kids' mindsets and their willingness and ability to support peers who are mistreated. If students believe they can make a difference, and if they feel capable of doing so, they are more likely to take action when someone is being picked on.[18]

This is why it's so important to teach kids specific steps they can take to support peers who are mistreated—to serve as upstanders rather than looking on as bystanders. In addition, it's essential to provide frequent opportunities for kids to role-play what they're learning. This practice helps them take action. Making time for practice and reinforcement will help students feel more prepared, confident, and capable, and they will be more likely to apply these strategies where it matters most—in real life.

The NIH study also gave the following key actions that educators can use to foster upstander behavior:[19]

- *Clearly communicate* that kids are expected to include and support anyone who's mistreated.
- *Show kids how* to include, support, and encourage others so they feel confident doing so.
- *Encourage the understanding* that bullying is wrong and that helping others is the right thing to do.

Kids also have a lot to say about what works to prevent bullying based on their personal experiences. The Youth Voice Project survey looked at data from more than 13,000 students. While it focused on students in fifth through twelfth grades, its valuable findings on bullying and victimization can be applied to students of all ages. This study's conclusions challenge some long-held ideas and shed light on the strategies that work best. Here's some of what the survey revealed.[20]

The single most helpful strategy for kids who are targets of bullying:
Seek support from an adult at school or from a friend. (Despite how helpful this strategy is, only 33 percent of the kids surveyed told an adult.)

Another highly effective strategy for kids who are targeted:
Don't think like a victim. Kids who told themselves that the bullying wasn't their fault, and that nothing was wrong with them, proved to be more resilient in the face of bullying.

The least helpful strategies for kids being targeted:
- Telling or asking the person bullying them to stop.
- Telling the person how they felt.

The most helpful things bystanders can do to support kids who are being bullied:
- Walk with them and spend time with them at school.
- Help them get away.
- Help them tell an adult.
- Distract the person or people bullying them.
- Give them advice and hope.
- Encourage them.
- Talk to them at school and show them that others care.
- Call them at home to give support.
- Hear their concerns without judgment.

The most important *adult* strategies to help kids who are bullied:
Kids surveyed by the Youth Voice Project also said that the three most helpful things any adult can do are:
- Listen to them.
- Encourage them.
- Check back later and over time to see if they're okay.

The least helpful things adults might do:
- Say, "You should have . . ."
- Tell a student that the bullying wouldn't have happened if he or she had acted differently.
- Tell a student to stop tattling. (This was the most harmful adult action.)

Other recommendations for adults:
- Reduce or eliminate the following messages in bullying prevention: "Stand up for yourself" and "Just pretend it doesn't bother you."
- Teach kids ways to support and include those who are being picked on or excluded, rather than to confront the person doing the bullying.
- Build a school climate that encourages inclusion and belonging for all.
- Give kids skills that foster connectedness and resilience. When kids feel connected to each other and to their school as a whole, bullying is less likely to occur, and kids are more likely to respond proactively when it does happen.

The lessons in this book will help you integrate all of these recommendations and tools. Communication, problem solving, and emotional management are just a few of the many prosocial skills you will find explored throughout the book.

Additional Data on What Impacts Kids Positively

Anyone who teaches knows how "contagious" emotions and behaviors are. If you've ever spent a year with a conflict-ridden class where bullying is prevalent, you probably know the feeling of throwing your hands up in frustration as bickering and meanness infected the atmosphere in your room.

But there's good news, too: Positive emotions and behaviors also are contagious. Dr. Nicholas A. Christakis, a researcher at Harvard Medical School, explains, "Emotions have a collective existence—they are not just an individual phenomenon." He goes on to say that how you feel depends "not just on your choices and actions, but also on the choices and actions of people . . . who are one, two, and three degrees removed from you."[21]

People one, two, and three degrees removed . . . as in a class. And when positive emotions and behaviors are sparked in a class, they spread. Christakis and his research partner, James Fowler, hypothesize that "behaviors spread partly through the subconscious social signals that we pick up from those around us, which serve as cues to what is considered normal behavior." Another likely cause of social contagions is mirror neurons in our brains, which cause us to mimic what we see in others.[22]

We've all seen that mimicking effect as a mood or message spreads through a classroom or social group, often through seemingly small gestures such as facial expressions, looks exchanged between students, eye rolls, and other body language. When we create a school climate where positive interactions are the standard, and negative interactions the exception, kids benefit in a variety of ways. According to a report published in the *Harvard Educational Review,* there is "powerful evidence that school climate affects students' self-esteem." Kids both learn better and feel better about themselves in an atmosphere of safety and respect. The report stresses that positive school climate supports the acquisition of "essential academic and social skills, understanding, and dispositions."[23]

Similarly, Search Institute in Minneapolis conducted a comprehensive review of studies on the impact of a caring educational environment on kids.[24] This review found that safe, supportive schools foster in students the following critical outcomes:

- higher grades
- higher engagement, attendance, expectations, and aspirations
- a sense of scholastic competence
- fewer school suspensions
- on-time progression through grades
- less anxiety, depression, and loneliness
- higher self-esteem and self-concept

These findings affirm the importance of making concerted efforts to build empathy, kindness, social skills, upstander behaviors, and conscience in students. Consider the following, as well:

- A 2013 review of school climate research concluded that "school climate has a profound impact on students' mental and physical health." This review also reported that "feeling safe in school powerfully promotes student learning and healthy development," and that schools with positive climates have less aggression and violence, as well as "reduced bullying behavior."[25]

- A meta-analysis of school programs involving 270,034 students found that kids who were engaged in social-emotional learning "demonstrated significantly improved social and emotional skills, attitudes, behavior, and academic performance."[26]

"How we behave matters because within human society everything is contagious—sadness and anger, yes, but also patience and generosity. Which means we all have more influence than we realize."
—Elizabeth Gilbert

By assiduously fostering empathy, conscience, and kindness along with teaching kids how to work out conflicts, deal with anger, and be upstanders for those who are bullied, I believe we can start reversing the trend of youth cruelty. At the same time, we can create a more peaceful atmosphere in our schools, ultimately setting the foundation for a healthier future for all of our children. Think of it as creating a contagion of kindness, compassion, and respect that spreads through your entire class and lasts all year—a contagion that dramatically reduces bullying and conflict.

About This Book

At the core of this book are 126 easy-to-use lessons that have been carefully designed to help you create an atmosphere free of bullying, where kids can learn and thrive. These twenty-minute activities require very little preparation and include key strategies to foster empathy and appreciation of differences, prevent bias-based bullying behaviors, and reinforce a culture of care and respect. The intent is to make it realistic and realizable for you to integrate bullying prevention, conflict resolution, and social-emotional skill building into your already busy school day.

How the Book Is Organized

"Conducting the Lessons and Working with Students" (pages 7–15) provides background information to help you use the book and instill its concepts and skills effectively. It includes information on how to help kids mediate conflicts, top ways of preventing bullying and conflict, and techniques for implementing the book's lessons into the daily routine.

Following that, the book is divided into two main parts:

Part One: Instilling "Get-Along" Skills and Attitudes. These fifteen Core Lessons are the cornerstone of *No Kidding About Bullying.* They introduce the concepts and skills that are the basis for all the other lessons in the book. See page 8 for more information about the Core Lessons.

Part Two: Getting Along and Building Respect. Here you will find 107 lessons arranged in seven topic areas:

- Fostering Kindness, Compassion, and Empathy
- Managing Anger
- Preventing Conflict
- Responding to Conflict
- Addressing Name-Calling and Teasing
- Dealing with Bullying
- Accepting Differences

The structure for each lesson begins with a list of the key character traits and skills the lesson reinforces, a quick activity summary, and "Students will," which highlights specific things students will learn. Each lesson also includes:

Materials. The materials you will need to conduct the lesson, including reproducible handouts, are listed here. Other materials are easily obtained, such as chart paper or drawing materials.

Preparation. This is included as needed.

The Lesson. Each lesson begins with an introduction followed by discussion, the main activity, and a wrap-up. The activities vary and may include role plays, large- or small-group tasks, writing, drawing and other creative arts, and learning new information.

Follow-Up. Most lessons include a follow-up activity or suggestion to reinforce and help you monitor how students are doing incorporating the skills and concepts.

Extensions. Many lessons include optional extensions. These are often activities that require more time and have students do creative projects, practice skills, or share what they are learning with others.

Reproducible Forms. Most activities include handouts. These are noted in the materials list and can be found at the end of each lesson; they are also included in the digital content for this book. Unless otherwise noted, you will need to print or copy a handout for each student prior to the lesson.

At the back of the book are several additional resources:

Review Lessons. Use these short lessons anytime to revisit and reinforce concepts from the other lessons.

Pre- and Post-Test. This brief assessment, also in the digital content, lets you measure students' attitudes and use of skills before and after taking part in *No Kidding About Bullying* lessons.

Survey About Conflicts. A blank form is provided so you can conduct your own survey with students in your class or school; the survey also is included in the digital content.

References and Resources. This is a selection of recommended books, websites, and other resources you may find helpful.

Index. With the index, you can look up a particular topic (such as calming strategies, gossiping, or physical bullying) or character trait (such as respect, collaboration, or self-control) and find lessons with that focus.

Digital Content. The digital content includes all of the reproducible forms from the book, additional resources for leading the lessons, and forms for sharing information with parents. The parent forms provide background about the concepts children are learning and suggestions for ways parents can support this at home. See page 291 for instructions on how to access the digital content.

Using the Book in Your Setting

Yours may be one of the many classrooms using the Olweus Bullying Prevention Program, Second Step, Responsive Classroom, or another social and emotional learning model. The activities in *No Kidding About Bullying* can easily be integrated with programs like these. If you're not using any particular curriculum to build social skills, this book will be an important tool for introducing them.

Depending on your needs, you may use as many or as few lessons as you like. Use them as a full curriculum from start to finish or as a shorter unit. In the latter case, conduct the Core Lessons first and follow up by focusing on a particular section (such as Managing Anger) or by conducting several activities from each section. You can also turn to specific lessons when you have an incident of bullying, unkindness, or conflict you want to address promptly.

Using the lessons first thing in the morning is ideal. If you're already doing morning meetings, you can weave these lessons in after the greeting. If another time of the day works better for you, that's fine, too. The whole idea is to make the lessons work for you and your setting. Three times a week will give you maximum results. Even doing one lesson a week will make a big difference. The more you do, the better.

Although designed with a classroom in mind, this book can easily be used in other settings, including youth groups, faith-based programs, before- or after-school settings, counseling groups, scouting, camps, or any other environment where children are served. You will find the book useful if you are a classroom teacher, resource teacher, school counselor, youth group director, community program leader, camp counselor, religious educator, or parent.

Each lesson can be conducted in twenty minutes. You can spend more time if you wish, and reinforce concepts as time permits by using the follow-ups and extensions. Several lessons in each section address similar topics in different ways, helping you reinforce important skills and practices. There are also review lessons, including "10-Minute Time Crunchers."

Conducting the Lessons and Working with Students

Before you begin, acquaint yourself with the following seven tools to enhance the experience you and your students have with the *No Kidding About Bullying* lessons:

Circle. The lessons in this book will be most effective if done in a circle. This helps with listening, focus, and empathy. One of the most basic ways people connect is by looking at each other's faces when speaking. So many children spend hours each day behind a cell phone, computer screen, or video game; they're often more connected to a screen than to each other. As a result, some kids may have become oblivious to each other's feelings and may find face-to-face interactions awkward. By seating your students in a circle, you can get them used to looking at the person who is speaking. Coach them to look around the circle when it's their turn to speak, and to wait to begin speaking until everyone is looking back at them.

Cueing kids to look at each other and tune in to what's being said can drastically improve communication skills and develop a greater sense of connectedness. The good listening and respectful attitudes fostered in the circle can also spill over into the rest of the day and make it easier to teach.

Globe. For many lessons, I strongly recommend having a globe handy. If you can, pick up the soft kind that's a cross between a ball and a pillow. You can order these through AAA, Amazon, or many other places online. Here are three ways to use your globe as you conduct the lessons:

1. Let it serve as a visual reminder that we are part of the larger world. Hold up the globe periodically to remind kids that our actions make a difference and everything we do affects the people around us. They can make the world a better place starting right in their own classroom. Peace begins with each person.

2. Use it as a "talking object" to pass in the circle when you do the activities in this book. The person holding the globe is the only one to speak. When he or she is finished, the globe is passed to the next person.

3. If you have a soft globe, you can use it as a ball to throw during review activities (for more on review activities, see the digital content), allowing you to review concepts easily and quickly.

Working in pairs. Many lessons in this book have children working in pairs and, in some cases, small groups. These interactions enable kids to immediately put into practice many cooperative behaviors they are learning: listening, compassion, kindness, openness to another's ideas. Studies have shown that using pairs and cooperative learning in teaching situations improves students' ability to learn new concepts.[27]

My favorite way to get students into pairs is to prime them by saying, "In a moment we're going to partner up. Your most important job is to make sure no one is left out. Look around and make sure everyone is included." I always follow this up with immediate acknowledgment of kids who make sure no one is left out, especially if they forgo sitting with a friend to be a partner to someone who doesn't have one. If I see students start rushing to be with friends instead of looking around to see if someone needs a partner, I stop the whole process and give a gentle reminder.

Assuming you have your kids in a circle, another way to get them to partner up is to randomly ask one child to raise his or her hand. After that, every second child raises a hand, alternating so half the students have hands raised. Kids with raised hands turn to the person on their right; this person becomes their partner. If there's an odd number, have one group triple up, or have the extra child be your partner.

Once students are in pairs, whether in chairs or seated on the floor, have them sit "knee to knee"—directly facing one another with their knees facing but not touching. This enables good eye contact and less distraction.

Charts. Many activities include creating a chart for or with students. Among these, there are seven that I recommend laminating and keeping up all year long as a visual reminder of the most important bullying prevention concepts in this book:

- **Our Agreements for a Get-Along Classroom:** Keep this chart somewhere in the front of the room for easy reference, high enough for everyone to see, but not so high you can't reach the agreements with a pointer. (This chart is introduced in Lesson 1.)
- **Respectful Listening:** This chart can be used all day long for every subject you teach. Display it where kids can't miss seeing it. (Introduced in Lesson 2.)
- **Peace Pledge:** You'll probably be using this every morning, so keep it in easy access for kids to view. You might want to have a different child lead the class in the pledge each day, so post it in a spot a student can stand next to. (Introduced in Lesson 6.)
- **Win/Win Guidelines for Working Out Conflicts and Rules for Using the Win/Win Guidelines:** Place these near your Peace Table or Peace Place (see page 9). Post them so they're readily accessible when two students sit down together to work out a conflict. (Introduced in Lesson 8.)
- **Stop, Breathe, Chill:** This is another good chart for your Peace Table area, but if space is limited, any place in the room will do. (Introduced in Lesson 9.)

- **No More Hurtful Words:** This is a pledge for students to live by and for you to refer to whenever they need a reminder to be kind. (Introduced in Lesson 22.)
- **Ways to Chill:** This chart can go in any spot where it's easily seen, even up high at the top of a wall. It will serve as a constant reminder of all the things students can do to calm down when angry. (Introduced in Lesson 40.)

Other charts recommended in lessons throughout the book can be left up as long as you need them, whether that's a day or two after you've completed the lesson or longer as a reinforcement. If possible, save any charts you take down. They can serve as helpful reminders of concepts you might want or need to review as the year goes on.

Student journals. Journals are used throughout the lessons in a variety of ways: for responding to a topic, airing personal experiences, brainstorming ideas, and more.

Provide students with notebooks to use as their journals. Have students decorate and personalize the cover. Keep a journal yourself and do the same exercises your students do. This will broaden your own understanding of the concepts in this book and expand your ability to empathize with what kids are going through. If you choose to share any of your journal entries with your students, it may help them open up even more.

Automatic writing. Some of the lessons employ automatic writing, a technique that can spark spontaneous thought and release ideas. In automatic writing, students should let their words flow out freely and land on the paper like coins spilling out of a bag. Neatness, grammar, and spelling don't count. After stating the given prompt, direct students to "write, write, write" for about three minutes straight without lifting pencil from paper until you say "Stop."

Automatic writing is about the unfolding of what's inside. Let students know that sometimes they may be surprised at what comes out. Whether they keep what they write confidential or share it with you and others is always up to them.

Students who have difficulty writing can draw their response, speak their words into a recorder, or dictate their words to you, a classroom aide, or another student if this is comfortable for them.

Role plays. Role playing is a key learning strategy in *No Kidding About Bullying*. Role playing allows students to practice the bullying prevention and conflict resolution skills they are learning, making it easier to apply them in real-life situations.

Often the role plays provided are based on the Survey About Conflicts and interviews we conducted with students. Your students' own experiences will also make good sources for role plays, so invite these wherever you feel it is appropriate.

Ask for volunteers to play the parts. If not enough students volunteer, take a part yourself. Do not have students act out aggressive behaviors or demonstrate the use of aggressive words, as acting out negative behaviors can reinforce them. Instead, describe what happened, then have students act out the resolution. The purpose of the role plays is to give students practice implementing the strategies they're learning.

If the actual situation being role-played resulted in a physical fight, allow only pantomimed movements.

Teach students these ground rules for role plays:

- Students who participate should never reveal personal information they're not comfortable sharing.
- No physical contact or swearing is allowed.
- Actors should not use real names.

If student actors get off track or start to act silly, stop the role play and remind them of its purpose and the ground rules.

Key Practices and Skills: The Core Lessons

The Core Lessons that make up Part 1 introduce the most critical skills and attitudes for creating a bully-free environment. Some of the strategies in Part 1 will be reintroduced in Part 2, but are included early on so you can start the year with them. The Core Lessons were designed to help you do the following:

- create agreements for a peaceful, "get-along" classroom
- foster empathy, kindness, and acceptance
- teach respectful listening
- build trust and collaboration
- introduce the Win/Win Guidelines for Working Out Conflicts
- introduce the anger-management strategy Stop, Breathe, Chill
- foster responsibility for one's actions

These initial lessons also include some important practices that will help you maintain an atmosphere of respect and kindness throughout the year: breathing for calmness, the process of visualization, a Peace Pledge to be recited each day, a ritual for setting aside upset feelings when entering the classroom, and the class Peace Table or Peace Place.

Deep Breathing

I recommend starting the activities in this book by leading students in a few rounds of deep breathing. Most kids like this practice. Taking a few deep breaths together is a ritual they learn to look forward to. Doing so helps them focus and sets a tone of calmness. Research shows that six deep abdominal breaths can lower the blood pressure.[28]

It's important that you get the feel of deep abdominal breathing before you teach it. See Lesson 4 (pages 28–29) for a thorough introduction to deep breathing. Practice so you're comfortable with the process.

Once you've taught it to your kids, you can use deep breathing throughout the day as a transition between lessons or as a way of lowering anxiety, tension, or nervous energy in your room. You can add visualization (see next section) to the breathing, especially as a way of calming before tests.

The Process of Visualization

A number of the lessons incorporate visualization. This is a highly effective tool to help kids mentally rehearse situations where they need to calm themselves, manage anger, talk out a conflict, resist bullying, or use other strategies taught in this book. According to psychology professor and researcher Dr. Barbara Fredrickson, "Visualization has been shown to activate the same brain areas as actually carrying out those same visualized actions. That's why visualization has been such a powerful tool for winning athletes. Mental practice can perhaps be just as effective as physical practice."[29]

Students are introduced to visualization in Lesson 9. Lesson 37, pages 94–96, provides a more structured introduction along with a visualization script.

Leave It at the Door

We've all seen it happen. A child comes to school filled with anger, fear, or stress, then spends the day acting out. Leave It at the Door (Lesson 7) gives you a method you can use all year long to alleviate this. Many kids are under enormous stress. We don't always know which children in our classroom may be sitting with heavy burdens weighing on their hearts. The "Leave It at the Door" box is a place where kids can write down and discharge intense or difficult feelings the minute they walk into your classroom.

The purpose of this exercise is not to minimize or stuff down feelings, but to help students transition to the school day so they can get along with classmates and learn. If students choose to let you read what they wrote (which is always optional), you then have an added window into their lives. If a child reveals something that requires follow-up or additional intervention, you can get the student the needed help. Should a student reveal serious family issues, any kind of abuse, feelings of depression, or thoughts of harming oneself, talk to your school counselor, nurse, or principal.

Having a tool for processing and communicating what's going on can be the lifeline that pulls a child out of hidden hurt or sadness. By letting out what's troubling them, kids often are more able to learn, and more apt to get along with peers rather than bully them.

Note: Make sure the box is sealed and has only a narrow slit at the top so no one but you can take out

what anyone else has written. Stress to students that everything they place in the "Leave It at the Door" box will be seen only by the teacher—no one else. Also, give your students the option of writing "Do not read" on their papers if they want to unload with absolute confidentiality. Emphasize that no one but the teacher is ever allowed to remove anything from the box. Place the box on a shelf in your clear view. If you have concerns that anyone in the class might try to take out something another child has written, keep the box on your desk instead of by the door.

Peace Table

A Peace Table gives students a place in the room where they can retrieve their grounding when angry or upset. It's also a place to talk out conflicts. Set up a Peace Table in a corner of your room. On and near it have objects kids can use to calm themselves and restore composure: a Koosh ball, headsets with soothing music, books, stuffed animals, writing paper, markers, pencils, clay, and more. Near the Peace Table, hang posters and drawings that nurture calmness. Post the Win/Win Guidelines for Working Out Conflicts and Rules for Using the Win/Win Guidelines (see page 36). Some teachers make flip cards with the Win/Win Guidelines for kids to hold when they're working out a conflict. Get students in the habit of going to the Peace Table to calm down and to talk things out when conflicts arise.

If space is an issue, create a Peace Place. Some teachers use a bean bag chair for this purpose. Put it in a corner and hang the Win/Win Guidelines and Rules nearby. Put together a Peace Box containing calming objects and place it next to the bean bag chair. A movable study carrel or screen is also a good idea if kids want privacy. "Quiet headphones" can block out noise for kids who tend to get overstimulated.

Physically moving away from the source can help kids "move" mentally and emotionally when they're angry or upset. Unhooking from the energy of anger, sadness, or frustration by squeezing a soft ball, listening to music, or writing in a journal helps kids learn that they have the ability to release and transform negative feelings in a healthy way. Giving kids the place and tools to do this helps make self-soothing and problem-solving intrinsic, rather than extrinsic. When we put the locus of control inside the child, we give the student a powerful tool to use throughout life.

Using the Win/Win Guidelines for Working Out Conflicts

Kids who know how to work out conflicts are less likely to bully. That's one of the many reasons why teaching conflict resolution is so important. The ultimate goal is that kids will be able to use the Win/Win Guidelines independently when they have a conflict. However, it takes time to develop that comfort level. Many lessons in the Preventing Conflict and the Responding to Conflict sections of this book (pages 119–188) are devoted to role-playing conflicts real kids reported in the Survey About Conflicts and in interviews with students in schools. The more role plays they do, the more natural it will feel for your students to use the Win/Win Guidelines to resolve their own conflicts, rather than fighting, name-calling, or tattling.

You can help mediate students' conflicts using the Win/Win Guidelines. One caveat: be sure to teach the guidelines before using them as a mediation tool. The guidelines, described on this page, are introduced individually in Lessons 8–14, and reviewed as a process in Lesson 15. See pages 36 and 47.

Note: The Win/Win Guidelines should not be used in bullying situations. Putting a bullied child face-to-face with the child who bullied him or her can be overwhelming and can cause a sense of intimidation and fear. See pages 11–12 and the Dealing with Bullying lessons (pages 217–260) for ways to address bullying.

Mediating Kids' Conflicts with the Win/Win Guidelines

It is best to mediate with no more than two students at a time. If a conflict involves more than two people, try to determine the two who are at the heart of the conflict. Then help them begin to resolve it, following the six guidelines:

1. **Cool off.** Separately, have each child take time out, get a drink of water, or do something physical to let off steam. Make sure both kids have cooled off completely before going to the next step. When it comes to conflicts, the number one mistake adults make is trying to get kids to talk out the problem while they're still mad. When tempers are calmer and tears are dried, sit down with the kids and go on to the second guideline.

2. **Talk it over starting from "I," not "you."** Tell students they're both going to have a chance to say what's bothering them, but they're going to need to listen respectfully to each other without interrupting. Then ask each child to state what's on his or her mind, starting from "I," not "you." Example: "I'm mad 'cause you grabbed my pencil without asking" is a lot less inflammatory than "You're so mean. Give it back!"

3. **Listen and say back what you heard.** Guide kids to do this for each other: "Justin, can you repeat back the main idea of what Mario just said?" Let them know that "saying back" doesn't indicate agreement, but shows respect, builds understanding, and makes it easier to work out the problem.

4. **Take responsibility for your role in the conflict.** In the majority of conflicts, both people have some

degree of responsibility. Ask each student, "How were you even a little bit responsible for what happened?" Stay neutral here. This part needs to come from them. If a student is unwilling to take any responsibility at all, try gently coaxing by saying, "Is there something really small that you might have done, too?" If this step starts to stymie the whole process, move on to the next step.

5. **Come up with a solution that's fair to each of you.** Ask, "How can the two of you work out this conflict?" Or, "What can you do so this doesn't happen again?" Then wait. Don't give kids solutions. It's important that they come up with their own. If the conflict is a recurring or ongoing one, have them write down the solution and sign it.

6. **Affirm, forgive, thank, or apologize.** Ask, "Is there anything you'd like to say to each other?" Or, "Would you like to shake hands?" If an apology is in order, ask, "Do you feel in your heart that you can give an apology?" If not, ask students to consider offering an apology at another time. Forcing apologies makes for inauthentic gestures and doesn't truly support the overarching goal of getting along better.

At the beginning of conflict resolution and throughout the process as needed, remind students of the Rules for Using the Win/Win Guidelines:

1. Treat each other with respect. No blaming or put-downs.
2. Attack the problem, not the person.
3. No negative body language or facial expressions.
4. Be willing to compromise.
5. Be honest.

Incorporating and Reviewing "Get-Along" Classroom Agreements

In Lesson 1, Introducing the Concept of a "Get-Along" Classroom, you and your students will create a chart called "Our Agreements for a Get-Along Classroom." These agreements are a contract that everyone signs and promises to follow. They form a scaffold for the entire year and are a working document that you and your class should revisit every few weeks. Here are five ways you can review the agreements and keep them alive:

"How are we doing?" check-in. Direct students' attention to items you think they need to work on. For example, you might ask them, "How do you think you're doing on listening when someone speaks?" Encourage students to be honest. When there are areas of challenges, lead a brief discussion on ways to deal with them. Then hold students accountable. Check back in a few days to see if suggested improvements have been followed through on.

"Pat on the back" check-in. Ask students where they have shown improvement individually or as a group. Acknowledge them for improvements made and for positive steps along the way. Have kids acknowledge each other, too.

Goal setting. Have students choose items on the "get-along" classroom agreements they want to improve on. Have them write the items in their journals. Talk about steps they can take to reach their goal. Goals can be for individuals or for the entire class. Encourage kids to be "support partners" for each other. For example, if Joey's attention drifts a lot and his goal is to be a better listener, Amalia may agree to be his support partner, sitting next to him during lessons and giving him an agreed-upon silent signal when he loses focus. Support partners can also encourage and affirm when progress is made.

New student review. When a new child joins your class, have your students lead a complete review of your "get-along" classroom agreements, answering questions from the new student and talking about how the class is living the words of the agreements.

Share with family adults. As suggested in Lesson 1, copy the agreements from your wall chart and send them home with a cover letter. At your back-to-school open house, introduce your "Agreements for a Get-Along Classroom" and let parents know how you're using them.

Four Critical Ways for Teachers to Prevent Bullying

1. Model, teach, and reinforce kindness, compassion, and empathy.
By taking the time to teach kindness and compassion, you lay the foundation for a classroom free of bullying. Three sections of this book will help you do this:
• The Core Lessons (pages 19–47)
• Fostering Kindness, Compassion, and Empathy (pages 51–81)
• Accepting Differences (pages 261–278)

What you model is key. As Albert Schweitzer once said, "Example is not the main thing in influencing others, it is the only thing." When he wrote these words, he had little idea that inside the human brain are millions of mirror neurons that cause us to mirror each other's behaviors, emotions, and facial expressions. Neuroscientists have discovered that this is why we tend to smile back when someone smiles at us, or frown when we see someone frowning. Mirror neurons are the reason kids' attitudes and behaviors are so contagious.[30]

Mirror neurons are also among the reasons that teachers and other adults have even more influence than we realize. Mirror neurons are functioning all day long. Plus, kids watch us for clues about how to behave, even when

we think they're not. There have been times I've heard kids say things like, "I know my teacher doesn't like Mr. So-and-So. I see the look on her face every time he walks by." This attests to the need to be mindful of our body language and facial expressions as well as our words.

For some kids, we may be the most influential role models they have, so we need to hold ourselves to a high standard. When we tell kids to treat others with respect and they see us doing this ourselves, we make a powerful impact for the good. Their mirror neurons are sparked to follow our lead.

2. Make kids part of the solution, and hold them accountable.
When kids have a role in coming up with their own rules and agreements, they are far more motivated to abide by them. That's why it's important to start by having your students define the kind of atmosphere they want to have in the classroom, then come up with agreements for creating it (Lesson 1).

It's also critical to hold students accountable. Kids can be good at parroting back the right answer when it comes to respect, kindness, and acceptance. They often "talk the talk," but don't "walk the walk." Getting kids to "walk the walk" requires frequent check-ins on how they're applying what they're learning. For example, after you teach an anger management or assertiveness strategy, tell students you're going to want to hear how they apply it in real life. Mark a date in your plan book, and make sure you take five to ten minutes to check in with kids when that date arrives. Reinforce skills and concepts by conducting additional role plays for a given lesson or for other lessons that have the same focus.

Be sure to tell family adults about the *No Kidding About Bullying* program you are introducing in your classroom. Share information early in the year, and let parents know you'll be contacting them from time to time to see how their kids are applying what they've learned. Then keep in touch via email, text, your class website, or by sending information home with students.

3. Teach kids concrete strategies they can use when they're angry and in conflict.
Giving kids acceptable ways to deal with conflict and anger can significantly cut back on bullying. A study by bullying researchers Justin Patchin and Sameer Hinduja found that kids who are angry and frustrated are much more likely to bully others and that in order to reduce bullying, we need to give kids positive, healthy ways of dealing with conflict and anger.[31] Other research has shown that teaching kids how to regulate their emotions, control anger, and improve moral reasoning can decrease aggressive behaviors like bullying for the long-term.[32]

Stop, Breathe, Chill (explained in Lesson 9) is one of the top strategies this book provides for managing anger. Many lessons that follow it show how to use this strategy when conflicts arise. Using Stop, Breathe, Chill yourself and sharing some personal examples with students can make the practice come alive for kids. The more they hear about your real-life applications, the likelier they are to follow in your footsteps. Sharing how you handled challenges in angry situations can give your students the confidence to keep trying rather than give up when they meet challenges of their own. The journey to managing anger and conflict is never easy. It requires us to be mindful of our old patterns and willing to change them. The role modeling you provide in this regard will be invaluable to your kids.

In terms of helping kids resolve conflicts, the key strategy is the Win/Win Guidelines, introduced in the Core Lessons. Following this, the Responding to Conflict section has twelve detailed lessons designed to help kids apply the Win/Win Guidelines in their lives. There are lots of actual conflicts described by students from our survey for your students to role-play, discuss, and brainstorm solutions to.

4. Never look the other way when bullying takes place. Kids need to know that bullying and other acts of cruelty will not be tolerated. Sometimes adults downplay or dismiss the damage bullying can do, saying that bullying has always existed or that it's just part of life. But that doesn't make it acceptable. And over time, bullying has changed, becoming harder to detect and control since the advent of cyberbullying. Ignoring or minimizing bullying of any kind only allows it to grow. As educators, we must hold kids accountable for cruel behavior. Not doing so reinforces these actions by sending a silent signal that cruelty and bullying are okay.

Most schools have some system of consequences for misbehavior as well as bullying response protocols. In the digital content for this book, you will find information regarding using these protocols. Also see the References and Resources on pages 285–287 for sources of schoolwide bullying prevention programs.

The Dealing with Bullying section (pages 217–260) contains nineteen lessons that give specific ways to help kids recognize different forms of bullying. It also teaches kids what to do if they or others are bullied and shows how to be an upstander, as opposed to a bystander, when bullying takes place. If bullying is going on in your classroom, don't rely solely on this section; the lessons on kindness, compassion, and acceptance are equally important, if not more so.

In fact, research reveals that kids who are bullied have certain social challenges in common. *The Journal of Clinical Child and Adolescent Psychology* reports that these students often have difficulty in at least one of the following three areas: reading nonverbal cues, understanding the meaning of social cues, and coming up with options for resolving conflicts.[33] Lessons throughout *No Kidding About Bullying* are designed to help kids

improve in all of these areas through role play, empathy building, and activities that require them to observe and respond to the reactions of others. Students with poor social skills can improve in these areas when provided with positive role models, effective strategies, and opportunities to practice social interactions.

Acknowledging and Affirming Students

John Milton once wrote, "Good, the more communicated, more abundant grows." One of the most powerful tools we have for making good things grow in our students is catching kids in the act of doing things right and affirming them for their positive acts. When you see students being kind, respectful, caring, or accepting, acknowledge it. Kindness is the antithesis of bullying. The more kind acts we can catch kids in the act of performing, the more we eliminate the roots of bullying.

Be like a detective on the lookout for kind words and actions. When you see kids cooling off when angry, talking out conflicts, or expressing compassion, acknowledge them. For students who feel embarrassed by compliments, make it private. Whisper your acknowledgment or jot it on a note. And make it specific: "Ahmed, I noticed how you helped Joe pick up his books when he dropped them. You didn't laugh, even though other kids did. That was a very kind thing to do. How did that feel for you?" By asking this question, you further reinforce the positive act.

Start and end lessons on a tone of affirmation by sincerely acknowledging individuals or the class as a whole for positives you've observed. Be sure to spread your acknowledgments out, so each child gets a chance to hear something positive at some point. It can be harder to find things to compliment with some kids than with others, so take note of progress made, moves in the right direction, sincere attempts to improve—the small, subtle things that often go unnoticed.

One of my favorite examples of positive change sparked by acknowledgment was with an intense fifth grader I'll call Miko. Miko was in a group I ran for at-risk kids who bullied and got into fights. He started the year angry, reactive, and quick with his fists. Although Miko constantly mumbled put-downs and gave nasty looks to other kids in the group, he had a lot of positive qualities. One day I took him aside and told him how much I enjoyed having him in the group—which I sincerely did—and shared all the positive things I saw in him: his intelligence, his strength, his vast potential. I asked him if he could try to let go of his reactions when kids in the group said or did things that got on his nerves. I told him he had the power to react less, and I said, "I have faith in you." His face completely changed when he heard those words. He admitted to me that he didn't know how to control his temper, so I showed him how to use Stop, Breathe, Chill.

Initially it was hard for Miko to contain his reactions when someone got on his nerves, but he started trying. When something was said that would ordinarily push his buttons, I would notice him consciously looking away (as opposed to giving a look) and breathing deeply. Each time he did this I'd acknowledge him privately. "You're gaining more control over your reactions," I would tell him, or, "You're really making an effort, and it's working." Often, he'd nod in agreement and give me a little smile. Over time, with consistent support and acknowledgment, Miko turned around. At the end of the year, he wrote these words:

> *"I love our program because it helped me so much with handling my problems. It really helped me calm myself down when someone or something bothered me. It taught me respect. I'm sure it would help others like me, too."*

Continuously catching Miko in the act of doing things right—even small steps and sincere attempts—helped Miko see his better self. He eventually learned that he had the ability to control himself, and when he did, he felt good. For kids who get in trouble all the time, this can be life-changing.

"It's not our job to toughen our children up to face a cruel and heartless world. It's our job to raise children who will make the world a little less cruel and heartless." —L.R. Knost

Also teach kids to acknowledge each other. Moment to moment, words and actions add up to the atmosphere that's created in our classrooms. If we're consistently affirming positive words and actions, our students often follow suit, noticing the positives in each other and affirming them.

You can prompt student-to-student affirmations fairly easily. "Is there something anyone would like to acknowledge someone for?" is a good question to ask when you complete activities in this book. Things you can prime your kids to notice are:

- kindness or respect in any form
- helpfulness
- patience
- listening attentively
- calming down when angry
- being an upstander

There are so many things worth acknowledging if our minds are primed to notice the positive. In the classroom, when we get in the habit of paying each other sincere compliments, something magical can take root. I've seen it happen over and over.

Anticipating Challenges

Confidentiality

Make sure students understand that they should not bring other people's personal information into group discussions or role plays. Remind students not to use real names when describing bullying or conflict situations. Coach them to say, "Someone I know," "This kid," "A person in our school," "Someone in my home," or "A relative of mine." This applies for writing assignments as well. Journals, too, need to be confidential. The only time a journal entry should be shared is when the writer chooses to share an entry with the teacher or the class during a lesson where optional sharing is designated.

What to Do If a "Red-Flag" Issue Comes Up

The lessons in this book may bring up some red-flag issues for kids. Bullying in and of itself can be one. Kids who are bullied can suffer from depression and even harbor suicidal thoughts. They may also have thoughts of harming someone else. If this or any other issue of major concern arises, talk to your school counselor, nurse, or principal. Discuss how to reach out supportively to the child's family adults and how to get further assistance for the child if need be. Sometimes just being there for the student yourself may be enough. I've known teachers who eat lunch with certain kids at least once a week, or invite them to help in the classroom and chat after school. Whatever avenue you take, consider the red flag a gift—this student is revealing that support is needed. Providing it can make all the difference in the world.

Finally, follow your school's policy for mandatory reporting of physical or sexual abuse.

Dealing with Disruptive Behavior

It's happened to all of us, and for some of us, it can happen every day: a student explodes, becomes defiant, or gets physical. What can we do? There's no magic formula, but there are some things that can help.

Calm yourself first. Immediately take deep abdominal breaths and silently say a calming statement (examples: "I can handle this," "Cool and steady," "I'll stay calm"). Then lower your voice instead of raising it. These steps will help lower your own stress and provide a model of calmness for the child who's acting out as well as for the rest of the class.

Convey the attitude, "I am on your side." When students think we don't support them, we lose the chance to connect and help correct their negative behavior. Kids, especially those who regularly get in trouble, need to believe we still care about them and believe in them even when they've lost control. Consequences can be given, but in the spirit of care and concern.

Let the student save face. Never back a disruptive child into a corner. If we threaten a child who's acting out, we can almost guarantee that he or she will choose a defensive or aggressive way out. ("You want me to go to the office. Try and make me!") Instead, phrase your response in a nonconfrontational way that doesn't further escalate the problem. Here's an example. Tina has just thrown an eraser at a student who made fun of her. You whisper to her: "Tina, I see you're upset right now. Why don't you take a break and get a drink of water?" If a consequence is in order, give it later, once Tina's volatility has subsided.

Make the child part of the solution. Ask, "What can *we* do to solve this problem?" Then come up with a plan together. Here's an example: Jessie always acts out during math lessons. After talking to him you discover that he doesn't get the math concepts you've been working on and his acting out is a mask for his feelings of frustration and inadequacy. Ask him what would help; then make some compromises and adaptations. Maybe Jessie can work with a partner, or maybe he can complete the few problems he understands and leave the rest till you can help him. Coming up with solutions together will return control to him, removing the sense of powerlessness that precipitated his acting out.

Use preventive maintenance. For some kids, calling out their name in front of the class is enough to set them off. Anticipate the anger triggers of kids who easily become disruptive, and do your best to avoid them. For example, if you know that embarrassment leads to outbursts, direct corrective comments to the child privately, or use a previously agreed upon signal. Here, too, involve the child in the solution. If Charlie is always interrupting lessons with inappropriate comments, speak to him privately, create a plan together, let him know you have faith in his ability to follow it, and affirm him when he does so.

Defuse potentially explosive situations. Here are a few phrases you might use with a student who's on the verge of a meltdown:

- "What do you need to do to take care of yourself right now?"
- "I can see you're very upset. Is there someone you'd like to talk to?"

- "I'm depending on you to have a level head."
- "Did that action help you or hurt you?"
- "How about taking a break."

Put physical safety first. If a child gets physical and can't be readily calmed down, follow your school's policy for dealing with student violence and keeping all students safe.

"Gay" Name-Calling

It's not uncommon for elementary-age kids to put each other down using homophobic terms. Many students who filled out our survey wrote about the heartache of having a homophobic label attached to them. This example came from an eleven-year-old boy:

> *"It started at lunch when everybody decided I was gay. So that's what they started calling me, and I'm not. They also called me freak because I don't buy lunch, and a nerd because I get straight A's. It's not solved. About a month ago this kid calls me a nerd and other names. So I go tell my mom. The next day his best friend hits me in the face because I told on his friend. Then I got mad and I wanted to hit him back, but I didn't. Now it's the end of the school year. It's like every day without crying is an accomplishment. Even some of my friends have turned on me. It just makes me want to die."* *

As this story painfully illustrates, students can be devastated by pejorative comments of this nature. Kids may use the term gay to label a child as homosexual. They may also use it as a kind of generic insult: "That's so gay!" But kids on the receiving end almost always take it as an embarrassing put-down. To respond to or prevent such incidents in your classroom, you can take the following actions:

- *Never* look the other way when homophobic comments are made. Kids need to know that speaking like this is never okay. Lesson 110 will help you address this issue.
- Ask your school to provide professional development training to help staff gain greater comfort in addressing LGBTQ issues and answering related questions from students.
- Help your students understand the common humanity all people share, including those who seem different from them. Use books and literature in your classroom that include diverse characters and families.
- Model and expect acceptance of, respect for, and kindness toward all people.
- Be willing to entertain questions regarding LGBTQ issues and people.

---

* While the students' surveys were anonymous, the teachers' were not. When a student's story indicated a critical need for help, every effort was made to alert the child's teacher.

Integrating This Book's Understandings Throughout the Day

The lessons in this book will live in their application. For systemic change to happen, it's critical to integrate the concepts and strategies presented in the lessons throughout the entire day. Here's how:

- Keep referring back to charts, signs, and quotes from each lesson, particularly your "Agreements for a Get-Along Classroom." Use them as living documents, tying them in to real-life situations in the classroom. For example, if one of your get-along agreements is "Treat others with respect," and something disrespectful happens, gesture toward the line in the chart about respect. Ask, "Was that respectful or not?" Remind students that every word and action counts. Before long, many kids will get in the habit of referring back to the charts themselves, keeping each other on track.

- Once again, affirm your kids for positive acts you witness. Continuously encourage students to affirm each other, too.

- Ask students to be aware of acts of respect, kindness, integrity, acceptance, and conscience performed by people they are learning about at school, whether these people are fictional characters or figures from history or current events. Highlight acts of goodness, and ask students to comment on them.

- When students go to lunch, recess, classes in other rooms, or other activities, remind them to keep abiding by their get-along classroom agreements. When they return, take a few minutes to hear how the activity went. Acknowledge positives, remediate negatives.

- At dismissal, remind your students to continue living what they're learning with their families, friends, and anyone else whose paths they cross. Follow up by checking in with them often about this.

- Invite guest speakers who reflect the values you are teaching. Teens who have overcome bullying or have been upstanders for others make good guests. So do

people who've learned how to manage their anger and deal with conflict. Kids enjoy and respond to real-life anecdotes and experiences.

- Refer to current events and ask students to speculate on how the values of respect, kindness, and compassion—or their opposites—might have made an impact on specific events of the day.

- Have students be on the lookout for examples of respect, kindness, compassion, acceptance, or conscience in the news, in movies, and on TV. Ask them to share examples they've come across. Have them go to MyHero.com for examples of everyday people doing extraordinary things.

- Look at conflicts in the news and have students talk about how those conflicts could be worked out using the strategies and concepts you are teaching.

Just about every lesson in *No Kidding About Bullying* zeros in on skills that not only help prevent bullying and conflict, but also help kids succeed in school. According to a survey of 8,000 teachers and parents by Dr. Stephen Elliott of Vanderbilt University, the following are among the top skills that help kids succeed in school:[34]

- listening to others
- taking turns when talking
- getting along with others
- staying calm with others
- being responsible for one's own behavior

In the pages ahead, you will find a wealth of activities that foster all of these skills. As you use them, be sure to share what's working for you in your classroom with your colleagues. Ask what's working for them. Find out what parents are doing at home to encourage their kids to show respect and kindness, manage anger, and resolve conflicts.

I also invite you to share your successes, challenges, and ideas with me. Please contact me in care of my publisher: help4kids@freespirit.com. I would love to hear from you.

In peace,
Naomi Drew

Notes

1. Azadeh Ansari, "FBI: Hate Crimes Spike, Most Sharply Against Muslims," CNN.com (November 15, 2016), cnn.com/2016/11/14/us/fbi-hate-crime-report-muslims.

2. National Crime Prevention Council, "Hate Crime," www.ncpc.org/topics/hate-crime.

3. The United States Department of Justice, "Hate Crimes," justice.gov/crt/hate-crimes-0.

4. Maureen B. Costello, "The Trump Effect: The Impact of the 2016 Election on Our Nation's Schools," Southern Poverty Law Center (November 28, 2016), splcenter.org/20161128/trump-effect-impact-2016-presidential-election-our-nations-schools.

5. Anlan Zhang, Lauren Musu-Gillette, and Barbara A. Oudekerk, "Indicators of School Crime and Safety: 2015," Bureau of Justice Statistics (May 2016), bjs.gov/content/pub/pdf/iscs15.pdf.

6. Cyberbullying Research Center, "Cyberbullying Facts" (2015), cyberbullying.org/facts.

7. Elizabeth Englander, "Cyberbullying Among 11,700 Elementary School Students, 2010–2012," Massachusetts Aggression Reduction Center (2012), vc.bridgew.edu/cgi/viewcontent.cgi?article=1005&context=marc_reports.

8. Harlan Luxenberg, Susan P. Limber, and Dan Olweus, "Bullying in U.S. Schools: 2014 Status Report," Hazelden Publishing (2015), violencepreventionworks.org/public/document/bullying_2015_statusreport.pdf.

9. Joseph G. Kosciw et al., "The 2015 National School Climate Survey: The Experiences of Lesbian, Gay, Bisexual, Transgender, and Queer Youth in Our Nation's Schools," GLSEN (2016), glsen.org/article/2015-national-school-climate-survey.

10. GLSEN and Harris Interactive, "Playgrounds and Prejudice: Elementary School Climate in the United States," GLSEN (2012), glsen.org/sites/default/files/Playgrounds%20&%20Prejudice.pdf.

11. Dorothy L. Espelage and Melissa K. Holt, "Suicidal Ideation and School Bullying Experiences After Controlling for Depression and Delinquency," Journal of Adolescent Health 53, no. 1, supplement (2013): 27–31.

12. Centers for Disease Control and Prevention, "Understanding Bullying Fact Sheet 2016" (2016), cdc.gov/violenceprevention/pdf/bullying_factsheet.pdf.

13. American Psychological Association, "Observing Bullying at School: The Mental Health Implications of Witness Status," School Psychology Quarterly 24, no. 4 (December 2009): 211–223.

14. Centers for Disease Control and Prevention, "Understanding Bullying Fact Sheet 2016" (2016), cdc.gov/violenceprevention/pdf/bullying_factsheet.pdf; Paul R. Smokowski and Kelly Holland Kopasz, "Bullying in School: An Overview of Types, Effects, Family Characteristics, and Intervention Strategies," Children and Schools 27, no. 2 (2005): 101–109.

15. National Center for Injury Prevention and Control, Division of Violence Prevention, The Relationship Between Bullying and Suicide: What We Know and What It Means for Schools (Chamblee, GA: Centers for Disease Control and Prevention, 2014), cdc.gov/violenceprevention/pdf/bullying-suicide-translation-final-a.pdf.

16. Deborah Lessne and Melissa Cidade, "Student Reports of Bullying and Cyber-Bullying: Results from the 2013 School Crime Supplement to the National Crime Victimization Survey," National Center for Education Statistics (April 2015).

17. Stephen T. Russell et al., "Adolescent Health and Harassment Based on Discriminatory Bias," American Journal of Public Health 102, no. 3 (2012): 493–495.

18. Robert Thornberg et al., "Bystander Motivation in Bullying Incidents: To Intervene or Not to Intervene?" West Journal of Emergency Medicine 13, no. 3 (August 2012): 247–252, ncbi.nlm.nih.gov/pmc/articles/PMC3415829.

19. Ibid.

20. Stan Davis and Charisse L. Nixon, Youth Voice Project: Student Insights into Bullying and Peer Mistreatment (Champaign, IL: Research Press, 2013). Reprinted with permission.

21. Pam Belluck, "Strangers May Cheer You Up, Study Says," The New York Times (December 4, 2008).

22. Clive Thompson, "Is Happiness Catching?" The New York Times Magazine (September 13, 2009): 28.

23. Jonathan Cohen, "Social, Emotional, Ethical, and Academic Education: Creating a Climate for Learning, Participation in Democracy, and Well-Being," Harvard Educational Review 76, no. 2 (2006): 201–237.

24. University Outreach and Engagement at Michigan State University. "Best Practice Briefs," no. 31 (December 2004): 5.

25. Amrit Thapa et al., "A Review of School Climate Research," Review of Educational Research 83, no. 3 (September 2013): 357–385.

26. Joseph Durlak et al., "The Impact of Enhancing Students' Social and Emotional Learning: A Meta-Analysis of School-Based Universal Interventions," Child Development 82, no. 1 (January/February 2011): 405–432, casel.org/wp-content/uploads/2016/06/meta-analysis-child-development-1.pdf.

27. Robert E. Slavin, Cooperative Learning: Theory, Research, and Practice (Boston: Allyn and Bacon, 1995), cited in Richard E. Nisbett, Intelligence and How to Get It: Why Schools and Cultures Count (New York: Norton, 2009): 72.

28. Hisao Mori et al., "How Does Deep Breathing Affect Office Blood Pressure and Pulse Rate?" Hypertension Research: Official Journal of the Japanese Society of Hypertension 28, no. 6 (June 2005): 499–504.

29. Barbara Fredrickson, Positivity: Groundbreaking Research Reveals How to Embrace the Hidden Strength of Positive Emotions, Overcome Negativity, and Thrive (New York: Crown Publishers, 2009).

30. Clive Thompson, "Is Happiness Catching?" The New York Times Magazine (September 13, 2009): 28.

31. Justin W. Patchin and Sameer Hinduja, "Traditional and Nontraditional Bullying Among Youth: A Test of General Strain Theory," Youth and Society 43, no. 2 (2011): 727–751.

32. Susan M. Swearer et al., "Reducing Bullying: Application of Social Cognitive Theory," Theory Into Practice 53, no. 4 (2014): 271–277, tandfonline.com/doi/abs/10.1080/00405841.2014.947221.

33. Robin Nixon, "Studies Reveal Why Kids Get Bullied and Rejected," Live Science (February 2, 2010), livescience.com/6032-studies-reveal-kids-bullied-rejected.html.

34. Frank M. Gresham and Stephen N. Elliot, The Social Skills Improvement System (Bloomington, MN: Pearson Assessments, 2008). Reported by Live Science in "10 Things Schools Don't Teach Well," livescience.com/4646-10-schools-teach.html.

Part One

Instilling "Get Along" Skills and Attitudes

Congratulations on beginning! The activities you are about to start are the gateway to a classroom free of bullying. These fifteen lessons introduce the most fundamental concepts and strategies for creating an atmosphere of respect, compassion, and kindness. Once you have conducted them, your students will have the beginning information and skills they need to take part in any of the other activities in the book.

Specifically, the Core Lessons will help you:

- Work with students to create agreements for a peaceful, "get-along" classroom

- Foster students' empathy, kindness, and acceptance

- Teach respectful listening and the use of I-messages

- Build trust and collaboration in your classroom

- Introduce the Win/Win Guidelines for Working Out Conflicts

- Introduce the anger-management strategy Stop, Breathe, Chill

- Foster students' sense of personal responsibility for their actions

The Core Lessons

The Core Lessons that comprise Part 1 introduce the most critical skills and attitudes for creating an environment without teasing, meanness, or bullying. Some of the strategies in Part 1 will be reintroduced and expanded upon in Part 2 lessons, but they are included early on so students will have the basic understandings and tools they need to begin getting along better as a class and to get the most out of future lessons.

It is best, but not absolutely necessary, to do all of the Core Lessons in order. However, to be effective, lessons 8–15 should be conducted in sequence. They are key introductory lessons on conflict resolution, an essential skill for all students.

1. Introducing the Concept of a "Get-Along" Classroom
2. Respectful Listening
3. Great Listeners in Our Lives
4. Deep Breathing
5. Integrity
6. Peace Pledge
7. Leave It at the Door
8. Peace Table
9. Stop, Breathe, Chill
10. Introducing I-Messages
11. Practicing I-Messages
12. Reflective Listening
13. Taking Responsibility in Conflicts
14. Brainstorming Solutions to Conflicts
15. Win-Win Guidelines for Working Out Conflicts

Lesson 1: Introducing the Concept of a "Get-Along" Classroom

respect • collaboration

Lesson 1 lays the groundwork for a "get-along" classroom that will last all year long.

Students will
- identify qualities of a "get-along" classroom
- recognize their responsibility for helping create a safe and supportive learning climate
- create and sign an "Our Agreements for a Get-Along Classroom" chart

Materials
- globe (see page 7)
- chart paper and markers
- handouts: "Our Agreements for a Get-Along Classroom" (page 21, one copy); parent letter (page 22)
- *optional:* art materials for a classroom display

Introduction. Welcome your students and express how pleased you are about being their teacher. Let them know that this is an important meeting, one that will help them start to create a peaceful year where they get along with each other and treat each other with kindness and respect.

Discussion. Ask students their number one hope for the coming year, months, or weeks. Briefly discuss.

Hold up the globe and tell students that just as we are connected to each other as members of the same classroom, community, neighborhood, and country, we're also connected as members of the human family. By learning to get along and respect each other in the classroom, we're preparing ourselves to get along with all kinds of people in all kinds of settings.

Ask: **What kind of world would you like to grow up in?** Students will likely say things like safe, peaceful, fun, and healthy. Write the words on the board.

Activity. Now ask: **How about here in our own classroom? How would you like it to be in here?**

On chart paper, write the title *"Qualities of a Get-Along Classroom."* List what students say. As each child shares, pass the globe.

Next, ask: **What are things each of us can do to create a get-along classroom?** Have students pass the globe as they speak. On chart paper, write the title *"Our Agreements for a Get-Along Classroom."* List the agreements they suggest, stating them in the affirmative where possible; for example, instead of "No hitting" write "Keep your hands to yourself."

As you list the agreements, ask students to give specific examples for each. For example, if someone suggests, "Treat each other with respect," ask what that means in terms of actions (avoid using putdowns even when you're angry, refrain from rolling eyes or laughing when someone makes a mistake or says something you disagree with, etc.).

Keep the list short (seven or eight agreements) and be sure to leave enough room at the bottom for everyone's signature, including your own. When the chart is complete, ask several students to lead in reading it.

Explain what a contract is and let students know that this agreement is a special kind of contract. Ask students to sign their names to the bottom of the chart. You might say: **By signing a contract we give our word of honor. This means we promise to do everything in our power to live up to the agreements we are signing our name to.**

Wrap-Up. Affirm students for working together to come up with agreements they can use all year long. Hold up the globe and remind students that getting along with others and creating peaceful relationships starts with each of us. Say: **If we want our world to become a more peaceful place, it has to begin right here.**

Follow-Up. Laminate the "Our Agreements for a Get-Along Classroom" chart and hang it prominently in front of the room where you can refer to it every day. This is a living document to be continuously integrated into the daily life of your classroom.

Copy the agreements from the chart onto the "Our Agreements for a Get-Along Classroom" handout and make photocopies to send home with a parent letter. Use the letter on page 22 or write your own.

Extension. Have students create and decorate a classroom bulletin board display that includes the "Our Agreements for a Get-Along Classroom" chart. Use the display to incorporate other key classroom charts you make in future lessons.

Our Agreements for a Get-Along Classroom

1. _____

_____

2. _____

_____

3. _____

_____

4. _____

_____

5. _____

_____

6. _____

_____

7. _____

_____

8. _____

_____

Date: _____

Dear Parent/Guardian,

Our class is committed to creating a classroom filled with peace, respect, kindness, and compassion: a "get-along" classroom. Attached are agreements we came up with together to help us do this all year long. Please ask your child to tell you about these agreements and why they're so important.

Many parents are looking for ways to reinforce respect, kindness, compassion, and peace at home, so periodically I'll be sending you information to help with this. You are an important part of the peaceful community we're working to create this year, and I welcome your involvement.

Thank you for your support. If you have questions or suggestions, please feel free to contact me at any time.

Sincerely,

_____

Contact me at: _____

_____

_____

_____

_____

_____

Lesson 2: Respectful Listening

respect • personal responsibility

Lesson 2 helps students understand the value of listening respectfully to others.

Students will

- recognize the differences between disrespectful and respectful listening
- learn guidelines for respectful listening
- practice listening respectfully

Materials

- chart paper and marker
- handout: "Respectful Listening" (page 24)

Preparation. On a piece of chart paper, copy the "Respectful Listening" guidelines from the handout.

Introduction. Invite a student to come to the center of the circle to role-play a scenario with you. (In your role, you will be demonstrating disrespectful listening, so be sure to choose a student who won't become upset by this.) Ask: **What's your favorite thing about school?** As soon as the student responds, act distracted, fidget, avoid eye contact, interrupt, and then take over the conversation and make it about yourself. After the role play, ask the student you role-played with how she or he felt about the way you were listening.

Now, ask the class to verbally list all the things you did as a not-so-respectful listener.

Next, start the role play over again with the same question. This time play the part of a respectful, attentive listener. Ask the same question as before, and when the student answers, show interest by leaning in, nodding, making eye contact, and staying focused. Paraphrase something she or he says and follow up with a relevant question. At the end, ask the student you role-played with how she or he felt this time.

Discussion. Ask the class to identify everything they observed you doing as a respectful listener. List these things on the board. Now show the chart you've prepared. Ask: **Is there anything we should add to this chart?**

Activity. Have students practice respectful listening in pairs, one partner as the Speaker and one as the Listener. Tell partners to sit directly across from one another looking at each other's faces. The Listener should ask the Speaker to describe his or her favorite things about school. The Listener then listens respectfully in the way that was modeled. Remind students to listen to each other as though no one else is in the room, giving their full attention to what's being said. After a few minutes, have students reverse roles.

Wrap-Up. Ask students to share what this experience was like for them. As each person shares, remind the student to look around the circle to see if everyone's listening before beginning to speak. Acknowledge respectful listening as it takes place. Pass out the "Respectful Listening" handout as a reminder of good listening habits.

Follow-Up. Laminate the "Respectful Listening" chart and hang it in a prominent place in the room. Refer back to it throughout the rest of the day, and use it daily.

Extension. Designate a day as "Respectful Listening Day." At the end of the day, do a brief check-in with the class to talk about how respectful listening affected their day.

Respectful Listening

Look at the person who is speaking.

Keep your body still, and focus your mind on what's being said.

Wait your turn to speak.

Listen with an open mind.

Take a deep breath if you have the urge to interrupt. Then focus your mind back on the speaker.

Lesson 3: Great Listeners in Our Lives

respect • personal responsibility

Lesson 3 helps students examine the impact great listeners have on others and honestly assess their own listening skills.

Students will
- share and discuss what makes a great listener
- recognize the role effective listening plays in helping people get along
- take inventory of their own listening strengths and weaknesses

Materials
- "Respectful Listening" chart from Lesson 2
- handouts: "A Great Listener in My Life" (page 26); "Check Your Listening" (page 27)
- student journals

Preparation. Prior to this lesson, pass out copies of the "A Great Listener in My Life" handout and have students complete it.

Introduction. Tell students that listening is the most fundamental way we show respect for others. Ask students how they feel when someone truly listens to them and cares about what they have to say. Share your own experience briefly.

Discussion. Ask students to take out their completed "A Great Listener in My Life" handouts. Have students pair up and share what they've written. Refer to the "Respectful Listening" chart, and remind students to use good listening as their partners share what they observed about great listeners in their lives.

Next, ask students to reconvene in the large circle and describe what the great listeners they observed do. Ask: **How does their respectful listening make other people feel?**

Activity. Pass out copies of the "Check Your Listening" handout and have students take a few minutes to assess their own listening habits. Encourage them to answer honestly. Then ask: **Which things on the list are you already good at? Which things do you need to work on?** Afterward, ask students to choose one or two listening goals to work on throughout the week. Have them write down their listening goals in their journals.

Ask: **How can being a good listener help people get along better?** Hold up or point to a globe and ask how our world would be different if people all over truly listened to what others had to say.

Wrap-Up. Close by reminding students that we each have the power to improve our listening, and when we do, our lives and relationships with others often get better.

Follow-Up. Be sure to revisit this activity at a later time so students can assess how they're doing with their listening goals.

A Great Listener in My Life

A person who is a great listener is: _____.

Here are some things I notice _____ doing when he or she listens to me or someone else:

_____

_____

_____

_____

This is how I feel when I'm talking with this person:

_____

_____

_____

_____

Here's what I plan to do to become a better listener:

_____

_____

_____

_____

Check Your Listening

**Take this self-test about your listening skills.
For each statement:**

Check the box if it is **true most of the time**.

If a statement is **usually not true** for you, leave the box blank.

❑   **1.**   I make eye contact with the person who is speaking.

❑   **2.**   I wait until the other person is finished before I start talking.

❑   **3.**   I focus on what the other person is saying instead of just thinking about what I'm going to say.

❑   **4.**   I let the other person speak without taking over the conversation and making it about me.

❑   **5.**   I care about what the other person has to say.

❑   **6.**   I try to understand what the other person is feeling.

❑   **7.**   When I have a conflict with someone, I try to listen to his or her side of the story.

❑   **8.**   I work on being a good listener in all my conversations.

How did you do?

If you checked at least 4 of the statements, you already have some good listening skills.

If not, you are not alone. Many people have not yet learned how to listen. The good news is that everyone can learn to be a better listener. It just takes practice. Be part of the solution by really listening to what other people have to say!

Lesson 4: Deep Breathing

personal responsibility • compassion

Lesson 4 shows students how to become calm and focused through deep abdominal breathing.

Note: This is a basic and essential strategy for fostering calmness. Use it with your students at the start of each day and as often as needed throughout. It also works well as a transition between activities.

Students will
- understand that feeling peaceful and calm inside helps them be more peaceful with others
- learn and practice deep breathing as a way to feel calm and peaceful

Materials
- handout: "Deep Breathing Instructions" (page 29)

Introduction and Discussion. Ask: **What does it mean to be a peaceful person? If you want to be peaceful with others, where does it have to start?** Discuss briefly, emphasizing that being peaceful with others starts by being peaceful inside ourselves.

Ask students if they ever find it hard to feel peaceful inside. Discuss. Then ask: **What do you do to calm yourself when you feel upset, angry, scared, or stressed?**

Activity. Tell students you're going to teach them an important strategy that's easy to do, yet powerful in its impact. Say: **This is a strategy professional athletes and performers use to feel calm, focused, confident, and peaceful before a performance or game. It's called deep abdominal breathing.**

1. Have students sit up tall without tensing, hands on lower abdominal muscles just below the navel.

2. Have them imagine a balloon in the lower abdomen that fills with air as they inhale. (Make sure no one has anything in their mouths before beginning. Food, gum, or another object could cause them to choke.)

   Together, take a slow, deep breath all the way down into the imaginary balloon. Together, hold the breath in gently for a few seconds. (This should be a gentle, quiet breath, not the kind kids take when they're about to swim under water.)

3. Now have students slowly, quietly, and gently breathe out, "deflating" the imaginary balloon as they exhale.

   Repeat three times, extending the length of each exhalation. (If kids giggle, tell them that this sometimes happens at first. Encourage them to do the breathing in a "mature" way, as an athlete or

a performer would. Remind them that learning to do abdominal breathing will help whenever they feel tense about anything, including tests.)

4. After three deep breaths, have students remove their hands from the lower abdominal area and take two more slow, deep breaths with their hands resting in their laps.

5. Now have them take a few regular cleansing breaths, rolling shoulders and neck to release any areas of tension.

Wrap-Up. Ask students how they feel. Discuss. For those who might have felt dizzy, tell them not to inhale quite as deeply next time. Kids with asthma may be especially prone to dizziness.

Affirm students for any positive behavior you observed during this lesson. Pass out the "Deep Breathing Instructions" handout and ask students to practice deep breathing when they go to bed tonight and when they wake up in the morning.

Follow-Up. When students next arrive at school, start the day with deep breathing. Consider starting every day with this exercise and using it during transition times, too—it's a very effective way to help kids refocus.

Extension. In his book *Peace Is Every Step*, Nobel nominee Thich Naht Hanh suggests using the following words with deep breathing: "I breathe in and I calm my body. I breathe out and I smile." Share these words with your students. They're comforting to say before beginning deep breathing. The smile that comes afterward helps set a tone of warmth and connection.

Deep Breathing Instructions

1. Sit up tall with your hands resting on the lower abdominal muscles, just below the navel.

2. Imagine a balloon in your lower abdomen that will fill with air as you breathe in. Take in a slow, deep breath, breathing all the way down into the imaginary balloon. Hold the breath gently for a few seconds.

3. Slowly, quietly, and gently breathe out, "deflating" the imaginary balloon as you exhale.

    Repeat this process of deep breathing three times. Each time, exhale a little more slowly.

4. After three deep breaths, remove your hands from your lower abdomen and place them in your lap. Take two more deep breaths.

5. Finish with a few regular "cleansing" breaths. Roll your neck and shoulders to help release tension.

Lesson 5: Integrity

personal responsibility • integrity • decency

Lesson 5 helps students understand the meaning of integrity and reinforces the importance of doing what's right, even when no one is looking.

Students will

- identify specific actions that indicate a lack of integrity
- list actions that constitute integrity
- reflect on the importance of being a person of integrity

Materials

- chart paper and marker
- student journals

Preparation. On chart paper, write the following: *"Integrity—Doing the right thing even when no one is looking"*

Introduction. Write the word *integrity* on the board. Ask if anyone knows what it means.

Show the definition and ask a student to read it aloud. Ask the class: **What does this mean to you?** Discuss, asking for examples.

Discussion and Activity. Ask students if they think it's important to do the right thing, even if they know they won't get caught doing something wrong. Encourage them to say what they really feel, not just what they think you want to hear.

Tell students: **Here's something a real student said: "I was part of a gossip club. We made up rumors about people and spread them around the whole school."** *

Then ask: **Does this show integrity?** Ask what's wrong with doing what this person did and how the people affected by the student's actions probably felt about it.

If students say, "What if they never found out who did it?" ask: **How do you think the student feels about herself inside when she thinks about what she did?**

Bring out the notion that when we do something that's not right, a part of us knows it, and we often feel guilty. Say: **Whenever we do something that could intentionally hurt another person, we're not showing integrity.**

Ask students to name some other things that show a lack of integrity (lying, bullying, stealing, cheating, disrespecting adults and peers, etc.).

Ask what often happens to adults who engage in these kinds of activities. Guide students to understand that when someone develops a pattern of doing things that are hurtful and dishonest, the person usually does get caught eventually. Ask what other negative things can happen (people not trusting you, losing the respect of others, lack of self-respect, getting in trouble, etc.).

Say: **At one time or another, even really honest people might do something that lacks integrity. This doesn't mean they're bad people, it just means they've made a bad choice. How do you feel about yourself when you do things you know aren't right?**

Ask students to think of things that show integrity (telling the truth, treating others with kindness and respect, not taking things that don't belong to you, listening to adults, etc.). List these actions on chart paper under the title, "Integrity is . . ."

Wrap-Up. Ask students to do three minutes of automatic writing in their journals on the topic of integrity. (See page 8 for details on automatic writing.) Here's a prompt you can start them with: **Give examples of what it means to be a person of integrity.**

In closing, remind students that even if they've done something that lacks integrity, every day is an opportunity to do better.

Extension. Ask students to observe their own behaviors throughout the day, asking themselves the question, "Am I acting with integrity right now?" Then, before they go to bed, have them write in their journals about what they observed in themselves.

---

* Quotes attributed to real students come from interviews and from responses to the Survey About Conflicts conducted by the author and publisher. See pages 1 and 282–284 for further information.

Lesson 6: Peace Pledge

respect • collaboration • personal responsibility

In Lesson 6, your class will create a Peace Pledge that can be recited at the beginning of each day.

Students will

- identify actions that help make their classroom a peaceful place
- work together to brainstorm ideas and distill them into a pledge to be used all year long

Materials

- globe (see page 7)
- chart paper and marker
- *optional:* art materials for creating classroom display; "My Peace Pledge" handout (page 32)

Introduction. Gather your class in a circle. Hold up or point to the globe. Remind students: **We are all part of the same human family. Having a more peaceful world starts right here in our classroom. Getting along with each other is the first step.**

Discussion. Tell students that today they'll be creating a Peace Pledge to say together at the start of each day. Ask how a pledge might help your class set the tone for a peaceful day in which people get along and treat each other with respect. Discuss.

Ask students to suggest things that might be included in the pledge. List ideas on chart paper. As a group, decide which are the most important and meaningful suggestions for the pledge.

Activity. Work together as a class to integrate ideas and create a Peace Pledge that kids can live by. Compose the pledge on chart paper, keeping it short and concise.

When the pledge is complete, ask several students to lead in reading it together. For each line, ask students how they can live the words through real-life actions. Ask students to name things from the pledge they are going to work on personally.

Wrap-Up. Compliment students for coming up with the Peace Pledge collaboratively and for other positive behaviors you noticed (attentive listening, acceptance of each other's ideas, fairness, creativity, patience, kindness, etc.). Ask if anyone in the group would like to acknowledge a classmate.

Follow-Up. Laminate the Peace Pledge and hang it in a prominent place in your room.

Let your students know that you'll be checking in with them to see how they're living the words of the Peace Pledge.

Extension. Create a bulletin board or other classroom display with the Peace Pledge at the center. Give students "My Peace Pledge" handouts. Have them write down and illustrate one thing they plan to do as peacemakers. Display individual Peace Pledges around the class pledge.

Sample Peace Pledge

We pledge to be peacemakers
Throughout the day
And at all other times,
To be kind to others
And follow the Golden Rule.

My Peace Pledge

In order to be a peacemaker, I pledge to

_____

_____

_____

Lesson 7: Leave It at the Door

empathy for self and others

Lesson 7 introduces the idea of a "Leave It at the Door" box—a container where students can "leave" problems when they walk into your classroom.

Students will

- learn a strategy for letting go of problems and stressful feelings
- understand that they can use the "Leave It at the Door" box throughout the year
- use the technique of automatic writing to discharge any negative feelings they presently have

Materials

- a box (or another container) large enough to contain student notes
- paper and pens or pencils

Note: Be sure to read all of the "Leave It at the Door" information on page 9 before conducting this activity.

Note: The purpose of this activity is to teach students a technique for letting go of problems and upset feelings they've brought to school, and to help them transition to a school day in which they can effectively learn and get along with others. It is not intended to minimize or deny feelings or issues that need to be addressed. If you think a child needs further help, speak with the child's parent or your principal, guidance counselor, or school psychologist. See page 13 for more information on what you can do if students share serious issues.

Preparation. Create a "Leave It at the Door" box by decorating a box and making a slot in the top. Attach a sign to the front that says, *"Leave It at the Door."* Place paper and pens or pencils near the box, along with a sign stating: *"You don't have to keep bad feelings inside. Let go of them here."*

Introduction. Affirm students for any acts of respect or cooperation you've seen. Ask if anyone would like to acknowledge another student in the group.

Discussion. Ask students if they ever arrive at school in a bad mood, angry, sad, or stressed. Let them know it's normal to have these feelings, and that you have them, too. Discuss this as a group, sharing your own story (frustration from sitting in traffic, an argument you had with a family member, etc.).

Ask students what they do to let go of bad feelings. Discuss. Remind them that there are many positive ways we can help ourselves manage strong emotions. Say: **Writing is one good way to *unload* negative feelings—to let go of them.**

Hold up the "Leave It at the Door" box and tell students that this is a place where they can put any negative feelings they might come to school with.

Point out the paper and pencils, and explain that they can write about any negative emotions they're feeling as soon as they walk through the door of the classroom.

Unloading their feelings on paper and putting them in the box can help them feel better. Let them know that no one in the class gets to read what's inside the box except you, and even that is only if a student wants you to read what he or she has written.

Activity. Give each student a piece of paper. Say: **Think of something you'd like to leave at the door right now. It can be something from this morning or any other time.** Give students about three minutes to use automatic writing to unload the feelings they'd like to leave at the door.

Encourage students to completely "unload" what's on their minds. Make sure they know that neatness and spelling don't matter. Emphasize that whatever they write will be confidential. Say: **If you would like me to read what you've written sign your name, fold your paper and put my name on top. If you don't want me to read it, crumple the paper and put it in the box. At the end of day, I'll destroy all the crumpled papers, and I'll read the ones addressed to me.**

After three minutes, ask students to finish writing and put their papers in the box. Tell students they can add something to the "Leave It at the Door" box at anytime, but you are the only one who is ever allowed to take anything out. Stress that you are expecting every person in the class to honor the confidentiality of the "Leave It at the Door" box. Place the box on your desk or on a shelf in your clear view.

Wrap-Up. Ask students how they felt "unloading" their thoughts on paper. Be aware that this process can open up unsettling feelings for some children.

If that happens, take a few minutes to talk privately with the child. Tell students that the "Leave It at the Door" box will be there every day all day and can be used whenever needed.

Follow-Up. This process can reveal useful information and give you deeper insight into your students. Save the notes addressed to you and follow up with a brief written or privately spoken response. If a child wants to talk to you further, consider meeting with him or her after class or at lunch. Providing this kind of support can make a big difference in how students feel at school.

Lesson 8: Peace Table

calming • working out conflicts

Lesson 8 introduces the Peace Table as a place where students can calm themselves when feeling stressed, angry, or upset. It's also a place to go to work out conflicts. This lesson also introduces "Win/Win Guidelines for Working Out Conflicts" and reinforces Guideline 1: *Cool off.*

Students will
- share what they already do to calm themselves when angry or upset
- learn other things they can do to calm down when angry or upset
- gain awareness that they have the power to resolve conflicts in a peaceful way

Materials
- small table and chairs
- calming objects (Koosh ball, books, age-appropriate stuffed animals, paper, crayons, markers, music and headphones, etc.)
- chart paper and markers
- handouts: "Win/Win Guidelines for Working Out Conflicts" (page 36); parent letter (page 37)
- *optional:* "Time at the Peace Table," a song by Paulette Meier on her *Come Join the Circle* CD (available at www.paulettemeier.com)

Note: You will find it helpful to read the "Peace Table" information on page 9 before conducting this activity.

Preparation. On chart paper, write the "Win/Win Guidelines for Working Out Conflicts" and the "Rules for Using the Win/Win Guidelines" (see page 36). Laminate them.

Set up the Peace Table in a place in your room where students can go when they feel upset. Place the calming objects you have assembled on or near the table. Hang the Win/Win Guidelines and Rules next to the Peace Table.

Introduction. Ask students what they do to help themselves feel better when they're upset, stressed, sad, or angry. Discuss. Direct students' attention to the Peace Table you've set up. Tell them the Peace Table will be available to them all year long as a place to go if they need to feel calmer or work out a conflict.

Discussion. Ask: **What is a conflict?** See if students can accurately define the word. Here is a definition: **A conflict is a misunderstanding, disagreement, or fight between two or more people. It can also be something that goes on inside yourself.** (For example: *Should I punch this person or walk away?*)

Ask students if they see many conflicts going on in their school and neighborhood. Ask them to briefly describe some of the conflicts they see. (Caution them not to use real names.) Discuss.

Ask students: **Do you think it's normal to have conflicts?** Allow their attitudes to surface. Then let them know that conflict is normal and natural, but what makes some conflicts bad is the way we choose

to handle them. Emphasize that every person has the power to choose fair and respectful ways of handling conflict. Tell students you're going to show them a very important strategy for working out conflicts at the Peace Table, or anywhere else.

Activity. Direct attention to the "Win/Win Guidelines for Working Out Conflicts" chart. Ask for volunteers to read each guideline, along with the rules for using them. For Guideline 6, briefly explain the meaning of *affirm.* Say: **When you affirm someone, you say something nice about the person. For example, "I'm glad we're still friends" or "I feel good about the way you listened to me."**

Tell students that Guideline 1, cooling off, is something they can always do at the Peace Table. Ask which objects on the table might help them calm down when they're angry or upset.

Ask what other objects they'd like to have on or near the Peace Table. Invite students to bring in objects they suggest.

Wrap-Up. Tell students you'll be going over every step of the Win/Win Guidelines very soon. Pass out individual copies of the "Win/Win Guidelines for Working Out Conflicts" and the parent letter. Ask students to display the guidelines at home and explain them to their families.

Extension. End with the song "Time at the Peace Table."

Win/Win Guidelines for Working Out Conflicts

1. Cool off.

2. Talk it over starting from "I," not "you."

3. Listen and say back what you heard.

4. Take responsibility for your role in the conflict.

5. Come up with a solution that's fair to each of you.

6. Affirm, forgive, thank, or apologize.

Rules for Using the Win/Win Guidelines

1. Treat each other with respect.
   No blaming or put-downs.

2. Attack the problem, not the person.

3. No negative body language or facial expressions.

4. Be willing to compromise.

5. Be honest.

Date: _____

Dear Parent/Guardian,

Our class is committed to creating a "get-along" classroom filled with peace, respect, kindness, and compassion. Attached are "Win/Win Guidelines for Working Out Conflicts" that we are using in school. Please ask your child to tell you about these guidelines and what she or he is learning about them.

The guidelines can be used by people of all ages in many different settings. Reinforcing the guidelines at home will encourage your child to use them. I hope you will post them and use them whenever conflicts arise. The more you practice them, the more natural they will feel.

Thanks as always for your support. If you have questions or suggestions, please feel free to contact me.

Sincerely,

_____

Contact me at: _____

_____

_____

_____

_____

_____

Lesson 9: Stop, Breathe, Chill

personal responsibility • anger management • self-control

Lesson 9 introduces "Stop, Breathe, Chill," a powerful strategy for managing anger. It reinforces Win/Win Guideline 1: *Cool off.*

Note: This lesson builds on skills learned in Lesson 4. Complete Lesson 4 before introducing this one.

Students will
- identify body sensations, feelings, and thoughts they have when they get angry
- learn the terms *reptilian brain* and *neocortex* and how they relate to anger
- learn how to shift from the angry part of the brain (reptilian brain) and get to a calmer place
- understand that the front of the brain (neocortex) is their place of power, especially when conflicts occur

Materials
- "Win/Win Guidelines for Working Out Conflicts" chart from Lesson 8
- chart paper and markers
- handout: "Stop, Breathe, Chill" (page 39)

Preparation. On chart paper, write the words *"Stop," "Breathe,"* and *"Chill"* in a column.

Introduction. Point to Win/Win Guideline 1: *Cool off.* Tell students that today you're going to give them a very powerful strategy that will help them cool off, control their anger, and work out conflicts more peacefully.

Discussion. Tell students: **Here is something a real student said: "Sometimes I react without thinking and hurt the people who make me mad. I want to learn how to handle my anger better."**

Ask students if they can identify with this statement. Briefly discuss.

Now share another statement from a real student: **"I try to walk away when I'm in a conflict, but inside my body I feel really mad, so I can't."**

Ask: **How does your body feel when you get mad?**

Say: **Think about where the anger "lands" inside you. Does it land in your heart, causing it to pound? How about your stomach?** Have students point to the places in their bodies as they respond.

Say: **Sometimes anger can cause tightness in the neck or shoulders, pounding in the head, heat in the face, shakiness in the hands.** (Point to each place on yourself as you refer to it.) **Anger is fueled by two things: the feelings we feel in our bodies and the thoughts we think in our heads.**

Now ask students to recall angry thoughts they've had. Ask for one or two volunteers to share.

Activity. Tell students that these thoughts and body sensations come from the *reptilian brain.* Point to the base of your skull; have them do the same. Then say: **The *reptilian brain* is the part that takes over when** we get angry. It causes us to react. When we react, we do things without thinking, sometimes things we regret. But there's another part of our brain that helps us think straight and *choose* a response. Touch the front of your forehead and have students do the same. **The front of the brain is called the *neocortex*. It is our place of true power.**

Refer to the "Stop, Breathe, Chill" chart. Say: **When anger strikes, if we stop, breathe, and chill, we can get *out* of our reptilian brain, and *in*to our place of power. Let's try it now.**

Have students close their eyes and think of a time they got mad. Say: **Recall where the anger landed in your body. Remember your angry thoughts.** Give students a minute to do this.

Then say: **Now picture a big red stop sign, and silently tell yourself to STOP.** (Pause.) **Take some slow deep breaths.** (Breathe with them.) **Feel the oxygen calming your body and mind.**

Stopping and breathing takes you out of the reptilian brain into the front of the brain, your place of power. (Have students point to each place.)

Ask: **What can you do to chill out after you stop and breathe?** Write suggestions on the board.

Wrap-Up. Pass out copies of the "Stop, Breathe, Chill" handout. Ask students to take it home and think of other things they can do to chill out when they're angry—after they stop and breathe. Have them write their ideas in the space provided on the handout and bring it to the next lesson.

Follow-Up. Take a few minutes to discuss students' "Chill" ideas. You'll find additional ideas in several of the Managing Anger lessons (pages 83–118).

Stop, Breathe, Chill

1. Stop

Picture a big red stop sign, and silently tell yourself to **STOP.**

2. Breathe

Take some slow deep breaths. Feel the oxygen calming your body and mind.

3. Chill

Do an activity that helps you relax. You might:

drink some water	draw a picture	skateboard
look out the window	go for a walk	talk with a friend
play a game	play an instrument	write in a journal
exercise	shoot baskets	talk to a teacher
listen to music	color or paint	read a book
gaze at the sky	watch a movie	stretch
talk to a parent	spend time with a pet	_____
_____	_____	_____
_____	_____	_____

Lesson 10: Introducing I-Messages

respect • responsibility • collaboration • conflict resolution

Lesson 10 introduces I-messages as a neutral, nonaggressive way of expressing one's feelings or concerns when conflicts arise. It reinforces Win/Win Guideline 2: *Talk it over starting from "I," not "you."*

Students will

- understand the purpose, use, and value of I-messages
- understand that I-messages are always intended to be respectful, never sarcastic or hurtful
- practice using I-messages through role-play

Materials

- "Win/Win Guidelines for Working Out Conflicts" chart from Lesson 8
- student journals

Introduction. Point to Win/Win Guideline 2: *Talk it over starting from "I," not "you."* Tell students that today they're going to learn about I-messages—an important skill for working out conflicts. Say: **First, let's look at the way many people often react when they're in a conflict.**

Ask for two students to come to the center of the circle and role-play a conflict in which one takes a pencil from the other without asking. Have them argue, and make statements starting with "you." ("You better give it back or else," etc.)

Discussion. Now ask the class what made this conflict get worse. On the board, list some of the things that escalated the conflict. Emphasize that blaming, name-calling, and starting from "you" *escalate* conflicts—make them grow. Tell students that starting from "you" puts people on the defensive—makes them want to defend themselves and lash out at the other person.

Say: **Starting from "I" lets us state what's on our minds respectfully without blame or put-downs. When we start from "I," that's called an I-message. I-messages let people be *assertive* (speak up for themselves) without blame or put-downs.** Emphasize that the way an I-message is delivered is just as important as the words. Sarcasm is never okay.

Ask students to turn the following "you-message" into an I-message: **"You just cut in front of me. You're mean."** Possible I-message alternatives are:

- "I was here first. Please don't cut in front of me."
- "I don't like when people cut in front of me. Please get behind me."
- "I don't appreciate being cut in front of. Please move."

An easy way to teach I-messages is to have students start sentences with "I didn't like it when . . ." and then elaborate without blame. Example: "I didn't like it when you told my secret. I thought you understood that this was just supposed to be between us. Please don't do it again."

Notes About I-Messages: It's not necessary for kids to state how they feel when they use I-messages. While I-messages have traditionally included statements of feelings ("I feel hurt when . . ."), many experts now believe that a more neutral form of I-messages is preferable. Starting with "I feel" often leaves the person delivering the words vulnerable and open to more hurt. (For example, the respondent might reply, "You feel hurt. Good!") I-messages can also be followed by a request, as illustrated above.

The word *you* can be included in I-messages ("I didn't like when *you* grabbed the pencil out of my hand"). But *you* should not be used in an accusatory or blameful way.

Activity. Have students partner up and think of an I-message for the following scenario: **Your friend insists that you play soccer at recess today. You want to play softball.**

After a few minutes, ask students to share some of the I-messages they came up with. Here are a few possibilities:

- "I don't think it's fair that we always have to play soccer. How about playing softball for a change?"
- "I don't really want to play soccer today."
- "I don't like it when you try to force me to play something I don't want to play."

Have students share some of the I-messages they came up with. Help them assess whether the I-message respectfully got their point across.

Wrap-Up. Commend students on the effort they've put into coming up with I-messages. Remind them to use I-messages when real conflicts arise.

Follow-Up. Have students think about a conflict they recently had. Ask them to think of I-messages they might have used during the conflict. Have them list a few in their journals.

Extension. One of the most important I-messages is, "I have something on my mind." This opens the door to airing concerns or hurts that have been tucked away. Encourage students to think about something they'd like to discuss with a friend or family member, but haven't had the courage to broach. Tell them to rehearse—or even write down—what they'd like to say. Then suggest they approach the person by saying, "I have something on my mind."

Lesson 11: Practicing I-Messages

respect • personal responsibility • collaboration

Lesson 11 gives students more practice in formulating and delivering I-messages. The lesson reinforces Win/Win Guideline 2: *Talk it over starting from "I," not "you."*

Students will
- formulate I-messages for common conflicts
- understand that the way an I-message is delivered is just as important as the words that are spoken

Materials
- "Win/Win Guidelines for Working Out Conflicts" chart from Lesson 8

Introduction. Review what you taught in the last lesson, particularly that I-messages need to be delivered in a respectful way free of blame, put-downs, or sarcasm. Ask why I-messages are more effective for resolving conflicts than "you-messages." (You-messages put people on the defensive and make conflicts escalate; I-messages help us state what's on our mind respectfully so we can talk out conflicts.)

Activity. Say: **When you use an I-message, it's not just about the words you speak. It's also about how you say them.** Demonstrate an I-message with arms crossed and a hostile look on your face. Ask students what message your face and body are delivering.

Now have students form pairs and come up with I-messages for the following scenarios. (Students might also suggest scenarios for this activity.) Have them practice delivering the I-messages assertively and with *neutral* (not aggressive) body language. After each scenario, stop and ask a few partners to stand and deliver I-messages they came up with.

I-message scenarios:

- Someone in class makes fun of your shoes.
- You drop the ball during a game and someone calls you a name.
- You approach two classmates at recess and one of them says, "You can't hang out with us."

After each I-message is delivered, ask the class if it sounded both assertive and respectful. Were the person's body language and facial expression neutral and respectful?

Wrap-Up. Encourage students to use I-messages throughout the day, always being aware of *how* the words are being spoken. Remind them that body language, tone of voice, and facial expression are just as important as words.

Follow-Up. Ask students to create I-messages to deliver to someone in their lives. Have them practice saying the words in a mirror, observing their own body language and facial expression.

Lesson 12: Reflective Listening

Lesson 12 introduces reflective listening and gives students the opportunity to practice it. The lesson reinforces Win/Win Guideline 3: *Listen and say back what you heard.*

Students will

- understand what reflective listening is and how it is used
- practice using reflective listening in a non-conflict situation

Materials

- "Win/Win Guidelines for Working Out Conflicts" chart from Lesson 8

Introduction. Ask students for examples of situations where they've used I-messages at home or in school. Ask: **How is it going?** Discuss briefly.

Tell students: **If we really want to resolve a conflict, the way we listen is as important as what we say. When someone gives us an I-message, we need to listen carefully and then *paraphrase* (say back) the main idea of what the person said. When we do this, we show that we care enough to listen, even if we disagree. Listening is the most powerful thing we can do to resolve conflicts.**

Discussion. Now point to Win/Win Guideline 3: *Listen and say back what you heard.* Ask: **Is this what people generally do when there's a conflict?** Ask students what they tend to do when the other person is speaking. (Many people think about what to say next, interrupt, or argue.) Speak honestly about what *you* tend to do. The more honest you are, the more it gives kids permission to be honest, too.

Activity. Explain that listening and saying back the main idea of what was said is called reflective listening; reflective listening can be used anytime, not just in conflicts. Say: **Now you're going to try using reflective listening in a neutral situation—one where there isn't a conflict. The more you practice reflective listening in regular conversations, the easier it will be to use when conflicts arise.**

Have a volunteer come to the center of the circle and help you demonstrate. Say to the volunteer: **Describe what you most like to do after school.**

Listen attentively, make eye contact, then paraphrase what the student says. You can start with the words "I'm hearing you say . . ." or "So. . . ." Afterward, ask the student if you got it right.

Now have students form pairs and face each other directly. Have each pair choose a Speaker and a Listener. Have the Listener ask, "Can you tell me about what you most like to do after school?" Caution Speakers not to let their response get too lengthy. Tell Listeners to listen with their full attention, as though no one else is in the room but the person they're listening to. When the Speaker is finished, the Listener needs to say back the main idea of what the Speaker said. If the Listener gets it wrong, the Speaker should repeat what he or she originally said, and the Listener should try again.

After a minute or two, have partners switch roles, so each one gets to be both Speaker and Listener.

Wrap-Up. Ask students how it felt to have someone truly listen to what they had to say. Discuss. Ask how reflective listening can help when it comes to working out conflicts.

Follow-Up. Tell students to practice reflective listening throughout the day; let them know you'll check in with them about how it went in the next lesson. Encourage them to try reflective listening at home and notice its impact on the people they listen to.

Lesson 13: Taking Responsibility in Conflicts

respect • personal responsibility • integrity • conflict resolution

Lesson 13 helps students understand that when conflicts arise, both people are usually responsible in some way, and that blaming only escalates conflicts. The lesson reinforces Win/Win Guideline 4: *Take responsibility for your role in the conflict.*

Students will

- examine a conflict they had and reflect on ways they may have been "even a little bit" responsible for some part of it
- role-play a conflict in which blaming prevents a peaceful outcome
- replay the conflict with people taking responsibility rather than blaming

Materials

- student journals
- "Win/Win Guidelines for Working Out Conflicts" chart from Lesson 8
- handout: "Responsibility Log" (page 45), several copies for each student

Introduction. Point to Win/Win Guideline 4: *Take responsibility for your role in the conflict.* Say: **One of the most important things we can do to work out conflicts is take responsibility for our part, even if we did something small.**

Discussion. On the board write the words *blaming* and *taking responsibility.* Ask: **What's the difference?** Discuss, guiding students to think about how often they blame rather than take responsibility in conflicts.

Discuss how common it is to blame rather than look at our own behavior and take responsibility for how we might have contributed to the conflict. Share this actual dialogue by a real sixth grader (not her real name) that illustrates this, playing each of the roles yourself:

Allysa: *My big sister is really mean to me.*
Teacher: What does she do?
Allysa: *She never lets me in her room, and I like to go in there.*
Teacher: Do you ask permission first?
Allysa: *No. I just go in.*
Teacher: And then she gets angry with you?
Allysa: *Yeah, and she calls me names.*
Teacher: Why do you think she gets so mad?
Allysa: *Because she's mean.*
Teacher: Is there something you're doing that brings out her anger?
Allysa: *Hey, this isn't my fault. My sister's supposed to be nice to me.*

Teacher: Sounds like you're putting all the blame on her. How are you responsible for the problem, too?
Allysa: *I shouldn't have to be responsible. I'm the youngest. She's the oldest and she should know better.*

Ask students if they can see themselves in any part of Allysa's story. Discuss. Bring out the point that Allysa is avoiding taking responsibility for going into her sister's room without permission, and she's trying to pin the entire blame on her sister with the excuse of being younger. Ask: **Have you ever made excuses for something you shouldn't have done?** Invite examples. Nearly all of us do this at one time or another, so share a situation where you blamed rather than taking responsibility.

Ask students to think about a conflict in which the other person blamed them and refused to take responsibility for anything that went wrong. Discuss a few examples, reminding students not to use names or refer to anyone in the class. Ask students how it felt to be blamed. Ask: **Did blaming cause the conflict to get better or worse?**

Say: **Now think of a time when *you* did the blaming.** Elicit one or two examples. Ask students if blaming the other person made the conflict get better or worse. Guide students to understand that blaming *escalates* conflicts—makes them grow bigger and worse—and prevents them from getting solved.

Now give students a moment to think about a conflict they've recently had. Say: **In almost all conflicts,** both people are responsible in some way. Can you think of a way you might have been *even a little bit responsible* for what happened? Share an example from your life to help kids open up about their own conflicts.

Tell students that taking responsibility is an act of courage, one that will help them better resolve any conflict that might come up. Say: **Taking responsibility for our part in a conflict can give the other person the courage to do the same.**

Activity. Ask for two volunteers to role-play the following conflict in a negative way. Ask them to use you-messages, blame each other, and refuse to take responsibility for their part:

Carl and Janie worked together on a class project. They just got it back, and discovered they

only earned a C because an important part of the project had been left out.

When the role play is completed, ask the class to comment on what made the conflict escalate. Ask each role player how it felt to be blamed. Now have them reenact the conflict, this time taking responsibility for whatever they each did, even if it was something small.

Wrap-Up. Ask students: **Which role play turned out better? Why?** Ask how taking responsibility helps us resolve conflicts.

Follow-Up. Have students keep a "Responsibility Log" for the next week. Provide them with a few copies of the handout on page 45 so they can practice taking responsibility for their role in conflicts.

Responsibility Log

Taking responsibility helps people resolve conflicts. Use this sheet to help yourself take responsibility for your part in conflicts.

A conflict I had: (Briefly describe what happened in the conflict.)

_____

_____

_____

_____

Is there some way I was even a little bit responsible? Describe.

_____

_____

_____

_____

What could I have done differently?

_____

_____

_____

_____

Lesson 14: Brainstorming Solutions to Conflicts

respect • personal responsibility • conflict resolution

Lesson 14 helps students understand that every conflict has many solutions, and if students are committed to working out conflicts, they can find fair solutions. The lesson reinforces Win/Win Guidelines 5 and 6: *Come up with a solution that's fair to each of you* and *Affirm, forgive, thank, or apologize.*

Students will
- work together with a partner to come up with fair solutions to conflicts
- recognize that conflicts can have a variety of possible solutions

Materials
- "Win/Win Guidelines for Working Out Conflicts" chart from Lesson 8
- student journals

Introduction. Tell students that every conflict has many solutions. Point to Win/Win Guideline 5: *Come up with a solution that's fair to each of you.* Say: **Today we're going to get some practice coming up with possible solutions to conflicts.**

Discussion. Ask: **How many of you get into conflicts with people over who's right and who's wrong?** Allow for a show of hands. Tell students you're going to share a story about two sixth graders whose friendship is about to fall apart over this issue. Read the following:

Tom and Jarrett always get into conflicts about who's right and who's wrong, and they're losing their patience with each other. Today it happens again. Tom says the book they've been reading in class is totally lame; Jarrett thinks it's really interesting. They start arguing over their opposing viewpoints, each trying to prove that the other is wrong. As usual they both end up walking away angry and frustrated.

Activity. Have students role-play Tom and Jarrett's conflict.

Now ask the class: **What are some possible solutions to this ongoing conflict?** List their solutions on the board under the title "Brainstorming Solutions." Some examples may include:

- Agree to drop the subject and do something else when disagreements come up.

- Refrain from discussing things they don't see eye to eye on—agree not to talk about them.

- Agree to hear each other out and try to understand the other person's point of view.

- When there's a point of disagreement, use one of the following phrases: "You have a right to your opinion," "I see it differently, but that's okay,"

"Even though I disagree, I respect your right to see things in a different way."

Have students partner up, discuss, and list in their journals at least five possible solutions to the following conflict.

Amy and Todd walk to school together each day. Todd is always on time, but Amy never is, so they often end up getting to school late. Amy is late again today.

Wrap-Up. Ask students to share the solutions they came up with. List their suggestions on the board. Refer again to Guideline 5: *Come up with a solution that's fair to each of you.*

Now refer to Guideline 6: *Affirm, forgive, thank, or apologize.* Have partners turn to each other, state which solution feels like a fair one, and imagine they have just worked out their conflict. Now have them either affirm (acknowledge), forgive, thank, or apologize to each other. Examples of affirming are, "I'm glad we're still friends." Or, "I appreciate the way you listened to me when I spoke." If apologies are given, they should be sincere.

Follow-Up. Have students write in their journals or talk to a trusted person about an ongoing conflict in their lives and consider possible solutions. Ask students to talk to the person they're in conflict with, brainstorm solutions together, and decide on a solution that's fair to both of them.

Extension. Keep a Question Box in your room. If students have conflicts they can't find solutions to, have them write about the conflict and put their paper in the box. Several times a week, have other students randomly select a conflict from the box, sit down with the person who wrote about it, and brainstorm solutions together.

Lesson 15: Win/Win Guidelines for Working Out Conflicts

respect • personal responsibility • conflict resolution

Lesson 15 reviews the Win/Win Guidelines and lets students practice using them through role plays.

Note: This lesson builds on skills and attitudes learned in Lessons 9, 10, 11, 12, 13, and 14. It's important to have completed these activities before conducting this one.

Students will
- role-play a conflict in the "old way—" negatively
- role-play a conflict using the Win/Win Guidelines
- understand that it's possible to resolve conflicts more peacefully when they use the Win/Win Guidelines

Materials
- "Win/Win Guidelines for Working Out Conflicts" and "Rules for Using the Win/Win Guidelines" charts from Lesson 8
- chart paper and marker
- globe (see page 7)

Preparation. Ask students to bring their copies of the "Win/Win Guidelines for Working Out Conflicts," distributed in Lesson 8 (page 36), to this lesson.

Introduction and Discussion. Ask students how they've been using the Win/Win Guidelines that they've learned in the last six lessons. Discuss. Be prepared for some students to complain about challenges they've encountered. Emphasize that challenges are normal. After more practice and role-playing, using the guidelines will start to feel more natural.

Activity. Ask for two volunteers to role-play a conflict. You can have students choose a conflict that's fairly common and role-play that one, or use this idea: **Person A shared a secret that Person B wanted kept private.**

First, have students role-play the conflict in a negative way instead of using the Win/Win Guidelines. Before they begin, prime the rest of the class to note what the role players do that escalates the conflict. After the role play, ask: **What made this conflict get worse?**

Direct attention to the Win/Win Guidelines for Working Out Conflicts and Rules for Using the Win/Win Guidelines. Choose a few students to read each of the rules aloud. Explain any that need clarification.

Now have volunteers replay the conflict, this time using the guidelines and rules:

Guideline 1. Tell role players to start by cooling off (taking some deep breaths, getting a drink of water, walking away for a few moments, etc.).

After the role players have cooled off, direct them to go through the remaining guidelines:

Guidelines 2 and 3. Have the role players take turns telling each other what was bothering them, starting from "I," not "you." As one person gives an I-message, the other should listen and briefly paraphrase what was said: "I'm hearing you say that_____."

Guideline 4. Ask each student how he or she might be "even a little bit" responsible for the conflict.

Guideline 5. Ask the role players to brainstorm a number of solutions, then come up with one they can agree upon. Ask the class to suggest solutions, too.

Guideline 6. Ask role players to either affirm (acknowledge), forgive, thank, or apologize to each other. Resist making students apologize if they're not ready. Forced apologies are not effective.

Ask the class to evaluate why the conflict ended better when the role players used the Win/Win Guidelines. Discuss.

Wrap-Up. End the Lesson by acknowledging your students for their openness to change and respectful, effective listening. Hold up or point to a globe and remind them that each time they try to work out conflicts respectfully, they're doing their part to make the world a little more peaceful.

Follow-Up. Check in with students occasionally on how they're doing as they use the Win/Win Guidelines. Provide refresher lessons on the guidelines, referring back to Lessons 9–14 as needed.

Extensions. Ask students to create a rap or cheer that tells how to use the Win/Win Guidelines or have students create a comic strip that shows people working out a conflict using the six guidelines.

Getting Along and Building Respect

All of the activities in Part Two of *No Kidding About Bullying* build on the fundamental bullying prevention skills and understandings introduced in the Core Lessons of Part One. Part Two has 107 lessons designed to help you create a get-along classroom that can last all year. Lessons in this section are organized into seven topic areas:

- Fostering Kindness, Compassion, and Empathy
- Managing Anger
- Preventing Conflict
- Responding to Conflict
- Addressing Name-Calling and Teasing
- Dealing with Bullying
- Accepting Differences

Fostering Kindness, Compassion, and Empathy

Fostering kindness, compassion, empathy, and conscience is your most powerful tool for preventing and alleviating bullying. Current research tells us that the prime motivator for bullying is a need for power. Kids who bully tend to be impervious to the feelings of others. By teaching, modeling, and expecting kind and empathetic behavior, we can create an environment where bullying becomes an "uncool" thing to do. This section also introduces the concept of being an upstander, one who stands up for those who are picked on.

Lesson 16: Creating Your Place in Other People's Memory Banks

respect • kindness • compassion • personal responsibility

Lesson 16 introduces the concept of a "memory bank"—the part of us that holds memories of the way we've been treated by others.

Students will

- understand that the way we treat people today creates memories of us that can last a long time, sometimes forever
- define two qualities they want to be remembered as having

- take greater responsibility for their words and actions

Materials

- small box (or other container) with a lid labeled "Memory Bank"
- notecards or slips of paper that students (and you) will put in the Memory Bank

Preparation. On chart paper, write: *"Our words and actions today create memories that will fill others' memory banks tomorrow."*

Introduction. Gather students in a circle. Affirm them as a class and individually for positive ways they've been treating one another. Ask students to think about acts of respect, kindness, or helpfulness that have taken place in the classroom recently. Ask if anyone would like to compliment a classmate. If no one does, give one more affirmation yourself.

Discussion. Hold up the Memory Bank you made. Explain that it represents the "memory bank" each of us has inside. Tell students that things we say and do now will go into people's memory banks, sometimes forever. Say: **Kind words and actions create positive memories. How about mean or hurtful words and actions—what kind of memories of us do they create?**

Share a positive memory of someone who showed kindness toward you. Next share the following negative memory from a real teacher:*

"Even though decades have passed, when I remember the person who bullied me, I still cringe. It gives me a stomachache. I can remember names he called me, his cruel laughter when I would walk by. The sight of his face in my mind brings me pain. If I were to see him today it would still bother me, even though we are both adults now."

Ask students to name some of the feelings this teacher holds in her memory bank about the person who bullied her. Write the feelings on a notecard or slip of paper and put it into the Memory Bank.

Now ask students to think of a positive memory that's stored in their memory banks of someone who was kind to them. Call on a student to share briefly.

Next ask students to think about their own place in other people's memory banks. Ask them how they would like to be remembered by others. Choose a few children to share aloud.

Display the statement you prepared. Say: **Our words and actions today create memories of us that will fill others' memory banks tomorrow.** Remind students that we have the power to create positive memories of ourselves through kind words and actions. Ask: **If we treat someone in a hurtful or unkind way, how will we be remembered?**

Activity. Pass out notecards or slips of paper and ask students to write two positive qualities for which they would like to be remembered (examples: caring, helpful, honest, fair). Get them started with this prompt: **"In future years, I want people to remember me as being _____ and _____."**

Have students read aloud the two qualities for which they would like to be remembered. Then have them put their papers in the Memory Bank. Ask what they can do now so people will remember them for the qualities they just named. List specific actions on the board.

Wrap-Up. Compliment students for any positive actions you observed during this lesson (honesty, kindness, good listening, sensitivity, etc.). Emphasize that these actions are creating good memories of them in people's memory banks.

---

* Quotes attributed to real teachers or students come from interviews and from responses to the Survey About Conflicts conducted by the author and publisher. See pages 1 and 282–284 for further information.

Lesson 17: How Do You Want to Be Remembered?

respect • kindness • compassion • personal responsibility

Lesson 17 asks students to define how they want to be remembered by peers over time and encourages them to be kind in word and action. This lesson is a follow-up to Lesson 16.

Students will

- envision how they want to be remembered by others ten years from now
- write about how they want to be remembered by others
- reflect on changes they need to make to be remembered in positive ways

Materials

- small box (or other container) with a lid labeled "Memory Bank"
- handout: "Creating My Place in Other People's Memory Banks" (page 54)

Introduction. Hold up the Memory Bank. Ask students what it represents (the place where we hold either positive or negative memories of others based on the way they treated us). Ask for a few students to share the qualities they would want to be remembered by. Tell students how you would like to be remembered by them, and describe what you're doing now to make that happen.

Activity. Ask students to close their eyes or look down. Say: **Imagine it is ten years from now. The people who know you now are remembering you back in (this year's) grade. What would you like them to be able to say about you? How would you like to be remembered by them?**

Give students a minute or two to envision this. Then have them open their eyes, get into pairs, and share what they envisioned.

Pass out the "Creating My Place in Other People's Memory Banks" handout and go over it briefly, making sure students understand each section. Allow five to ten minutes for students to complete the handout. If anyone needs more time, have them finish it later in the day.

Discussion. Ask for several volunteers to share what they wrote. Be sure to have them include actions they can take now to be remembered in a positive way by those who know them presently.

Wrap-Up. Ask students if they have any compliments for people who listened respectfully. End by reminding students that every moment is an opportunity to create positive memories of ourselves in other people's memory banks.

Follow-Up. When you see students acting in kind, compassionate ways, point out that they're creating positive memories of themselves in other people's memory banks. If you observe hurtfulness or meanness, ask, "What kind of memory might you be creating right now?"

Creating My Place in Other People's Memory Banks

Imagine it is ten years from today and people who know you are thinking about the person you were in the grade you're in now. Write a paragraph describing how you would like other people to remember you. Include the qualities you would like them to remember about you. Also include things you hope they will be able to say about you years from now.

_____

_____

_____

_____

What can you do now to be remembered in the ways you described above?

_____

_____

_____

_____

What changes do you need to make so people will remember you in the way you hope they will?

_____

_____

_____

_____

Lesson 18: Choosing Kindness

kindness • respect • empathy • personal responsibility

Lesson 18 focuses on the need for kindness and empathy and guides students to choose kind actions over hurtful ones.

Students will
- describe how it feels to be treated unkindly
- understand that kindness is a gift they can give to each other every day

Materials
- handout: "What Real Kids Have to Say About Being Mean" (page 56)
- "Our Agreements for a Get-Along Classroom" chart from Lesson 1

Introduction. Gather students in a circle. Affirm several kids for acts of kindness and respect you've recently observed. Ask students if they think it's more common for kids to treat each other in kind ways or mean ways.

Discussion. Distribute handouts and read or have a student read the statistic at the top. Ask: **Does this sound right to you? How mean do you think kids are to each other?**

Read or have a student read the quoted story from the handout. Invite responses from students. Ask: **Has anything like this ever happened to you?**

Activity. Have students pair up. Ask them to think of a time they were treated in a mean way, sharing with their partner what happened and how it made them feel. Caution students not to use real names.

Next have students complete the bottom of the handout. After several minutes, have students share their experiences with the class, either reading what they wrote or talking about it. Ask them to describe how they felt when they were treated unkindly.

As students identify feelings, list them on chart paper under the heading "Being Treated Unkindly Makes People Feel . . ." After students share, ask for someone to lead in the reading of the chart.

Refer to your get-along classroom agreements and ask: **How can being kind help us create and keep the kind of get-along classroom we all want? Why is it important to constantly remember how our words and actions affect others?**

Wrap-Up. On the board or on chart paper, write: "A gift we can all give each other is kindness." Say: **Giving kindness isn't just "acting nice." It's more about treating others the way we want to be treated.** Ask students to focus on kindness for the rest of the day and to give the gift of kindness to each other as often as they can.

Follow-Up. Post the "Being Treated Unkindly Makes People Feel" chart and the statement "A gift we can all give each other is kindness." Keep referring back to each. As the day goes on, affirm kids for any kind acts you witness. Have students affirm each other, too. (You'll notice that after a while they'll do this automatically.) If you see an unkind act, ask, "Was that kind or unkind?" Sometimes just asking the question is enough to hold kids to account.

Relate the concept of kindness to characters in literature you read for the remainder of the day, or to people in articles and books used in other content areas.

Throughout this week and the next, when students go to lunch, remind them to keep giving the gift of kindness to everyone they come in contact with. When they return, take a few minutes to hear how it went. At dismissal, remind your students to continue giving the gift of kindness to their families and anyone else they cross paths with.

Note: It's possible when a student is nice to someone that the person may respond negatively. If a student reports this happening, help the student think about potential reasons behind the negative response. Could the person be angry about an unresolved problem between the two of them? If so, suggest the student talk to the person, find out what's going on, and see if they can work it out. Might the person be showing off and trying to impress friends by acting tough or be having a bad day? Or maybe the person has a completely unrelated problem. Encourage students to try not to take situations like these personally. Talk together with students about possible ways to handle specific situations, and encourage them to continue to give the gift of kindness to others.

What Real Kids Have to Say About
Being Mean

In a national survey of more than 2,100 students in grades 3–6:

73% (1,584 students) said they thought other kids are **somewhat** to **very mean.**

Here's what one student wrote:

"I'm a new kid at this school. At the beginning of the year everyone knew I was different. I am. Anyway, this is what happened: I tried to make friends with a few kids in my class, but they weren't interested. One kid really didn't like me. He whacked me on the back of the head and screamed at me. Later he did it again and yelled. The next day he did it again. I told him if he tried it again I would tell. He finally stopped. But then other kids were doing other things to me. It made starting in a new school really hard. Being the new kid is really hard. Being picked on makes it even worse."

What do YOU have to say about being mean?

How do you feel when someone is mean to you? What can we do to stamp out meanness?

_____

_____

_____

_____

_____

_____

_____

Lesson 19: Take a Stand for Kindness

kindness • respect • empathy • personal responsibility

In Lesson 19, students reflect upon the importance of kindness and consider ways to be an "upstander"—someone who stands up for people who are mistreated.

Students will
- come up with words and actions they can use as upstanders who help kids who are being picked on or mistreated
- role-play a scenario in which upstanders intervene on behalf of a child who is being mistreated

Materials
- chart paper and marker
- handout: "The Courage to Be an Upstander" (page 59)
- globe (see page 7)

Introduction. Ask students to think of a time when someone they know was treated in a mean way. Ask for examples, cautioning kids not to use real names or other identifying factors. Suggest they start with, "Someone I know" or "Someone I saw out on the playground."

Ask students what they, personally, could have done to help. Say: **When you stand up for someone who's being mistreated, you're being an** *upstander.* **Sometimes it can be hard to be an upstander alone. Pairing up can give us the courage to speak up when we might otherwise be too afraid.**

Discussion. At the top of a piece of chart paper write: "Be an Upstander." Ask students what they can say or do to help someone who's being picked on. List their suggestions. Guide students to understand that upstanders are both respectful and direct, always making sure not to bully the person who's committing the hurtful act. Give the following example of an appropriate comment upstanders can use when they intervene: "Hey, it's not cool to treat someone that way." Ask for other suggestions and write them on the board.

Tell students that it's fine to address the person who's being mistreated, rather than the one who's doing the mistreating. Give the following example of a phrase they can use when they intervene: "Do you need some help? Why don't you come with us?" Ask for other suggestions and write them on the board.

Activity. Have students get into groups of four to role-play a scenario in which one child falls down on the playground and another person laughs, makes mean comments, and tries to get bystanders to join in. Have one child play the role of the person who

falls down, another play the role of the person who's being mean, and the other two act as upstanders who intervene together. Circulate as groups role-play, and give help where needed.

Afterward, have students reconvene in a circle. Ask how the role plays went. Ask: **What did the upstanders do? What did they say? Did their words and actions help? If the kid who was acting mean said nasty things to the upstanders, what did the upstanders do in response?** Emphasize that sometimes upstanders will need to say what they have to say and then walk away. Sticking around and arguing back and forth with the person who acted mean will only add fuel to the fire. It is best for upstanders to speak up assertively, then turn and walk away with the student they helped. They can say something like, "We're not going to listen to this." Discuss, and ask a few students to demonstrate. Emphasize that they should walk away tall and proud with heads held high.

(This is very important because some students think walking away shows weakness; it's critical to help them see walking away as a sign of strength. I often remind students of how Martin Luther King Jr. walked away, head held high when people hurled threats and racial epithets at him. Dr. King demonstrated the epitome of walking away tall and strong, walking away with dignity, not weakness.)

Ask students why it takes courage to be an upstander, especially when others are acting mean.

Then ask: **When you consider being an upstander for someone who's being mistreated, what might make it hard to actually do?** Briefly discuss, emphasizing that the more students practice being upstanders, the easier it becomes.

Note: Upstanders should never physically intervene. Make sure students know that if a fight is going on, or if kids are physically attacking another child, it's important to immediately seek the assistance of an adult. Stress that seeking help is not tattling or snitching. It's supporting the right every person has to be safe.

Wrap-Up. Point to the globe. Remind students that every time we are kind in word and deed, we send ripples of peace out into the world. Being an upstander is one of the highest forms of kindness we can give.

Follow-Up. Distribute the "Courage to Be an Upstander" handout and ask students to complete it on their own or with a classmate. Discuss students' handouts at the beginning of a future lesson.

Note: The handout asks students to learn about Miep Gies, a Dutchwoman born in 1919 who helped Anne Frank and her family stay in hiding from the Nazis during World War II.

The Courage to Be an Upstander

1. On the internet, in an encyclopedia, or at the library, look up Miep Gies. Gies was a courageous upstander. What did Miep Gies do?

_____

_____

_____

_____

_____

_____

2. What might stand in your way of being an upstander for someone who's being mistreated? What can you do to overcome whatever might be in your way?

_____

_____

_____

_____

_____

_____

_____

_____

_____

Lesson 20: It's Cool to Be Kind

> **kindness • compassion • integrity • personal responsibility • decency**
>
> Lesson 20 helps students equate "coolness" with kindness, compassion, and integrity.

Students will
- learn a new way of looking at the word *cool*
- understand that being an upstander is a very high form of "coolness"
- role-play being an upstander

Materials
- *optional:* markers, colored pencils, or crayons

Preparation. On chart paper, write the following:

> "**C**ompassionate
> **O**utrageously kind
> **O**ften an upstander
> **L**ives with integrity"

If you wish, have a student illustrate this chart ahead of time.

Introduction and Discussion. Ask: **What does being cool mean to you?** (Students may say things like being popular, having the right clothes, etc.) If someone does not suggest it, introduce the idea that there are other ways to be cool, especially when it comes to how we treat others. Ask: **Do you know someone who's cool because they're kind, fair, and treat people with respect?** Allow for responses. Say: **This form of coolness is the most powerful of all.** Give an example of someone you respect who's cool, kind, and caring.

Activity. Show students the "COOL" chart. Ask for a volunteer to read it aloud. Ask: **What does it mean to be compassionate?** Share the following definition: **Being compassionate means understanding the feelings of others and feeling what they feel in your own heart.** Clarify that feeling compassion doesn't mean feeling sorry for someone. It means feeling what the person is feeling: happiness, sadness, embarrassment, or any other emotion.

Ask students to think of a time a friend was sad and they felt their friend's sadness. (Example: A friend is grieving the loss of a beloved pet and you choke up when they tell you about it.) Ask students to think of a time when someone was extremely happy, and they felt happiness for that person.

Refer to the chart and ask: **How about outrageously kind—what does that mean?** Invite an example or share a story from your life.

Next, point to "Often an upstander." Ask students what an upstander does. Ask for an example.

Point to the final phrase, "Lives with integrity," and ask students the meaning of integrity. Share the following definition: **Showing integrity means doing the right thing, even when no one is looking.**

Wrap-Up. Direct students' attention to the chart again and ask how this definition of *cool* differs from the one many people hold. Ask for a few volunteers to act out a situation where one or two people show outrageous kindness, integrity, and compassion by being upstanders for a classmate who's being picked on. Ask how standing up for others is a way of being cool.

Extension. Have students create posters using the COOL acrostic introduced in this lesson. Ask them to illustrate the posters with examples that reflect what the four letters stand for.

Lesson 21: Redefining Cool

kindness • compassion • integrity • respect

Lesson 21 helps kids further redefine coolness, equating it with kindness and other positive qualities. This lesson is a follow-up to Lesson 20.

Students will

- see the link between "coolness" and admirable qualities like compassion, kindness, and courage
- understand that it's never cool to be cruel, even though popular images often equate the two
- be encouraged to disavow cruelty

Materials

- "COOL" chart from Lesson 20 (page 60)
- photo of someone you admire and respect (a person you know, or someone of note, such as Martin Luther King Jr. or Eleanor Roosevelt)
- chart paper and marker
- drawing paper, markers, and crayons for each student
- *optional:* large mural paper

Introduction. Review the COOL chart, then show the picture you brought in of someone you admire and respect, linking the qualities this person has with words on the chart. Include other words like courage, creativity, and uniqueness if they apply. List these qualities on chart paper entitled, "The New Definition of Cool."

Discussion. Ask students to think of a cool person they respect and admire. Have them name some of the positive qualities this person possesses. Add them to the list.

Ask if it's ever cool to be cruel. Discuss, guiding students to understand that it is never cool to be cruel to another person. Write the following words on the board: "Being cruel is never cool."

Ask students to think about people in popular culture who are regarded as cool, but are actually cruel (such as certain video-game characters, violent movie heroes, etc.). Reiterate that cruelty cancels out coolness.

Encourage students to think of more qualities that can go on "The New Definition of Cool" list (intelligent, think for themselves, etc.).

Activity. Ask students to draw a picture of a cool person they admire and respect. Beneath it, have them write the following caption: "I respect _____. He/she is cool because _____."

Wrap-Up. Remind students that the qualities discussed today are what make people truly cool. End by reiterating that it's never cool to be cruel.

Follow-Up. Create a bulletin board or display with the heading "A New Definition of Cool" that incorporates the pictures students made.

Extension. Lay out mural paper, markers, and crayons. Ask a student to write "Cool Is:" in the center of the paper in large colorful letters. Then have the class colorfully write all of the qualities listed on the "New Definition of Cool" list plus others that might apply. Have them create corresponding illustrations. Somewhere on the mural should be the words, "Being cruel is never cool." When the mural is complete, hang it in the hallway. Let students know that this mural can help other kids in the school redefine what it means to be cool. Encourage them to be role models for the new definition of cool.

Lesson 22: Words That Hurt

PART TWO
Fostering Kindness, Compassion, and Empathy

compassion • kindness • conscience • respect • personal responsibility

Lesson 22 fosters compassion by guiding students to reflect upon the impact of hurtful words and actions.

Students will

- reflect on the impact of name-calling, mean words, and hurtful gestures
- understand that hurtful words have no place in a get-along classroom

Materials

- handout: "What Real Kids Have to Say About Mean Words" (page 63)
- student journals
- *optional: The Misfits* by James Howe; poster paper and markers

Preparation. Write or type the quote from *The Misfits* (see Discussion, below) so you can display it for the class.

On chart paper, write the title *"No More Hurtful Words"* Beneath it, write: *"I pledge not to use words, jokes, or gestures that hurt others or put them down in any way."*

Introduction. Begin by asking volunteers to read aloud quotes about name-calling and put-downs from the handout. Ask students if any of the things kids said ring true for them. Discuss. Also talk about how they feel when they see other kids being put down or called names.

Discussion. Display the quoted passage, below, from *The Misfits* by James Howe, which gets right to the heart of why mean words and names hurt so much. In the book, these words are spoken by a boy who is overweight and unpopular, but still has the courage to run for president of the student council. He says these words in his speech to the whole student body:

> "Sticks and stones may break my bones, but names will never hurt me. Anybody who believes that has never been called a name. This is what I think about names. I think that names are a very small way of looking at a person. Another thing I think about names is that they do hurt. They hurt because we believe them. We think they are telling us something true about ourselves, something other people can see even if we don't."
>
> —Bobby Goodspeed, in *The Misfits* by James Howe

Ask students to respond to Bobby Goodspeed's words. Then ask: **Are there other actions or gestures that can hurt our feelings even if not a single word is spoken?** (Examples might include being laughed at or having people roll their eyes when you walk by.)

Ask: **In order to have a get-along classroom, why is it especially important that we not use hurtful words and gestures? What can we do as a class to put an end to different forms of hurtfulness?**

Activity. Allow three minutes for students to do automatic writing (see page 8) in their journals on how they've been affected by name-calling. Ask them to think about what they can do if they have the urge to say or do something hurtful to another person.

Wrap-Up. Direct students' attention to the pledge on the chart paper (and on their handouts). End by having everyone say the pledge together.

Follow-Up. Post the pledge in front of the room, referring to it daily.

Extension. Put students in pairs and pass out the poster paper and markers. Have students create posters entitled, "No More Hurtful Words or Actions." When posters are complete, have students hang them throughout the school.

What Real Kids Have to Say About
Mean Words

In a national survey of more than 2,100 students in grades 3–6, kids reported the top three things that made them mad, caused conflicts, and led to fights: **being teased or made fun of, name-calling, rumors and gossip**

Here are some things kids said:

- "People call me names and make me, oh, so very mad."
- "I hate it when people call me loser, idiot, retard."
- "I cry when someone calls me names."
- "Someone called my friend stupid, slow, disgusting, and useless. No one stood up for her. It was horrible."
- "It stresses me out when people say mean things about my family."
- "Something that made me really mad was when this kid called me weird and gay. It led to a physical fight."

What do YOU have to say about mean words?

How do you feel when people make fun of you or call you names? Do you ever do this to people? If so, why?

_____

_____

_____

_____

Take the Pledge!

I pledge not to use words, jokes, or gestures that hurt others or put them down in any way.

_____

signature

Lesson 23: Standing Up for Those Who Are Mistreated

kindness • compassion • respect • personal responsibility • decency

Lesson 23 helps students think of ways they can support peers who are called names or teased in other ways and practice being upstanders.

Students will
- be guided to choose kind actions, particularly when others are being unkind
- role-play being upstanders in situations where someone is being treated with meanness or intolerance

Materials
- chart paper and marker
- handouts: "8 Ways to Be an Upstander" (page 65); "Kindness Worksheet" (page 67)

Preparation. On chart paper, write: *"I am only one; but still I am one. I cannot do everything, but still I can do something. I will not refuse to do the something I can do."* —Helen Keller

Introduction and Discussion. Ask students if they've ever chosen to be kind to someone everyone else was being mean to. Ask if they've ever been an upstander for someone who was being mistreated. Discuss, acknowledging how hard this can be.

Show the Helen Keller quote and invite a student to read it. Ask: **What is "something we can do" when someone's being called names or made fun of by others? Why does it take courage to choose to be kind when others aren't or to stick up for someone when no one else does?**

Activity. Present the following scenarios, or scenarios students suggest. After reading each scenario aloud, ask students to suggest ways they could support the person who was mistreated. List students' responses on chart paper. Title the list "Kind Choices We Can Make When People Are Unkind." (**Note:** Current research has found that supporting people who are being bullied or picked on is more effective than saying something to the people who are mistreating them.) Now have students role-play each scenario, demonstrating how they would support the person being picked on.

- Mehmet gives the wrong answer to a question the teacher asks. Other kids start to snicker and make faces.

- Hannah comes to school wearing a shirt with a big stain on it. Her hair is all tangled and looks like it hasn't been washed in a while. A few kids hold their noses as she walks by.

- Jason has trouble reading. He stumbles over some simple words that most of the class can easily read. Someone makes a joke about Jason's reading. A few kids start to laugh.

- Kai tends to be awkward around other kids. Sometimes she talks too loud. People find her annoying. She always ends up sitting alone at lunch.

Distribute the "8 Ways to Be an Upstander" handout and review the ways to help people who are picked on. Encourage students to come up with other upstander actions to add to the handout.

Wrap-Up. Affirm students for acts of kindness, compassion, and good listening you observed during this lesson. Ask whether anyone would also like to acknowledge a classmate for any positive actions or attitudes.

Follow-Up. Have students complete the "Kindness Worksheet." Note that the worksheet will be used in Lesson 24.

8 Ways to Be an Upstander

1. Choose not to be a passive bystander. Doing nothing allows the mean behavior to continue.

2. Choose not to join in when people are picking on or laughing at someone.

3. Try distracting the person or people who are teasing someone. Find a way to change the subject or shift the focus to something else.

4. Ask the person who's being targeted to join you in something that will get him or her away from the people who are being unkind.

5. Show you care: Say something kind, supportive, and understanding to the person who was mistreated.

6. Ask the person being mistreated how he or she is doing. Listen with compassion and don't judge what he or she says.

7. Offer to walk the person to class. Also check in later to see how he or she is doing. You could call, email, or write a note. Consider doing this multiple times. Let the person see that you care.

8. Help the person and tell an adult what's going on.

What else can you do? _____

_____

_____

_____

_____

_____

_____

Lesson 24: Thinking About Kindness

kindness • compassion • respect • personal responsibility • decency

Lesson 24 asks students to reflect on their willingness to be kind, even when others aren't.

Students will

- reflect on how kind they've been to others and how others have been kind to them
- reflect on the challenges of being kind when others aren't
- role-play intervening when an act of unkindness takes place

Materials

- handout: "Kindness Worksheet" (page 67; see Preparation, below)
- globe (see page 7)

Preparation. Prior to this lesson, pass out copies of the "Kindness Worksheet" and ask students to complete it ahead of time and bring it to this lesson. Encourage students to answer the questions with complete honesty. Let them know you'll be completing the worksheet, too.

Introduction. Have students bring their "Kindness Worksheets" to the circle. Tell them you're going to be asking them to share their answers, and that you'll be sharing, too. Remind students not to use people's real names when they share, and to be as honest as possible.

Discussion. Discuss each question on the handout together:

- How kind have I been today?
- What acts of unkindness have I witnessed?
- What did I think when I saw the unkind acts taking place?
- What did I do when I saw the unkind acts taking place?
- What can I do if something like this happens again?
- What acts of kindness have I witnessed?
- What acts of kindness have I performed?

Talk together about realistic challenges kids face in trying to be kind when others aren't. For example, kids may say, "I wanted to say something when my friends were picking on somebody, but I didn't because I was afraid they might get mad at me." Or, "I'm afraid if I say something, I'll get picked on, too." Help students come up with viable solutions.

Activity. Ask for several volunteers to role-play the following scenario:

Jeffrey is in a wheelchair. When Nick and Kalil see him they call him names and make fun of him. They try to get their friends to join in. Nora and Chris are upset by this unkindness. They decide to be upstanders for Jeffrey.

After the role play is complete, debrief with the class. How did the role play go? Ask Jeffrey: **How did you feel when Nora and Chris intervened?** Ask Nora and Chris: **How did you get the courage to be upstanders?** Ask Nick and Kalil: **How did it feel to have people step in when you were being mean?** Ask the class if they can picture themselves being upstanders for someone who's being mistreated.

Wrap-Up. Hold up or point to a globe. Ask students how our world might be different if people were kinder to each other. Challenge students to be kind in word and deed throughout the rest of the day.

Extension. Have students make a Kindness Commercial that they can deliver in person, in writing, over the school intercom, or on video. Arrange for them to take their commercial "on the road" to other classes and schools.

Kindness Worksheet

Answer each question honestly. Use the back of this sheet or extra paper if you need more room.

How kind have I been today? _____

_____

_____

What acts of unkindness have I witnessed? (Don't use real names.)_____

_____

_____

What did I think when I saw the unkind acts taking place?_____

_____

_____

What did I do when I saw the unkind acts taking place? _____

_____

_____

What can I do if something like this happens again? _____

_____

_____

What acts of kindness have I witnessed? _____

_____

_____

What acts of kindness have I performed?_____

_____

_____

Lesson 25: Listening with Care and Openness

respect • personal responsibility

Lesson 25 gives students the opportunity to practice listening with an open, caring heart and mind when someone else speaks.

Students will

- review the elements of respectful listening
- practice using respectful listening and paraphrasing what they hear
- understand that listening respectfully shows care for others

Materials

- "Respectful Listening" chart from Lesson 2 (page 23)
- handout: "How I Learned to Listen" (page 69)

Introduction. Review the "Respectful Listening" chart. Ask students how it feels when someone really cares about what they have to say and listens with an open heart and mind. Briefly discuss. Tell your students how you feel when you are listened to in this way.

Tell students they will have the opportunity to practice listening with care and respect during this lesson.

Activity and Discussion. Ask for two volunteers to come to the center of the circle. Ask one student to describe to the other a birthday he or she celebrated that was especially happy. Tell the student who listens to do so with complete focus as though there's no one else in the room. When the first child finishes talking, have the child who listened paraphrase the main idea of what was said. The listener can start paraphrasing with the words "I'm hearing you say" or "It sounds like" and can also name the feeling the other person conveyed. Here's an example: "I'm hearing you say that your ninth birthday was the best ever. Your mom took you and five of your friends roller skating and then out for pizza. You sound really excited about it."

Ask the student who shared the birthday story how it felt to be listened to with such care and interest. Ask the listener: **What was it like to really care and pay attention while you listened?** Ask everyone: **What would it be like if people listened in this way more of the time?**

Have a volunteer read aloud the story on the handout about a student who realized she wasn't such a good listener and decided to become one.

Ask students to respond to the story.

Now have students pair up to practice respectful listening. Have pairs choose a Person A and Person B. Person A will ask Person B the question from the role play: "Can you tell me about a birthday you celebrated that was especially happy?" (Alternatively, Person A can ask another question you and students choose.) Person A needs to listen with total focus and then paraphrase the main idea (starting with "I'm hearing you say" or "It sounds like"). Person B can repeat anything important that might have been missed. If that happens, tell Person A to paraphrase it again. Then have partners switch roles so both get the chance to speak and listen.

Wrap-Up. Ask students how it felt to be listened to with care and respect. Ask how being good listeners might help them at school and in other parts of their lives. Discuss. Affirm students for good listening you observed.

Follow-Up. Tell students to continue practicing respectful listening throughout the day, including at home. Refer to the bottom of the handout and encourage them to notice the effect of their listening on others.

How I Learned to Listen

People used to always get annoyed with me, and I couldn't figure out why. One day it happened again—the kid who sat next to me seemed to get mad at me out of the blue. So I got up the courage to ask him why he was mad at me. He said it was because I was always interrupting. He said, "Every time I talk, you cut me off and start talking about what you want to talk about. You don't seem to care about what I have to say."

He was right. I always wanted to do the talking. I didn't have the patience to listen. The truth hurt, but I guess I needed to hear it. That night when I went home I started noticing how often I'd get the urge to interrupt. It was hard for me to stop. No wonder people kept getting mad at me!

I made up my mind I would change, but I didn't know how. So I decided to watch people who were really good listeners and see how they did it. I thought of this kid in my class named Saj and remembered how, whenever anyone talked to him, he always listened with complete interest. It felt so good to be around him.

I started paying more attention to what Saj did so I could learn from him. I noticed a couple of things right away: He was really patient and he never interrupted. He always looked right at you when you talked to him, like you were the only person in the room. His eyes never drifted over your head.

So I started trying to do what he did. I would think about how Saj listened whenever I was with anybody. I had to work hard to catch myself when I wanted to interrupt.

I'm doing a lot better now, and I have more friends. I like myself better now that I know how to truly listen.

Respectful Listening Challenge

Throughout the day, try to listen as well as Saj did.
Tune in to the people you're listening to.
Show you care.

At the end of the day, think about the effect of your respectful listening on others and on yourself.

Lesson 26: Being Excluded

empathy • kindness • acceptance • personal responsibility • decency

Lesson 26 helps students see that excluding others is hurtful and encourages them to include kids who are left out.

Students will
- reflect on what it feels like to be excluded
- use reflective listening to hear and understand the feelings of another
- understand the importance of including others

Materials
- student journals
- *optional: Blubber* by Judy Blume

Introduction. Read aloud the following story a boy wrote in the Survey About Conflicts:

"Early in the school year no one I knew would play with me. I didn't know why. I asked if I could play with other people. They said no. I wandered around school looking for somebody to play with. No one would play with me. So I sat on the ground talking to myself. Fall and winter passed, still nobody."

Activity. Have students do several minutes of automatic writing in their journals about a time they were left out (or what it might have been like for the boy who wrote the story).

Ask students to pair up and read (or talk about) what they wrote. Ask them each to reflect back (paraphrase) the main idea of what the other person said. For example, "It sounds like you were really upset and lonely when your friends left you out."

Discussion. After students have shared with partners, have them reconvene in a circle. Ask them to share some of the thoughts and feelings that came up in this activity. Share your own feelings, too.

Ask: **What actions can each person take so no one in our class feels the way the boy who wrote the story felt?** Discuss. Then ask: **What can we do on the playground when someone isn't picked for a team or gets left out of games?**

Encourage students to talk about some of the real issues that come up for them when it comes to including someone they don't really want to include. As they speak, ask the class to think about viable solutions and practical actions they can take.

Wrap-Up. End by affirming students for acts of respect, kindness, compassion, and good listening you've observed. Ask if anyone in the group would like to acknowledge a classmate.

Extension. Have your students read *Blubber* by Judy Blume. In this book, Linda gets picked on and excluded by Jill and other kids in the class. Things change when the tables are turned on Jill, forcing her to find out what it's like to be the one who's left out. Available in Spanish: *La ballena.*

Lesson 27: Put-Ups, Not Put-Downs

respect • kindness • compassion • decency

Lesson 27 helps students learn to use *put-ups*—sincere words of acknowledgment and encouragement.

Students will

- understand the meaning and purpose of put-ups
- contrast the impact of put-downs and put-ups
- generate ideas for put-ups they can give to each other

Materials

- chart paper and marker
- student journals
- *optional:* brown construction paper, other construction paper, scissors, crayons or markers

Preparation. On chart paper, write: *"Put-ups, not put-downs."*

Introduction and Discussion. Ask students how they feel when put-downs are used against them. Ask: **How do you feel when you see put-downs being used against others?** Discuss.

Ask students how they feel when someone says positive, complimentary, or encouraging words to them. Discuss.

Introduce the idea of *put-ups*—words and phrases that are positive, encouraging, and complimentary. Guide students to understand that a put-up should always be sincere and deserved: something the person giving it truly means and the person receiving it truly deserves, as opposed to a fake compliment. Demonstrate by giving a put-up to a student, such as: "Your listening has improved so much recently" or "I notice how you always offer a helping hand."

Ask for a few examples of put-ups from students. Encourage them to resist superficial statements like "Nice shirt," focusing instead on a person's positive actions, personal qualities, or character traits. Caution students that true put-ups are never used in a sarcastic way. Doing this turns put-ups into put-downs.

Refer to the words you wrote on the chart paper, "Put-ups, not put-downs." Ask a student to read them aloud. Ask: **Would this be a good policy for our class? Why?** Discuss.

Activity. Put students in pairs. On paper or in journals, have students brainstorm as many put-ups as they can think of.

After about three minutes, have students share their put-ups with the class. List these on a chart entitled "Put-Ups." If no one comes up with "Nice try," suggest it yourself. Encourage kids to use this put-up when classmates make mistakes.

Wrap-Up. Tell your class the put-up chart will be posted as a reminder of things they can say each day. Acknowledge students for their teamwork and ideas and for any acts of kindness, compassion, and respectful listening you observed during this lesson.

Follow-Up. After the lesson, laminate the "Put-Ups" chart and post it prominently in the room. Keep using the put-ups listed on the chart, and remind students to do the same.

Extension. Have kids make a "Put-Up Tree" out of brown construction paper. Hang it on a wall in your room. Pass out leaves to every member of the class. Have them write a generic put-up (as opposed to a put-up directed at a specific person in the class) on each leaf. Hang the leaves on the tree. Refer to it often.

Lesson 28: Personal Put-Ups

respect • kindness • compassion • decency

In Lesson 28 you'll be affirming every student and giving students the opportunity to affirm each other.

Students will
- understand the importance of affirming each other with put-ups
- each receive a personal put-up from their teacher
- give personal put-ups to each other

Materials
- notecards
- student journals
- *optional:* chart paper and marker

Preparation. Prior to this lesson, on a notecard write a brief personal put-up for every child. It can be as simple as "You have a wonderful smile." Put the child's name at the top and sign your name at the bottom.

Introduction. Have students gather in a circle. If you haven't done Lesson 27, introduce the idea of put-ups now—words and phrases students can say to each other that are positive, encouraging, sincere, and complimentary. Put-ups might be about things someone's good at, talents or skills they possess, or positive qualities such as kindness, helpfulness, or a good sense of humor.

Activity. Tell students that you appreciate each and every one of them, and today you're going to give every person in the class an individual put-up. Go around the circle, affirming each student by name. Make direct eye contact with every child as you do this. Afterward, give all students their written put-ups.

Next, tell students they will now do a put-up activity with a partner. Explain that the activity is an opportunity for them to be kind and accepting toward their partner, whoever she or he might be. Have each student turn to the person he or she is sitting next to and face the person directly. Say: **Look at your partner. Think of something positive you've noticed about this person. Maybe he or she has shown kindness toward others or has a special talent. Maybe the person is helpful or caring or has a great sense of humor. Tell your partner the positive thing you've noticed about him or her. Look directly at your partner as you give your put-up.** Remind students: **Even if you're not friends with each other, do your best to think of at least one positive thing you've sincerely noticed about this person. Be generous with kindness.**

Discussion. After the activity, ask students how it felt to be affirmed with a put-up. Share how you felt as you watched your students giving each other put-ups. Ask students: **How does it feel when our classroom is filled with put-ups and we show care and kindness toward each other?**

Wrap-Up. Encourage students to keep affirming one another daily with personal put-ups. Tell them that put-ups contribute to the peace and kindness everyone wants to have in the classroom and in the world.

Follow-Up. Encourage students to give personal put-ups to other people in their lives, such as family members and friends. After they've given personal put-ups, suggest that they think or write in their journals about the impact of the put-ups upon the people who received them and upon their own lives.

Extension. Have each child randomly select the name of another classmate and write a letter of affirmation—a put-up letter—to the person whose name they chose. Prior to writing, take a few minutes to brainstorm with the class a general list of positive qualities people might possess. If time allows, you can also model on chart paper how to write a letter of affirmation to someone you don't know extremely well. Example:

Dear Kim,

I think you're a really caring person.

Last week when James forgot his markers you offered to share yours. And last week when Katie didn't have a snack you gave her part of yours. You are very kind, and I wish more people were like you. I'm glad you're in our class.

Sincerely, Mei Lee

Lesson 29: Rumors Are Unkind

respect • empathy • kindness • decency • personal responsibility

Lesson 29 fosters the understanding that rumors can poison the atmosphere around us. The lesson helps build a sense of personal responsibility when it comes to resisting spreading rumors.

Students will

- understand the negative impact of rumors
- understand the need to always avoid spreading rumors
- come up with words that can be used to deflect the spread of rumors

Materials

- colored construction paper
- chart paper and marker
- handout: "Rumors Are Unkind Reflection Sheet" (page 74)

Preparation. Prior to the lesson ask a pair of students to trace and cut out the outlines of one another's feet, each set on a different color construction paper.

Introduction. Compliment your students for any positive things you've observed in the areas of respect, acceptance, empathy, or kindness.

Tell them that today you're going to be addressing the issue of rumors. Distribute the handout and ask a student to read the statistic it cites from the Survey About Conflicts: 64 percent of students listed rumors and gossip as the top cause of conflicts in their lives.

Ask students if they think rumors are a big problem. Discuss briefly.

Activity. Demonstrate the trajectory of a rumor by playing a short game of telephone. Whisper a rumor about a pretend person into the ear of the first student. Let the rumor spread through the circle.

Have the last person come to the center of the circle and stand on one set of footprints and share with the class whatever the rumor "morphed" into.

Have another student pretend to be the person the rumor was about. Have him or her come to the center of the circle and stand on the other set of footprints facing the first person.

Ask the second child to imagine what it would really be like to have had this rumor spread about him or her. How would it feel? Ask the child to look into the eyes of the other person and describe those feelings.

Ask the first child to paraphrase what was just said, reflecting back the main idea and feelings the other person conveyed. ("I'm hearing you say that . . .")

Discussion. Ask: What do you think about the rumor we all took part in spreading? Discuss briefly.

On the board, write, "Rumors hurt." Ask students to think about how rumors and gossip create conflicts. Discuss, reminding students not to use real names if they relate personal stories. Ask: What do you think is the right thing to do if someone comes to you with a rumor? What can you say if someone gossips or tells you a rumor about someone else?

Have students pair up and think of at least two responses that can be given to someone who approaches them with a rumor. Model one possible response before they begin: "I'm uncomfortable hearing this. Please don't tell me any more." Encourage students to start from "I," not "you."

After about five minutes have students share some of the responses they came up with for deflecting rumors. List them on chart paper under the title "Stamp Out Rumors."

Wrap-Up. Ask students to imagine what their classroom and school would be like if rumors were completely abolished. Call on a few students. Then ask: Who does creating a rumor-free environment start with? Whose responsibility is it to make sure rumors don't get spread?

Follow-Up. Have students complete the "Rumors Are Unkind Reflection Sheet," being as honest and thorough as they can. Note that the handout will be used in Lesson 30.

Rumors Are Unkind
Reflection Sheet

In a national survey of more than 2,100 students in grades 3–6: **64% of students** surveyed listed rumors and gossip as the top cause of conflicts in their lives.

> **Here's what one student wrote:**
>
> "There were rumors being spread about what people were wearing and how they looked. This girl I know was making fun of my friend because her teeth were crooked. It kept getting worse. I don't think it's fair to make fun of people who don't look exactly like everybody else. Everyone is different."

What do YOU think about rumors?
Answer the following questions.

1. In the quoted story above, how do you think the people who were talked about felt? How would you feel if you were one of them?

   _____

   _____

2. Have you ever spread a rumor? What happened?

   _____

   _____

3. Have you ever had rumors spread about you? How did you feel?

   _____

   _____

4. When it comes to rumors, what can you do to be part of the solution?

   _____

   _____

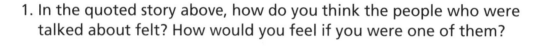

Lesson 30: Stamp Out Rumors

respect • empathy • kindness • decency • personal responsibility

Lesson 30 empowers students to take responsibility toward stopping the rumor cycle. The lesson is a follow-up to Lesson 29.

Students will
- reflect on the impact of rumors in their lives
- role-play being an upstander for someone about whom rumors are being spread
- know how to be a part of the solution to rumors and gossip

Materials
- "Stamp Out Rumors" chart from Lesson 29 and markers
- completed handout: "Rumors Are Unkind Reflection Sheet" (page 74)
- *optional: Mr. Peabody's Apples* by Madonna

Preparation. Make sure students have completed the "Rumors Are Unkind Reflection Sheet" prior to this lesson. Have them bring their sheets to the circle at the start of the lesson.

Introduction. On the board write: "Rumors _____." Ask for a volunteer to come to the board and fill in the blank. (Acceptable answers can include: hurt, are unkind, make people mad, cause conflicts, etc.)

Discussion. Ask students to share the most important things they learned from the last lesson on rumors.

Have students take out their completed handouts. Go through each question and ask for volunteers to share their responses and reflections. Discuss.

Ask students if they've had the opportunity to apply what they learned about stopping the spread of rumors. Caution students not to use real names when sharing. Acknowledge that stopping the spread of a rumor can be harder when it's about someone you don't like. Help students recognize and understand that stopping *all* rumors is important.

Activity. Tell students they're going to have the chance to role-play a conflict that was sparked by a rumor spread about real kids. Read the following:

"I was in a conflict when this girl emailed my friend and said all this mean stuff about us. Then she started telling the whole school all the things she'd written in the email, and these terrible rumors about us got started. It went so far that my friend and I finally went to the principal. The rumors stopped after the principal had us talk everything out."

Call on students to role-play the scene. Have a child play the role of one of the girls about whom the rumors were being spread. Have another child play the role of the girl who started the rumors. Have two more kids play the roles of upstanders who work to stop the rumor from going further when approached by the girl who is spreading it. Refer to the "Stamp Out Rumors" chart for examples of things the upstanders can say to stop rumors.

Wrap-Up. Refer back to the "Stamp Out Rumors" chart. Ask students if there are any other words or actions that can be added. Remind them that you'll be checking in from time to time to see how they're doing in regard to helping stop the rumor cycle.

Extensions. Have students work with a friend to make "Stamp Out Rumors" posters. Display the posters in the classroom and around the school.

Share the children's picture book *Mr. Peabody's Apples* by Madonna. Although the format of this book may seem more suited to younger students, its retelling of a 300-year-old story depicting the impact of a single rumor has universal appeal.

Lesson 31: What Is Conscience?

respect • decency • integrity • compassion • personal responsibility

Lesson 31 helps students understand the meaning and purpose of conscience.

Students will

- understand the meaning of conscience
- reflect on why it's important to listen to the voice of one's conscience
- be better able to listen to the voice of their conscience, choosing right over wrong

Materials

- chart paper and marker
- handouts: "What Real Kids Have to Say About Struggling with Conscience" (page 77); "Doing What Is Right" (pages 80–81); "Conscience Interview" (page 78)

Preparation. On chart paper, write: *"Conscience—A feeling or knowledge of right and wrong that guides us to do what is right."*

Introduction. Write the word *conscience* on the board. Ask students what it means. Then share the definition you've prepared. Have a student read it aloud. Then paraphrase, saying: **Conscience is a kind of goodness inside each of us that can guide us to do the right thing.**

Discussion. Distribute copies of the "What Real Kids Have to Say About Struggling with Conscience" handout and read or have a student read the real story from the Survey About Conflicts. Ask: **What did this boy's conscience first guide him to do? Why didn't he continue to follow his conscience? How did the boy feel at the end of the story?**

Ask students: **How does it feel to ignore what the goodness inside us guides us to do?** Discuss.

Ask students if there's a different way the boy who wrote the story could have handled this situation. Then ask: **Were the boy's friends in the story really true friends? Why or why not?** Guide students to understand that the boy who wrote the story ignored the voice of his conscience for the sake of kids whose actions were not those of true friends.

Activity. Ask students to pair up. Have them think of a time when they struggled with conscience, describing to partners what happened and how they felt. Ask students to write about their experiences on the handouts or in their journals. After about five minutes, have students reconvene in a circle.

Ask students to share their experiences, either reading what they wrote or talking about it. Caution them not to use real names.

Wrap-Up. Ask students: **How does it feel to follow your conscience, even when it's a hard thing to do?** Emphasize that when people listen to the voice of their conscience, they usually end up feeling at peace with themselves, even if they had to make a hard choice. Encourage students to notice what their conscience is telling them in the days ahead.

Follow-Up. Have students complete the "Doing What Is Right" handout. Note that the worksheet will be used in Lesson 32.

Extension. Distribute the "Conscience Interview" handout and encourage students to interview someone and discuss the quote about conscience. At the beginning of the next lesson you conduct, invite students to share some of the things they learned from their interviews about conscience.

What Real Kids Have to Say About
Struggling with Conscience

In a national survey of more than 2,100 students in grades 3–6, here is what one student wrote:

"There is this one kid *everyone* picks on but me. Sometimes I would defend him, but when I did my friends called me weird. They stopped accepting me. This kid now thinks he's my best friend and bugs me all the time.

"My friends finally started to accept me again. Now I pretend to tease the other kid so I don't lose all my friends again. But I feel bad because I really feel sorry for him."

Write about a time when you
struggled with your conscience:

_____

_____

_____

_____

_____

_____

_____

_____

Conscience Interview

"Each person has inside a basic decency and goodness. If he listens to it and acts on it, he is giving a great deal of what it is the world needs most. It is not complicated but it takes courage. It takes courage for a person to listen to his own good." —Pablo Casals

1. **Interview someone you trust and respect.** Read the Pablo Casals quote to the person. Ask him or her these questions:

   • What does the quote mean to you?

   • Do you know someone who listened to his or her own goodness and acted on it, even though other people did not? What happened?

   • Do you think it takes courage to follow your conscience? Why?

2. **After your interview,** write about something you learned from the person you interviewed:

   _____

   _____

   _____

   _____

   _____

   _____

   _____

   _____

   _____

   _____

   _____

   _____

Lesson 32: Listening to the Voice of Your Conscience

> **respect • decency • integrity • personal responsibility**

Lesson 32 gives students the opportunity to reflect on the importance of living by one's conscience.

Students will

- understand that the time is always right to do what's right
- be guided to take responsibility for choosing between right and wrong
- understand that they can make amends if they have done something wrong

Materials

- chart paper and marker
- handout: "Doing What Is Right" (pages 80–81; see Preparation, below)
- globe (see page 7)

Preparation. Prior to this lesson, pass out copies of the "Doing What Is Right" handout and ask students to complete it ahead of time and bring it to this lesson.

Introduction. Write the word *conscience* on the board. Review the meaning of it—a feeling or knowledge of right and wrong that guides us to do what is right. Have students take out their completed "Doing What Is Right" handouts and ask a volunteer to read the Martin Luther King Jr. quote at the top: "The time is always right to do what is right."

Discussion and Activity. Ask students what the quote means to them. Discuss.

Go over the questions on the handout one by one, sharing and discussing students' ideas and responses.

Students may struggle with question 6. Some kids think telling an adult is "snitching"—and that this violates a code of ethics. Help them see that seeking the aid of an adult when someone is being harmed, especially when other measures have failed, can keep someone from being hurt and may prevent other bullying situations.

Note: You will want to continue to address the complex issues that students face regarding bullying. Many of the lessons that remain in Part 2 will be helpful to you, especially those in the Dealing with Bullying section, pages 217–260.

Ask: **How do you feel when you don't follow your conscience?** Discuss. Point out that everyone makes wrong decisions at times, and that we each can recognize our mistakes and work to do better next time.

Ask: **What can you do if you choose not to follow your conscience and then feel guilty about it afterward?** Include in your discussion the importance of taking responsibility and apologizing if necessary. Ask students to think of a way they could make *amends*—do something to make things better—for something they did in the past.

Wrap-Up. Hold up or point to a globe. Say: **Having a more peaceful world depends on people of conscience doing the right thing. What do you think the world would be like if everyone listened to the voice of their conscience?**

Doing What Is Right

"The time is always right to do what is right." —Martin Luther King Jr.

1. Think of a book or movie where a person had to choose between doing what was right and what was wrong. What did the person do? Describe what happened.

_____

_____

_____

2. What did you think about the decision this person made?

_____

_____

_____

3. Think of a time when you were faced with a decision between right and wrong. (For example: to tell the truth or not tell the truth, or to admit a mistake or pretend nothing happened.) What happened? What did you decide to do?

_____

_____

_____

Doing What Is Right (continued)

4. How did you feel about the decision you made?

_____

_____

_____

_____

5. Why do you think it's important to listen to your conscience and follow it?

_____

_____

_____

_____

6. If you see someone being bullied or picked on, what do you think is the right thing to do? How can your conscience help you do the right thing?

_____

_____

_____

_____

Managing Anger

Teaching kids how to control their anger is an important way to help prevent bullying. Sometimes incidences of bullying are triggered by angry interchanges and resentful feelings that follow. By providing kids with real-life tools to use when anger strikes, we set the stage for more positive relationships while diminishing seeds of resentment that might otherwise germinate into full-blown bullying.

This section provides step-by-step anger-management strategies that are easy to use, highly effective, and become more and more natural for kids to apply each time they practice them. Breathing techniques, visualizations, and role plays are among the many activities you'll find in this section. You'll also find out how to help kids keep from getting physical when they're angry. Stop, Breathe, Chill (introduced in Lesson 9) is students' most powerful anger-management strategy. Reread that lesson for a step-by-step refresher before you begin the Managing Anger section.

Note: These lessons follow a sequence. Even if you don't use every lesson, conduct the ones you choose to do in the order they are presented.

Lesson 33: Things That Make Us Mad

personal responsibility • anger management • self-control

Lesson 33 builds students' awareness of their anger triggers and guides them to use calming strategies that will help them "unhook" from negative reactions.

Students will
- understand that anger is a natural emotion that everyone feels at times
- explore common anger triggers in kids
- review Stop, Breathe, Chill as a way of constructively responding to anger

Materials
- handout: "What Real Kids Have to Say About Anger Triggers" (pages 85–86)
- *optional:* student journals

Introduction. Ask students to raise their hands if they ever get angry. Raise yours, too. Ask kids what makes them angry. Discuss briefly, making sure they understand that anger is a natural emotion we all feel from time to time.

Say: **Even though anger in itself isn't a bad thing, sometimes people make bad or harmful choices when they get mad. What are some negative choices people make when they get angry?** (hitting, yelling, name-calling, etc.)

Then continue: **The good news is that it's possible to react more calmly when we're angry and to be more in control of the choices we make. How might your life be better if you could avoid making negative, hurtful choices when you're angry?** Discuss.

Ask students to suggest a few positive choices they can make in the face of anger (deep breathing, walking away, telling themselves it's not worth it to lash out, etc.).

Discussion. Say: **Being aware of what makes us angry is the first step in gaining more control over how we react.** Share something that makes you really angry. Then ask: **What makes you really angry?** Allow for a couple responses.

Distribute the handouts and read or have a student read the top three anger triggers students reported in the Survey About Conflicts. Ask: **What does *anger trigger* mean? Can you relate to boys' and girls' top three anger triggers? What are some other anger triggers?**

Go around the circle having students, one at a time, read aloud the quotes about anger triggers. Then ask: **Which of these quotes do you identify with most?** Allow a few students to respond. Discuss.

Put students in pairs and give them a few minutes to share about things that make them really angry, describing how they feel when they get mad. Afterward, have students reconvene in the large circle. Ask them to look at the handout and find the part that can help them calm down when their anger is triggered (Stop, Breathe, Chill). Tell students they'll be getting lots of practice using this and other calming strategies in future lessons.

Wrap-Up. Reiterate that anger is a natural emotion, one we all have, and there are ways we can get in better control of our reactions when anger is triggered. Remind students to use Stop, Breathe, Chill the next time they feel angry. Say: **Remember, the minute you feel the anger in your body and mind, hold up a big red stop sign in your head and silently say "Stop." Then take a few slow, deep abdominal breaths. Let's take some now.** (Breathe together). **Then do something else to help yourself chill out. What might that be?**

Follow-Up. Let students know you'll be checking in with them about how they're using Stop, Breathe, Chill in real life. When you check in with your students, tell them how you're using it, too.

Extension. In journals, have students write the words "Anger Bin" at the top of a page. Tell them to write out or draw their anger in the "Anger Bin" next time they feel it, describing or showing what happened and how they reacted. Remind them that whatever they record is just for them and not to be shared with peers. Have them also write about or draw what they can do to calm down.

What Real Kids Have to Say About
Anger Triggers

In a national survey of more than 2,100 students in grades 3–6, kids answered a question about what makes them angry. Here are some things they said:

It makes me angry when people . . .

- talk behind my back
- say I did something that I didn't do
- hit me and pick on me because of my size
- call me weak and say no one likes me
- make fun of me because I don't have a mom
- hurt others for no reason
- pick on younger kids
- make me feel like I'm invisible
- talk to me but won't listen
- make threats
- judge me 'cause I'm different
- are racist when they talk about people's families
- tease me and say I'm poor and have moldy food
- throw stuff at me and flip my tray over
- lie, write notes, and tell people not to be my friend
- exclude me, steal stuff from me, and make fun of me
- say my name wrong on purpose
- say I'm ugly and then say, "Kidding!" and laugh
- make little jokes that are funny to them and not to me
- think they're way better than someone else

What Real Kids Have to Say About Anger Triggers (continued)

Here are the top 3 anger triggers from boys and girls who took the survey:

Top 3 Anger Triggers for Boys

1. name-calling
2. being made fun of
3. hitting, kicking, and pushing

Top 3 Anger Triggers for Girls

1. name-calling
2. being made fun of
3. gossiping

When you feel yourself getting angry, here's how to get in better control of your reactions:

1. **Stop.** Picture a big red stop sign, and silently tell yourself to STOP.

2. **Breathe.** Take some slow deep breaths. Feel the oxygen calming your body and mind.

3. **Chill.** Do something that helps you calm down. You might:

   go for a walk   play an instrument   look out the window

   talk with a friend   drink some water

   play a game   exercise   draw

What else can you do to help yourself chill out?

Lesson 34: It's Okay to Be Angry, But Not to Be Cruel

compassion • decency • anger management • self-control

Lesson 34 helps students reflect on the impact of cruel words and actions and avoid using them when angry.

Students will

- gain greater sensitivity toward the feelings of others
- understand that using cruel words and gestures is never okay

Materials

- colored construction paper
- chart paper and marker
- handout: "What Real Kids Have to Say About Angry Reactions" (page 89)
- plain lined paper for brainstorming

Preparation. Prior to the lesson, ask a pair of students to trace and cut out the outlines of one another's feet, each set on a different color construction paper. Also, on chart paper, write the following: *"I have the right to feel angry, but that doesn't give me the right to be cruel."*

Introduction. Gather students in a circle. Share the statement you've written and ask a student to read it aloud. Ask: **What does this statement mean to you?**

Say: **Anger is a natural emotion all people feel. However, using mean words or hurting others when we're angry is never okay.** Tell students how it makes you feel as a teacher when you see kids saying or doing mean things to each other. Ask students how they feel when they observe cruel acts.

Discussion. Distribute the handouts and read or have a student read the quotes from kids who responded to the Survey About Conflicts. Invite comments from students about how it feels to be treated meanly by someone who is angry.

Pass out the plain paper. Say: **We've been talking about how it feels to be hurt by the anger of others. Think about times *you* directed cruel words or actions toward someone you were mad at.**

Have students take their plain paper to a private spot. Give them about two minutes to individually brainstorm a list of hurtful words or gestures they or others have used in anger. Let students know that each list is confidential. No one will see it but them.

At the end of two minutes, ask students to fold up their lists and put them on or in their desks.

Have students return to the circle. Ask them how it felt to remember these hurtful words and actions. Discuss, cautioning students not to use real names.

Activity. Tell students they're now going to have an opportunity to look more closely at the impact of mean words. Place the sets of footprints in the middle of the circle so students standing on them will face one another. Ask for two volunteers, Student A and Student B. Have them stand on the footprints facing each other.

Then say: **Student A, I want you to "put yourself in the shoes" of someone who says hurtful things when she or he gets mad. While you're on the footprints, you will *be* that person.**

Student B, your role is to "put yourself in the shoes" of someone who takes things to heart and gets hurt easily.

Then say to Student A: **Imagine Student B accidentally bumped into you when you were lining up. You're mad! React to Student B with mean words.**

After hearing the words, ask Student B to describe for the class how these words made him or her feel.

If time allows, repeat the process with two more students, having each put themselves in the shoes of someone who reacts quickly with mean words and someone who feels hurt or offended as a result. Use scenarios similar to these, or invite students to suggest scenarios:

- Student B tries to pass a football to a friend, but the ball goes too far and hits Student A. Student A shouts at Student B, telling the student that he/she is terrible at football and every other sport.

- Student B is wearing a sweater that is out of style. Student A says mean things that embarrass Student B in front of other people.

With each role play, ask Student B how it felt to have mean words directed at him or her. If a child says "I don't care," ask the class how they would feel if they were the recipient of these words. Talk about how you would feel, too.

Talk about how sometimes what might seem like "no big deal" to one person can actually be very hurtful to another person.

Wrap-Up. Conclude the activity by having students do a "No More Mean Words and Actions" ritual.

Have them take the lists they wrote at the beginning of the lesson, tear them up into small pieces, and throw them away. As they throw away the pieces, ask everyone to make a silent promise not to use cruel words or actions, even when they're really mad. Remind them to use Stop, Breathe, Chill and other calming strategies when anger rises up.

Extension. Set a Daylong Challenge: Ask the class to have a day without mean words, including at home. Remind them to take a few slow deep breaths if they feel like they're going to react to someone in a hurtful way.

What Real Kids Have to Say About
Angry Reactions

In a national survey of more than 2,100 students in grades 3–6, kids wrote about negative ways they deal with anger. Here are some things they wrote:

> • "I have anger issues. Sometimes I'm able to walk away, but sometimes I yell back and say mean things even though I know I shouldn't."
>
> • "Sometimes I get so mad I smack people and call them jerks."
>
> • "I want to know how to get along better, 'cause sometimes I can be kind of mean. Sometimes I'll push or hit. I want to stop doing these things. Once I get into high school I could get into serious trouble."

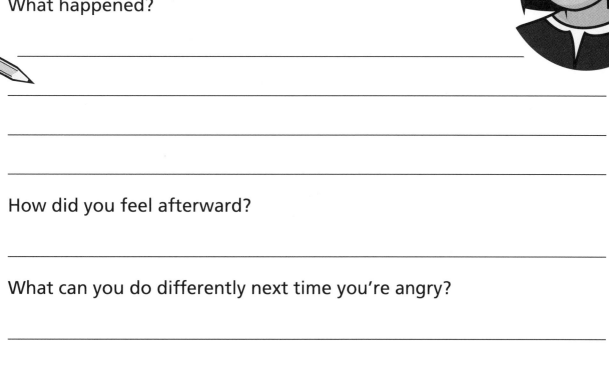

Write about a time you hurt someone (with words or actions) when you were angry.

What happened?

_____

_____

_____

_____

How did you feel afterward?

_____

What can you do differently next time you're angry?

_____

_____

Lesson 35: Responding to Anger

respect • anger management • self-control • personal responsibility

Lesson 35 encourages students to think about how they behave when they're angry and identify positive choices they can make in response to anger.

Students will
- complete a checklist of their positive and negative responses to anger
- evaluate whether responses they chose result in positive or negative outcomes
- identify healthy responses to anger they can work on developing

Materials
- handout: "When I Get Mad" (page 91)
- student journals

Introduction. Give each student a handout and go over it briefly. Then ask students to mark all of the responses to anger that they commonly have. If something they do isn't on the list, have them write it in at the bottom. Give students a few minutes to complete this.

Activity and Discussion. Have students get into pairs and talk about the items they checked off. After each item, have them ask themselves the question: **Did this choice make the situation get better or worse?** (Write the question on the board.) Have them discuss this together.

Next, have students reconvene in a circle. Ask them to share some of the things they do when they are angry. You share, too. Keep asking: **Did this choice make the situation (or problem) get better or worse? Did it help the relationship or harm it? Did it help you get along better with the other person or not?**

Now have students circle all of the positive responses to anger on the list. Have them choose two positive things on the list to work on in the coming weeks. Ask them to write the two things they chose in their journals as a reminder.

Wrap-Up. Go around the circle and have each student share one thing they plan to work on. Tell them what you plan to work on. Remind them that you'll be checking in with them about this during the week. Ask how doing this can help create a more peaceful classroom and world.

Extension. Ask students to remember a time they reacted to anger in a negative way. Tell them to think about what they did to make a situation between them and another person worse. Have them write or draw a journal entry about what happened, how they feel about it today, and what they would do if they could go back and change their reaction.

When I Get Mad

When I get mad at someone, I usually . . .

- ❏ push, hit, punch, or kick the person
- ❏ walk away from the situation to cool off
- ❏ use put-downs or name-calling
- ❏ take slow, deep breaths
- ❏ yell
- ❏ curse
- ❏ roll my eyes or give a nasty look
- ❏ do something positive that helps me calm down
- ❏ gossip about the other person
- ❏ get even with the person
- ❏ refuse to talk to the other person
- ❏ discuss the problem with a trusted adult

- ❏ ask the person to stop doing whatever is making me angry
- ❏ use Stop, Breathe, Chill
- ❏ stuff my feelings down and try to ignore them
- ❏ take out my anger on someone else
- ❏ ignore the person
- ❏ tattle
- ❏ talk to the person respectfully about how I feel
- ❏ _____
  _____
- ❏ _____
  _____
- ❏ _____
  _____

Think About It: Which of the checked items make the situation better?

Which work best? _____

_____

Two things I plan to work on:

1. _____

_____

2. _____

_____

Lesson 36: Peaceful Place Visualization

calming • personal responsibility

Lesson 36 introduces a visualization tool students can use to calm themselves when they feel angry, stressed, frightened, or upset. This calming technique can also help students relax and refocus before tests and during transition times.

Students will

- reflect on a place they've been where they felt calm and at peace
- learn a tool for calmness they can use daily, now and for the rest of their lives

Materials

- art and writing materials including paper, pencils, and markers
- handout: "Peaceful Place Visualization Script" (page 93)

Introduction. Tell students that today they'll be learning a very powerful way to feel calm inside, no matter what's happening on the outside.

Ask students to think of a place they've been where they felt happy, peaceful, relaxed, and safe. It can be a place close to home or far away. It might be a place from the past, like their grandmother's kitchen when they were little. (If students have difficulty coming up with a peaceful place, suggest they focus on a beach, park, or other natural setting.)

Call on students to share about their peaceful places. Share about yours. Make sure everyone in the class has come up with a peaceful place before going on with the activity.

Activity. Have students sit comfortably on the floor or in a chair; some kids may prefer to lie down on the floor. Tell students it's very important that they're completely silent during this activity. Ask them to close their eyes, cover them, or look down and take several slow, deep abdominal breaths.

Then read aloud the "Peaceful Place Visualization Script" (page 93), using a steady, calm voice.

When you finish reading the script, have students open their eyes. Ask how they feel. Allow a few students to share about the relaxing effect this visualization exercise had for them.

Assure any students who had difficulty envisioning their peaceful place that it often gets easier with practice. Let everyone know that doing this visualization on a regular basis can help them feel calmer and more relaxed, including before tests and other stressful events.

Ask students to take a few minutes to draw or write about their peaceful place. Encourage them to include as much vivid detail as possible. Drawing or writing in detail about their peaceful place will help them return to the vision of it whenever they need calmness.

Wrap-Up. Ask students to hang the drawing or story of their peaceful place in a spot where they'll see it every day. This can serve as a reminder of the peaceful place they hold inside. Their work can be displayed either in school or at home. Distribute the handout so students can use it at home.

Extensions. Suggest that students record their own voices reading the "Peaceful Place Visualization Script." Tell them they can listen to it before going to bed at night or at any time they feel stressed, upset, angry, or fearful.

Have students write a poem or haiku describing their Peaceful Place.

Peaceful Place Visualization Script

Close your eyes and breathe slowly and deeply. As you breathe, imagine your mind is a blank movie screen. Your screen is the color blue, a bright, soothing shade of blue, like the sky on a clear spring day. Allow this image to fill your mind completely.

Now project onto your screen an image of your peaceful place, a place you've been where you felt happy, relaxed, peaceful, and safe. Let this peaceful place completely fill the screen of your mind. Allow it to grow so large that the blue screen melts away and all that's left is the vision of your peaceful place.

Now, step into your peaceful place. Imagine being there right now. Look around and notice the colors. Now listen to the sounds of your peaceful place. *(Pause.)*

Breathe deeply and inhale the scent of your peaceful place. Allow it to fill your body, brain, arms, and legs. *(Pause.)*

Allow the good feelings you had when you were last in this peaceful place to completely fill your heart and spread out into every cell, the way rays of the sun give warmth to everything they touch.

If any distracting thoughts come up, put them on a cloud, and let the cloud float them away. Then gently bring your focus back to your peaceful place and let the good feelings soak into every part of you.

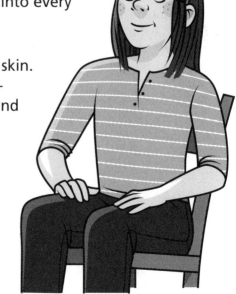

Now feel yourself becoming fully at ease in own your skin. Let yourself be filled with a sense of well-being, confidence, peace, and happiness. Keep breathing slowly and deeply. *(Pause.)*

When you open your eyes, you will bring with you a complete sense of calmness, relaxation, and happiness. Now open your eyes and take these good feelings with you wherever you go throughout the rest of the day.

Lesson 37: Using Stop, Breathe, Chill in Real-Life Situations

> **respect • anger management • conflict resolution • self-control**
>
> Lesson 37 reinforces the core skill of Stop, Breathe, Chill and gives students an opportunity to mentally rehearse applying it to an actual situation.
>
> **Students will**
> - review how stopping and breathing helps them think more clearly and respond with better judgment when they are angry
> - review and practice the Stop, Breathe, Chill technique and visualize themselves using it in a real-life situation
>
> **Materials**
> - sign from Lesson 34: *"I have the right to feel angry, but that doesn't give me the right to be cruel"* (see page 87)
> - "Stop, Breathe, Chill" sign from Lesson 9 (see page 39)
> - handout: "How Stop, Breathe, Chill Can Help" (page 96)
> - student journals

Introduction. Recognize students for any kind acts or words you have observed in recent days; also affirm acts of self-control in the face of anger.

Refer to the sign, "I have the right to feel angry, but that doesn't give me the right to be cruel." Ask why it's important to resist using cruel words when we get angry (or at any other time).

Share with the class these words from real students:

"My classmate made a face at me and I tried to control my anger, but I couldn't hold it in any longer. So I made a face back at her."

"I was in a conflict with my brother. He kept coming into my room without asking. The last time he did it I felt the anger swell up inside me. I told him to get out but he shook his head no. My anger started flowing out all over."*

Ask students if they can identify with either of the statements. Briefly discuss.

Ask students how they've been using Stop, Breathe, Chill as a way to control their anger. Respond to comments and questions. Also tell students how you've used this strategy.

Note: Don't be surprised if someone says, "I used Stop, Breathe, Chill, but I still felt angry." Explain that Stop, Breathe, Chill doesn't completely erase angry feelings. What it does is help us gain greater control over our reactions, even when we still have some anger inside. The angry feelings might be there for a while, buy they'll have less control over us.

Say: **Using Stop, Breathe, Chill actually changes the way our brains work. Let's review.** Ask students what part of the brain angry reactions come from (the reptilian brain). Have them point to the base of the skull.

Ask what part of the brain Stop, Breathe, Chill takes them to (the front of the brain—the neocortex).

Ask why the front of the brain is the place of true power. (It's the part that allows us to think straight and choose a response instead of just reacting.)

Activity. Say: **The more we practice Stop, Breathe, Chill, the easier it is to use in real life.** Tell students they're going to be doing a visualization that will give them practice now. Tell them that visualization is the same technique many Olympic athletes use to help themselves accomplish their goals. Have students close their eyes, or cover them and look down, and picture a time they got mad. Say: **Recall where the anger landed in your body. Recall your angry thoughts. Recall what you actually did.** Give students a minute or so to do this.

Say: **Now let's replay the angry event. This time, you'll see yourself handle it with more control. Picture what happened that made you angry. Now imagine a big red stop sign, and silently tell yourself to STOP so you don't say or do something you'll regret.** (Pause.) **Take some slow, deep abdominal breaths.** (Breathe with students.) **Feel your body and mind calming down.** (Pause.)

---

* Quotes attributed to real students come from responses to the Survey About Conflicts conducted by the author and publisher. See pages 1 and 282–284 for further information.

Picture yourself doing something else that will help you chill out a little more, like walking away or getting a drink of water. (Pause.)

Now, imagine yourself feeling more in control. Decide what you're going to do next. Do you want to work things out with the person you're mad at? Or do you want to just let the problem go? Whatever you choose, picture yourself doing it. (Pause.) See yourself feeling in control of yourself and proud of the choice you made.

Have students open their eyes and share what they envisioned. If any students say they weren't able to visualize what you asked them to, let them know that visualization gets easier with practice.

Wrap-Up. Acknowledge the class for the important work they did today. Ask how the world could change if people all over learned how to control their anger better. Let them know they are part of helping this happen.

Follow-Up. Have students read and discuss with a family member the "How Stop, Breathe, Chill Can Help" handout. Ask them to write or draw in their journals an example of how they are applying Stop, Breathe, Chill in their lives.

How Stop, Breathe, Chill Can Help
Ideas from Real Kids

Here are some things students have to say about how using Stop, Breathe, Chill helps them:

"I was playing basketball and a player from the other team shoved me. I was going to shove her back, but I *thought about the consequences* and decided to stop, breathe, and chill instead. I told myself this wasn't worth fighting over. And it wasn't. *I was able to help my team win instead of getting a foul for fighting.*"

"Stop, Breathe, Chill helped me with my annoying sister. She started getting on my nerves the other day and *I almost called her a name. But then I stopped, took some breaths, and reminded myself that she's only four.*"

"I used Stop, Breathe, Chill with my mother. She was yelling at me to clean my room, and instead of talking back, I stopped and breathed. Then I told myself to just do it. I was going to have to do it anyway. *I avoided a fight with my mom and I didn't end up getting punished.*"

"I was in the cafeteria when someone rolled their eyes at me. Usually I would roll my eyes back at them. This time I reminded myself to stop and breathe. Then *I chilled out by saying the name of my dog. That always calms me down.* I was able to just walk away and forget about it then, instead of getting into a big thing."

"In touch football, this kid pushed me and yanked the ball out of my hand. I was ready to fight him for it, but I knew I'd get in trouble for that. So *I stopped and breathed and decided to play even harder and better. I ended up scoring three touchdowns.*"

"Knowing how to stop, breathe, and chill really helps me handle my anger. I can control myself better now. *Before, I would do things when I got mad that I'd feel guilty about.* Sometimes I would get punished. Now I can calm myself down and make a better choice. *I feel better about myself now.*"

Lesson 38: Calming Statements

calming • anger management • self-control

In Lesson 38, students learn how calming statements can give them greater control over angry reactions.

Students will

- recognize that angry thoughts fuel angry feelings
- understand that calming thoughts can help diminish angry reactions
- come up with a personal calming statement to help them chill out whenever they feel angry

Materials

- "Stop, Breathe, Chill" sign from Lesson 9 (see page 39)
- handout: "Chill Out with Calming Statements" (pages 98–99)
- student journals

Introduction. Refer to the "Stop, Breathe, Chill" sign. Lead students in taking three slow, deep abdominal breaths.

Briefly review the way stopping and breathing helps people move to the place of power in their brain. Ask students: **Which part of the brain do angry reactions come from?** (The reptilian brain; point to the base of the skull.) **Which part of the brain helps us think straight and choose a response?** (The neocortex.) **Which part of the brain is our place of power?** (The neocortex; point to the front of the skull.) **How can we get out of our reptilian brain into the front of the brain?** (By stopping, breathing, and chilling.)

Tell students that they are now going to learn a very important skill for chilling out—a skill that will help them move out of the reptilian brain and into the front of the brain when they're angry.

Activity. Distribute the handout. Ask seven volunteers to stand and read aloud each of the seven paragraphs of the handout. Encourage them to read in the most expressive way possible, as though making a public service announcement on the radio or YouTube.

Afterward, invite questions and discuss what was just read. You might ask: **Have you noticed that when your anger is triggered, your mind is often filled with angry thoughts? How do these angry thoughts make you feel? Have you ever tried using a calming statement to help yourself calm down? How did that work for you?** Give an example of your own and ask for others.

Now have students work in pairs to come up with personal calming statements that they write in their journals. After several minutes, go around the circle and have each student say aloud his or her calming statement.

Wrap-Up. Encourage students to use their calming statement every time they feel angry or annoyed, including at home. Tell them you'll be using yours and you'll be checking in with them to see how it went.

Follow-Up. The next time the class meets, check in with students to ask how it's going for them to use calming statements.

Extension. Have students create their own public service announcements (PSAs) or skits to teach other students about calming statements and how they can help people chill when they feel angry. Arrange for students to share their PSAs during the morning school announcements or to present their skits to another class.

Chill Out with Calming Statements

One of the main things that fuels anger is the thoughts we think: "I can't stand that kid!" "I'm ready to blow my top!" Thoughts like these make us even madder. Sure, angry thoughts are going to pop into your head when you feel mad. But if you keep focusing on them, you're going to end up feeling more and more angry and out of control.

When your mind is full of angry thoughts, there's a helpful way you can chill out: Use a calming statement. Calming statements are words you silently say in your brain that help you cool down. A calming statement helps put you back in control of *you*. Every time you think or say a calming statement to yourself, the place of power in your brain will start to take over and help you feel calmer. You'll be better able to deal with the other person when you're in control of yourself.

Here's an example of a calming statement: "I can handle this." It's simple. It's positive. And when you say it to yourself, it makes you feel like you really can handle whatever you're faced with. A calming statement can also be a line from a song or poem. It can be a simple phrase that reminds you of a peaceful place, like "Ocean waves."

Calming statements are so powerful because they reprogram your brain. It's like your brain is a computer and the calming statement is the command you're giving it. Even if you don't believe your calming statement right away, it will still work. Really! Say it like you mean it, and trust your brain to do its job. The more you use your calming statement, the more you'll start to actually feel calm.

Chill Out with Calming Statements (continued)

Here are some other calming statements you might want to use:

"I can keep my cool."

"I am in control."

"I have the power to stay calm."

"Peace now."

"Chill."

Now it's your turn. Come up with your own personal calming statement. You can choose one of the statements from this handout or make up your own. Remember, keep it short and positive. Choose something that makes you feel good when you say it.

Write your calming statement in your journal and on a separate piece of paper, too. That way you can hang it in a place where you can read it every day. Repeat it often. Picture it coming true. After a while, it will! Whenever you're faced with anger, your calming statement will help you stay in control.

Lesson 39: Picture the Cake, Blow Out the Candles (10-Minute Time Cruncher)

self-control • calming • anger management

Lesson 39 gives students a fun tool they can use to calm down when they feel angry or upset.

Students will
- learn a simple, effective visualization and breathing exercise

Materials
- *optional:* drawing paper and markers

Introduction. Tell students that you're going to give them a fun way to calm themselves called "Picture the cake, blow out the candles."

Activity. Say: Pretend that your birthday is today, and it's the most wonderful birthday ever. Everything is exactly how you want it to be, including the cake.

Ask for volunteers to briefly share about the cake they imagine.

Say: **Now close your eyes and picture your cake. Picture the icing, the filling, and any special decorations you would like.** (Pause.) **Put your candles on the cake. Light them. Take a deep breath and blow out the candles.**

Say: **Okay, now let's do it again. Take a deep breath, blow out the candles.**

Say: **One last time . . . Take a deep breath, blow out the candles. Now open your eyes.**

Wrap-Up. After the activity, ask students how they feel. Kids often really enjoy this activity and may be smiling. Encourage them to "Picture the cake, blow out the candles" anytime they feel angry, stressed, or upset.

Extension. Have students draw their ideal birthday cake. Encourage them to hang their pictures in their rooms at home to remind themselves to breathe deep and blow out the air as a way of calming themselves.

Lesson 40: Other Ways to Chill Out

calming • anger management • self-control

Lesson 40 reinforces the core skill of Stop, Breathe, Chill and introduces students to three modes of self-calming, so they will have an expanded range of ideas to call upon when they're angry, stressed, or upset.

Students will
- learn the three modes of chilling out: physical, quiet and calm, or distraction
- brainstorm ways to chill using all three approaches
- individually identify specific ways they can calm themselves when angry

Materials
- "Stop, Breathe, Chill" sign from Lesson 9 (see page 39)
- chart paper and marker
- student journals
- *optional:* drawing materials

Preparation. On the board or chart paper, write the following quote: *"The best remedy for a short temper is a long walk." —Jacqueline Schiff*

Introduction. Refer to the "Stop, Breathe, Chill" sign. Lead students in taking three slow, deep abdominal breaths. Then ask students how it's been going for them to use Stop, Breathe, Chill and calming statements in school, at home, or outside. Discuss. Share your own story, including challenges you've faced.

Discussion. At the top of the chart paper, write "Ways to Chill." Ask students: **What are some ways you chill out when you feel angry?** Discuss briefly, listing ideas on the chart paper. Then say: **There are lots of ways to chill out. Some people prefer to do something physical.** Show the Jacqueline Schiff quote and ask students if taking a walk works for them. Invite more examples of physical activity that can help people chill out; add these to the chart.

Say: **Another way to chill out is by finding something calm and quiet to do, like going to a quiet spot and reading. What are some other calm, quiet ways to chill out?** Elicit more suggestions, such as listening to music or writing in a journal. Add them to the "Ways to Chill" chart.

Continue: **A third way to chill out is to distract yourself by channeling your energy into something completely different. It's kind of like changing the channel on the TV.** Invite examples of distraction activities, such as cleaning one's room, making or building something, or helping someone. List more distraction ideas on the chart.

Activity. Have students pair up and brainstorm at least six new ways they can chill out when angry, upset, or stressed at school or home.

After about three minutes, ask students what they came up with. Add their ideas to the "Ways to Chill" chart.

Ask students: **Which of the ideas on our chart can you do here in our classroom?** Put a star ★ by each one.

Wrap-Up. In their journals, have students write down three chill-out strategies that can work for them. Say: **Your job is to put this into practice in real life. When you're angry, remember to stop, breathe, and then chill using your calming statement or another one of the ideas you've chosen. Also, in your journals write down the names of two trusted people you can talk to if you're still angry. I'll check in with you in a few days to see how it's going for you.**

Follow-Up. Laminate the "Ways to Chill" list and hang it in a prominent place. This will be one of your most important working documents throughout the year, one that students can refer to whenever they need a healthy channel for anger or stress.

The next time the class meets, check in with students to ask how their methods of chilling out are working for them.

Extension. Have students make pictures or posters showing ways they calm themselves when they are angry. Create a bulletin board or hallway display under the heading "Chill Out."

Ideas for a "Ways to Chill" Chart

put cold water on your face	read
go to a quiet spot	draw
do some physical exercise	model clay
★ write out what's bothering you	clean out a drawer
listen to music	ride your bike
talk to a friend	play with your pet
★ look at a poster or picture	do push-ups or sit-ups
★ use a calming statement	★ squeeze a Koosh ball
★ talk to an adult	★ remind yourself that you're bigger than the problem
★ look at the sky	
★ think of something funny	take a bath or shower
throw a ball	★ put it in perspective—know this moment will pass
go outside and run	

Lesson 41: See Yourself Getting Calmer
(10-Minute Time Cruncher)

self-control • anger management • personal responsibility

Lesson 41 gives students the opportunity to mentally rehearse chilling out.

Students will
- envision putting chill-out strategies into practice with a real-life conflict

Activity. Make sure students are seated comfortably. Say: **Close your eyes or cover them. Breathe in slowly through your nose all the way down into the bottom of your stomach. Hold the breath in and slowly release it. Take another slow, deep breath all the way down, and let it calm your mind and body. Breathe out slowly.**

Picture yourself having an angry conflict with someone. (Pause.)

In your mind, tell yourself to stop. Take a slow, deep calming breath. Now say your calming statement in your head. Picture yourself telling the other person that you're going to take a moment to chill out; then you'll come back to talk things over. (Pause.)

Picture yourself doing something from the "Ways to Chill" chart. (Pause.) **Feel yourself getting calmer. You are more in control now. Picture yourself going back to talk about the problem.** (Pause.)

Now picture yourself talking it out and coming to a fair solution. (Pause.)

Now open your eyes. Welcome back. How did it go?

Wrap-Up. Briefly discuss with students what they learned from doing this exercise.

Lesson 42: Things We Do When We Get Angry

anger management • self-control • personal responsibility

Lesson 42 reinforces the important understanding that we each have the ability to choose a response rather than simply react when we get angry.

Note: Review Lessons 10 and 11 (pages 40–41) prior to conducting this lesson.

Students will
- evaluate the outcomes of negative choices they might still make in response to anger
- identify things they can do to gain greater self-control when angry

Materials
- handout: "What Real Kids Do When They're Angry" (pages 104–105)
- chart paper; black and red marker

Introduction. Say: You've been learning a lot of ways to better control anger. Change takes time, and sometimes it's hard to let go of old habits. Today we're going to evaluate how we're doing with managing anger now.

Discussion. Distribute the handout and ask volunteers to read the comments from students about what they do when they're angry. Have students pair up and discuss what they do now when they get angry, noting positive changes and places where they may be stuck in negative patterns.

After a few minutes have students share in the large group about things they do when they get angry, noting positive changes or negative choices that still remain. List students' answers on chart paper.

When the list is complete, point to each action, one at a time, and ask: **Does doing this tend to make things get better or worse? How?** Put a red X by each action that makes things worse.

Ask: **What negative things happen when we do the things marked by an X?** (Punishment, guilt, retaliation, disappointing people we care about, disappointing oneself, etc.)

Then ask: **What can you do to help yourself avoid the choices that make things worse?** List these on a separate sheet of chart paper.

Activity. Ask for three volunteers to role-play the following scenario:

Three students have to come up with an idea for a science project. Student A keeps interrupting. Student B feels ready to lose his or her temper and say something mean. Student C notices and decides to say something that might help.

Have the role players act out the scenario, first using one or more of the negative actions on the list. Then have them replay it, this time using some of the positive strategies they've been learning. If they need prompting, here are some choices the players might make:

- Student C might suggest that they all take a break.
- Student B might excuse him/herself, get a drink of water, and think about an I-message to say. He or she can return to the group and deliver the I-message.
- Student B might use Stop, Breathe, Chill to calm down and then talk about the problem.

After the role play, debrief with the class. Ask what made things get worse the first time the scenario was acted out. What made things work out better the second time? What other choices could the players have made that might have helped?

Wrap-Up. Remind students to use the strategies you've been practicing together at home, after school, and throughout the day. Let them know you'll check in with them to hear how it's going.

Acknowledge acts of respect, listening, and compassion you observed during this lesson. Ask students if anyone wants to acknowledge somebody else.

Follow-Up. Have students answer the questions on their handout, either in writing or in discussion with a partner.

What Real Kids Do
When They're Angry

In a national survey of more than 2,100 students in grades 3–6, kids wrote about negative ways they deal with anger. Here are the top 5 things boys and girls reported doing when they're angry:

Top 5 Things Kids Do When They Get Mad

Boys

1. Walk away or ignore/avoid the person or situation.
2. Fight or do physical things such as hit, kick, push, or shove.
3. Try to stay calm.
4. Tell an adult.
5. Tell the person to stop.

Girls

1. Walk away or ignore/avoid the person or situation.
2. Tell an adult.
3. Talk/work it out.
4. Tell the person to stop.
5. Try to stay calm.

Here are some other things students said they did when they're angry:

> "When I get mad sometimes I freak out."
>
> "I count to ten, take a deep breath, and try to relax."
>
> "When someone gets me mad I egg them on."
>
> "I try to stay calm and not get worked up."
>
> "I scream into my pillow when I get home."
>
> "I usually stomp away."
>
> "If someone makes me mad I call them names."
>
> "I just try to sort it out in my head."

What Real Kids Do When They're Angry (continued)

What do YOU do when you're angry?

_____

_____

_____

What helps?

_____

_____

_____

Is there something you still do in response to anger that you need to change? Explain.

_____

_____

_____

_____

What can you do to make this change?

_____

_____

_____

_____

Lesson 43: Breathe Out/Breathe In
(10-Minute Time Cruncher)

calming • anger management • self-control

Lesson 43 introduces a way to breathe out anger and breathe in calmness.

Students will
- learn and practice a technique called Breathe Out/Breathe In

Introduction. Tell students you're going to show them a different way of breathing that can help them release anger and chill out. It's called Breathe Out/Breathe In.

Activity. Ask students to remember a time they felt angry. Ask them to feel the anger in their bodies. Say: **Now, breathe out the anger you feel. Breathe it out as hard as you can.** Explain that they should not blow out, but rather exhale deeply with the mouth slightly open. Demonstrate this deep exhalation for students so they can see the difference.

Next, have students take a slow, deep inhalation from all the way down in the lower abdomen. Demonstrate this deep inhalation.

Ask students to repeat this cycle of breathing. Say: **Breathe out the anger again. Breathe in the calmness.** (Pause.)

Repeat Breathe Out/Breathe In one more time.

Wrap-Up. Together with students, pretend to wipe the angry energy out of the air, the way you would "wipe" the air if it were filled with smoke. Tell students they can use Breathe Out/Breathe In as another way to Stop, Breathe, Chill.

Lesson 44: How Are We Doing? (Review)

anger management • self-control

Lesson 44 is a check-in with students on their application of the anger-management strategies they are learning. It will enable you to provide support and encouragement where needed.

Students will

- review skills they have learned for calming down and choosing a response rather than reacting when angry
- consider positive changes they have made and can make in the future to deal with anger in a healthy way

Materials

- handout: "What Real Kids Have to Say About Helpful Ways to Deal with Anger" (page 108)
- chart paper and marker
- "Stop, Breathe, Chill" sign from Lesson 9 (see page 39)
- "Ways to Chill" chart from Lesson 40 (see pages 100–101)
- student journals

Preparation. On the board or chart paper, write the following quote: *"For every minute you are angry, you lose sixty seconds of happiness."* —*Ralph Waldo Emerson*

Introduction. Lead students in taking three slow, deep abdominal breaths.

Invite a student to read the Ralph Waldo Emerson quote aloud. Ask students: **What do these words mean to you?** Discuss briefly. Then ask: **What is the most helpful thing about managing anger you've learned so far?** Discuss, referring to the "Stop, Breathe, Chill" sign and "Ways to Chill" chart.

Discussion. Distribute the handouts and ask for volunteers to read the statements from real students about managing anger in positive ways. Ask kids to respond to the ideas.

Remind students that managing anger can be challenging for all of us. The important thing is to keep working at it. Then ask: **What challenges are you having with managing anger? What successes are you having?** Discuss, offering suggestions and inviting them from other students. Let them know what works for you.

Activity. Ask students to think of a time in recent days when they felt angry and didn't let it get the best of them. What did they do to keep their cool?

Ask them to think of a time they got angry recently and didn't handle it well. Have them take out their journals and do some automatic writing, using this prompt: **Describe the situation that made you angry. Describe how you reacted, then come up with some things you could have done differently.**

Afterward, ask for volunteers to share what they wrote. Discuss.

Wrap-Up. Acknowledge students for showing compassion, self-control, and respect toward their classmates. Remind them to continue using anger-management strategies at home.

Extension. Have students interview someone they admire and find out what the person does to manage anger, especially in moments when he or she feels really mad. Does the person have any special tips to share? Students can take notes in their journals and share any valuable ideas with the class.

What Real Kids Have to Say About
Helpful Ways to Deal with Anger

In a national survey of more than 2,100 students in grades 3–6, kids wrote about positive ways they deal with anger. Here are some things they wrote:

- "I either talk to a friend who understands me, or I tell stuffed animals if there's no one to talk to."
- "I go outside and say to myself, 'Don't lose control.'"
- "With physical fights, I walk away and say, 'I don't fight.'"
- "I walk away so me and the other person can cool down. Sooner or later we forgive each other."
- "I find my calming point."

What are YOU going to do to help yourself better deal with anger the next time you're annoyed or in a conflict?

_____

_____

_____

_____

_____

_____

_____

Lesson 45: Getting Past Reacting

anger management • personal responsibility • self-control

Lesson 45 helps students gain additional insight into managing anger based on the example of a middle schooler who gained greater control over hers.

Students will
- examine more ways of gaining greater self-control in the face of anger
- come up with an action plan for responding to anger

Materials
- handout: "What Real Kids Have to Say About Making Changes" (pages 110–111; see Preparation, below)

Preparation. Prior to this lesson, pass out copies of the "What Real Kids Have to Say About Making Changes" handout and ask students to complete it ahead of time and bring it to this lesson.

Introduction. Have students bring their handouts to the circle. Explain that you will be asking people to share ideas they included on their "What Real Kids Have to Say About Making Changes" sheets; remind students not to use people's names when sharing.

Read or have a student read the quoted story from the handout.

Have students look back at the story and underline one line that's particularly meaningful to them. Ask for a few volunteers to read aloud the line they chose and to explain why they chose it.

Discussion. Discuss each question on the handout together:

- How does this student stop herself from reacting in ways that will get her in trouble?
- What did the girl do when the boys she passed were saying mean things about the way she looks and dresses?

- What is the most important thing you learned from this story?
- What words can you tell yourself to calm down when you're getting angry?
- What activity can you do to "take a break" from a situation that's making you mad?
- What can you do when it feels very hard to stay in control of anger?

Activity. Ask why it's important to have an action plan for staying in control when anger strikes. Tell students they're going to have a chance to share their action plans (at the bottom of the handout) with a partner now. Group students in pairs to briefly discuss the action plans they came up with. They can add more to their handouts at this time.

Have students reconvene in a large circle and ask some students to share their action plans for gaining control over anger.

Wrap-Up. Affirm students for the work they are doing to manage anger, be more peaceful people, and get along together.

What Real Kids Have to Say About
Making Changes

In a national survey of more than 2,100 students in grades 3–6:

64% said they want to learn more about dealing with anger, conflict, and how to get along with others.

In the survey and in interviews, kids wrote about changes they're making to manage anger in better ways. Here is something a middle school girl shared:

"I used to yell and scream and curse if someone made remarks about me. Then I'd get in trouble and would get grounded and not be allowed to watch TV or go outside—all the things I like to do. It wasn't worth it.

"Now I'm trying to take everything step by step and think before I act. I'm starting to see a dramatic change in myself. Like today, these boys were talking mean about the way I dress and the way I look. I just kept walking. Once you get past that stage of reacting, you get to see who you really are. I know that inside I'm a kind, loving person. I don't need to do what everyone else does just to be cool."

What do YOU think about the girl's story?

How does this student stop herself from reacting in ways that will get her in trouble?

_____

_____

What did the girl do when the boys she passed were saying mean things about the way she looks and dresses?

_____

_____

_____

What Real Kids Have to Say About Making Changes (continued)

What is the most important thing you learned from this story?

_____

_____

What activity can you do to "take a break" from a situation that's making you mad?

_____

_____

What can you do when it feels very hard to stay in control of anger?

_____

_____

Action Plan

Make an action plan you can follow the next time anger strikes. List three things that can help you stay in control. Include words you can tell yourself that help you calm down.

_____

_____

_____

_____

_____

Lesson 46: Don't Get Physical

anger management • self-control • personal responsibility

Lesson 46 can help students learn how to manage anger when they feel on the verge of losing control and hurting or physically harming another person.

Students will

- understand why it is important not to get physical
- identify a variety of ways to keep from losing control when angry
- role-play ways to use temper tamers in anger-provoking situations

Materials

- handout: "What Real Kids Have to Say About Taming Their Tempers" (page 113)
- chart paper and marker
- student journals

Introduction and Discussion. Ask: **Why is it important not to get physical when we're angry?** Discuss. Ask what negative outcomes can result from physically hurting someone. (You can get in trouble, end up getting hurt, bring about retaliation, gain an enemy, etc.)

Note: Let students know that there are rare instances where people might have to defend themselves physically (for example, if someone attacks them and they have no other way out). But in most cases, physical responses should be avoided. Tell kids it takes more courage to stand tall and walk away from a fight than to let themselves be drawn into one.

Ask students what they do to avoid getting physical or saying things they'll later regret. Discuss briefly. Tell them what you did at their age.

Tell students that today you'll be discussing "temper tamers." Temper tamers can help them if they're really mad and feel like they're about to go out of control verbally or physically.

Pass out copies of the handout. Ask for volunteers to stand and read aloud the quotes from real kids. Tell students to follow along and underline the parts they find most useful.

After the quotes have been read, ask students to share what they found most helpful in the advice from other kids. Discuss.

At the top of a sheet of chart paper, write "Temper Tamers." Ask students to suggest temper tamers they can use to help themselves when their tempers are in danger of flaring and they're on the verge of lashing out physically. List their suggestions on the chart.

Activity. Have volunteers come to the center of the circle and role-play the following scenarios or scenarios they suggest. As time permits, have students enact the scenes more than once, using a different temper tamer each time.

- **You are working hard on controlling your temper. The kid who sits next to you makes a joke about a bad grade you just got on a test. You feel like throwing your pencil at her. What do you do to tame your temper?**

- **You are working on controlling your temper. You're on the playground, and someone backs into you as he's trying to catch a ball. You feel like pushing him down, but you want to control your temper. What do you do?**

Briefly discuss each role play, focusing on different temper tamers that were used and emphasizing the negative outcomes that were avoided as a result.

Wrap-Up. Have students choose three or four temper tamers and write them in their journals. Encourage them to use their temper tamers in real life when they are angry or losing control. Acknowledge students for the good work they are doing. See if anyone would like to acknowledge a classmate.

Extension. Tell students: **Think of a conflict in which you got so mad you completely lost it. Maybe you got physical, or maybe you said something cruel. Now think about what you could have done differently to tame your temper and maintain control of yourself. Create a comic strip showing the steps you would take.**

What Real Kids Have to Say About
Taming Their Tempers
Tips from Middle Schoolers

Here's what some middle school students said about ways they try to control their tempers:

"When someone gets me mad, I ask them why they said what they did. I try to understand. That usually helps us work it out. If I get really frustrated, I ball my fist up real tight and think what would happen if I react in a bad way. I know what might get me in trouble and I keep myself aware of the consequences."

"When someone gets me mad, I feel hyper and ready to hit. Things that help me calm down are going into the bathroom and taking a minute, sitting outside, or going in my room and playing my game when I'm home."

"If someone messes with me or calls me a name, I tell them to stop. I've learned how to manage my anger. I used to have a short fuse. I used to hit people real quick without thinking. Now I think things through first."

"I got a little squeeze ball. When I get mad, I squeeze it. Also I try to think of something else, something good from the past, like a place I went with my family when I was younger."

"If someone bothers you, walk away. If they're trying to hit you, you have the right to tell an adult. Don't worry about being called a snitch. Everyone has the right to protect themselves."

Lesson 47: Peace Shield

calming • self-respect • anger management

Lesson 47 introduces the concept of a Peace Shield*—a calming ritual students can use when faced with other people's anger.

Note: Be sure to complete Lesson 36, "Peaceful Place Visualization," prior to this lesson.

Students will
- learn a tool for calmness that can help them feel more safe and confident when someone is acting aggressively toward them
- visualize their own Peace Shields protecting them from other people's anger and hurtful behavior

Materials
- handout: "Peace Shield" (page 115)
- "Ways to Chill" chart from Lesson 40 (see pages 100–101)
- drawing paper and markers or colored pencils

Introduction and Discussion. Ask students how they feel when they are faced with an angry person. (Tell them not to use other people's names when describing situations of this nature.) Discuss.

Remind students of the reptilian brain, which is activated when people are angry. Tell students: **When someone else is mad, and you feel scared or angry in response, your fearful reaction starts in the reptilian brain, too. How do you feel when someone directs their anger at you? What happens inside your body?** (Fast pulse and heartbeat, hot face, etc.) **Which part of the brain helps you calm down and choose a response, instead of just reacting?** (The front of the brain or neocortex.)

Ask students what they're already doing to calm themselves and feel better when upset, hurt, or angry. If needed, remind them about Stop, Breathe, Chill; deep breathing; calming statements; and ideas from the "Ways to Chill" chart (Lesson 40). Tell students that all these things also help when they feel nervous, frightened, or threatened. Then say: **Today we'll learn about another technique you can use, called the Peace Shield.**

Activity. Read the "Peace Shield" handout aloud in a calming voice, pausing as needed for students to visualize. Afterward, ask students: **Were you able to picture your Peace Shield? How did it feel to imagine this invisible shield of protection?** Discuss.

Have students pair up and describe their Peace Shields to each other. Ask: **Can you think of ways your Peace Shield can help you at school and at home?** (For example, when someone makes them feel afraid by yelling, threatening, put-downs, etc.) Also describe how you are planning to use your Peace Shield. Without getting too personal, refer to situations they can relate to: being in the presence of a sharp-tongued neighbor or relative; having a conflict with someone who tries to put you down. Talk about locking in the power of your Peace Shield and focusing on the feeling of protection it gives you.

Wrap-Up. Remind students that they have the right and the power to protect themselves from people's anger, teasing, and other mistreatment. Say: **When you feel the need for protection from hurt, anger, or fear, remember to breathe deeply and put your Peace Shield in place. Feel it locking in your safety and locking out the harm that comes from bad feelings and mean words. The power of your Peace Shield will help you feel calmer and safer with people of any age who speak or act in aggressive ways.**

Encourage students to envision themselves surrounded by their Peace Shield whenever they feel the need.

Follow-Up. Give students their own copies of the handout. Have them draw a picture of themselves surrounded by their Peace Shield.

---

* Special thanks to student assistance counselor Virginia Abu Bakr for sharing with me the idea of the Peace Shield.

Peace Shield

Close your eyes. Take three slow, deep, calming breaths. Now go to your Peaceful Place. Let the good feelings you felt when you were there fill you up completely. Picture yourself standing tall and strong, feeling confident and happy. Now imagine yourself surrounded with an invisible shield of protection—a Peace Shield. Picture what the shield looks like to you. It is invisible to everyone else. Picture yourself surrounded by your Peace Shield. Picture it keeping you completely safe from harm. Your Peace Shield has the power to keep good feelings in and bad feelings out.

Take another slow deep breath. On that breath you are "locking in" the power of your Peace Shield. Feel this happening now. The power of your Peace Shield is yours forever.

Start every day by closing your eyes and putting your Peace Shield in place. When you feel the need to protect yourself from anger or hurt, breathe deeply and feel your Peace Shield protecting you. See it locking in your safety and locking out anger and meanness. Use your Peace Shield anytime, day or night.

Lesson 48: Using "Think-Alouds"
(10-Minute Time Cruncher)

anger management • personal responsibility • self-control • calming

Lesson 48 helps you demonstrate to students the thought process that takes place when implementing core skills and anger-management strategies.

Note: Conduct Lesson 47, "Peace Shield," prior to conducting this lesson.

Students will

- observe the process of thinking through and preparing to talk about a conflict
- review Stop, Breathe, Chill calming strategies and the Win/Win Guidelines for Working Out Conflicts
- understand that mental rehearsal and thinking things through are essential tools for dealing with conflicts

Materials

- "Win/Win Guidelines for Working Out Conflicts" chart from Lesson 8 (see page 36)
- "Stop, Breathe, Chill" chart from Lesson 9 (see page 39)
- "Ways to Chill" chart from Lesson 40 (see pages 100–101)

Introduction and Activity. Tell your students that today you are going to model thinking aloud about how to deal with anger and conflict. You can use or adapt the following:

Imagine that someone has just done something to hurt my feelings. I need to say something, but I know if I do it now, I'm going to make it worse because I'm very upset. I'm going to show you how I would think this through, and what I would do. This is called a Think-Aloud.

First, I'm going to Stop, Breathe, Chill. (Point to the chart.) I'm going to stop and feel what I feel. I'm noticing that my heart is pounding very fast and my face feels hot. I'm going to breathe in deeply and then breathe out the bad feelings. I'll do this three times. Do it with me. (Breathe together.)

Now I'm going to calm myself down by saying my calming statement: "I can handle this." I'm also going to splash water on my face to calm myself some more. (Pretend you're doing that now.) And I'm also going to remind myself that this isn't the end of the world.

Maybe I'll take some more deep breaths to calm even more. Do this with me. (Breathe together.) I think I'll do something else from my "Ways to Chill" list. I know—I'll think about something funny. (Close your eyes and smile to yourself.)

(Open your eyes.) I'm starting to feel better now. I think I'll also talk confidentially—privately—with my aunt about what happened. She's a helpful listener. That way I can let go of some more anger before I talk with the person who hurt my feelings. (Pretend you're making a phone call to your aunt.)

Okay, now I'm ready to think about what I'm going to say. Let's see, start from "I," not "you." (Point to step 2 of the Win/Win Guidelines.) Hmm. Okay. Here's what I'm going to say: "I felt bad when you made that mean remark to me."

Let me practice that in the mirror so I can feel comfortable saying it. (Pretend to face a mirror and repeat your I-message a few times.)

(Face forward.) **Good. Now I'll put on my Peace Shield so I feel safe and protected.** (Pretend you're putting on your Peace Shield now.) **Okay, now I'm ready to talk to the person who hurt my feelings.**

Role-play talking to the person who hurt your feelings. Have a student play that part. Go through the steps of the Win/Win Guidelines.

Wrap-Up. Ask if students have any questions. Encourage them to suggest other ways you could have made yourself feel calmer, stronger, and more ready to face the person. Reassure students that it takes time and practice to put all the skills together. Emphasize that the more they practice, the easier it will become.

Extension. Have students get into pairs and do Think-Alouds of their own in response to an imagined conflict. Say: **This will be practice for a time in the future when you feel yourself getting angry. In your Think-Aloud, use Stop, Breathe, Chill. Try to remember the different ways you can calm yourself down. Then think about an I-message you can use. Put on your Peace Shield to help yourself feel ready to face the person you have a conflict with.**

Lesson 49: Anger Management Role Play

anger management • conflict resolution • self-control

Lesson 49 shows how to use anger-management and conflict resolution skills in combination.

Note: Conduct Lesson 47, "Peace Shield," prior to conducting this lesson.

Students will

- review and practice anger-management skills introduced so far
- brainstorm and role-play solutions to a common conflict
- evaluate the impact of calming strategies and mental preparation

Materials

- "Win/Win Guidelines for Working Out Conflicts" chart from Lesson 8 (see page 36)
- "Stop, Breathe, Chill" chart from Lesson 9 (see page 39)

Introduction. Say: **Today we're going to see how to put all the anger-management skills we've been learning into practice when we're faced with an actual conflict. First let's put on our Peace Shields.**

Have students close their eyes or look down. Lead students in taking three slow, deep abdominal breaths. Then have them visualize themselves surrounded by their Peace Shields. Say: **The power of your Peace Shield is locked in; you are safe and protected behind it. Now picture someone standing in front of you calling you names. Picture the mean words bouncing off your Peace Shield. Feel yourself strong inside as you realize that no one's words can break through the power of your Peace Shield.** Pause and give students a few moments to envision in silence.

Now ask them to listen as you read aloud this story from a real student:

"These kids started teasing me about this girl they said I liked. Every day I would hear them say, 'Hey, how's your girlfriend treating you lately?' I told them to stop but they wouldn't. Then everybody started doing it. It kept getting worse and worse until finally I couldn't take it anymore."

Discussion and Activity. Ask: **What do you think this boy did next?** Discuss, being open to hearing negative or positive choices the boy might have made. Then ask: **What could he have done to make things better?**

Display or point to the "Stop, Breathe, Chill" and "Win/Win Guidelines for Working Out Conflicts" charts. Ask for two volunteers—one to play the child who started taunting the boy in the first place, and one to play the boy.

Before starting the actual role play, have the student playing the role of the boy who was taunted mentally prepare himself. Then have him demonstrate the following:

- using Stop, Breathe, Chill
- deciding what he's going to say before approaching the other boy
- rehearsing what he's going to say
- putting on his Peace Shield

See if the class has any other suggestions.

Now have him role-play approaching the other boy. Display or point to the Win/Win Guidelines. Guide the role players through the steps, with special emphasis on steps 1, 2, 3, and 5.

Win/Win Guidelines for Working Out Conflicts

1. Cool off.

2. Talk it over starting from "I," not "you."

3. Listen and say back what you heard.

4. Take responsibility for your role in the conflict.

5. Come up with a solution that's fair to each of you.

6. Affirm, forgive, thank, or apologize.

After the role play, discuss what happened. Ask: **How did it help to stop and breathe? What did the boy do to calm himself?** Ask the role player: **Did putting on your Peace Shield help? How?**

Wrap-Up. Remind students to use all the calming skills they've learned next time they are in a conflict in school or at home. Let them know that they will have more opportunities to practice using all of the Win/Win Guidelines for Working Out Conflicts.

Follow-Up. Put students into small groups and have them enact the same scenario or other scenarios you or the class come up with. Move from group to group, observing students, and providing coaching when necessary.

Lesson 50: Getting Help with Anger
(10-Minute Time Cruncher)

anger management • personal responsibility • calming

Lesson 50 helps students identify trusted adults they can talk to if they need support with anger or any other upset feelings.

Students will
- understand that talking to a trusted adult is a helpful thing to do when they're angry or upset about a problem
- determine at least two people they can go to for support

Materials
- chart paper and marker
- soft ball appropriate for throwing in class
- student journals

Activity. Say: **Talking out a problem helps people feel better and can also help them come up with solutions. It's important for each of you to have a trusted adult you can talk to when you're angry or upset.** Tell students who you used to talk to when you were their age. Also share about who you talk to now. On chart paper, list students' suggestions of trusted people they can talk to if they have a problem. Be sure to include parents or caregivers, other relatives, counselors, teachers, school social workers, youth group leaders, coaches, people affiliated with places of worship, neighbors, friends' parents.

Have students pair up and determine which trusted adults they can (or do) talk to when they're angry or upset about something.

After about three minutes, have them reconvene in a large circle. Throw the ball to a student and ask him or her to name a trusted person he or she can talk to. The student can say the person's role rather than actually naming the person. Have the student throw the ball to someone else who names a trusted person to go to. Continue until everyone has had a turn.

If a child doesn't have a trusted adult to go to, see the student after the lesson and help identify an appropriate person, perhaps someone at school.

Wrap-Up. At the front of their journals, have students write down the names of the two trusted adults they can go to for support. You may also want to share the toll-free phone number for Boys Town (1-800-448-3000), a support hotline for young people.

Preventing Conflict

Teaching kids how to resolve conflicts respectfully and fairly helps cut back on bullying. Although it's not possible to eliminate conflict completely, it *is* possible to significantly reduce the amount and severity of conflicts in your classroom and school. This section will help you foster in your students a greater willingness and desire to work out differences rather than fight. The lessons were designed to help you nurture an attitude of conciliation in students, opening their minds to working out conflicts peacefully, and to provide important tools that help them do this. The activities in the Preventing Conflict lessons lay the groundwork for the Responding to Conflict activities on pages 165–188. You will want to conduct at least some of these lessons before conducting those.

Be sure to have these charts (introduced in Lessons 2, 8, and 9) displayed: "Respectful Listening," "The Win/Win Guidelines for Working Out Conflicts," and "Stop, Breathe, Chill."

51. Top 10 Conflict Starters
52. Conflict Habits, Part 1
53. Conflict Habits, Part 2
54. Positive and Negative Choices in Conflicts
55. Observing Conflict
56. Responsibility vs. Blame, Part 1
57. Responsibility vs. Blame, Part 2
58. Willingness to Work Out Conflicts
59. Willingness Blocks
60. Examining Our Willingness Blocks
61. Let's Compromise (10-Minute Time Cruncher)
62. Basement or Balcony? Part 1
63. Basement or Balcony? Part 2
64. Staying in the Balcony
65. Introducing Assertiveness
66. Conflict Solver Interviews
67. Staying Respectful with Someone You Don't Like
68. The Dignity Stance
69. Staying Out of Physical Fights

Lesson 51: Top 10 Conflict Starters

conflict resolution • cooperation • personal responsibility

Lesson 51 invites students to survey peers on common causes of conflict and compare their findings to results from the Survey About Conflicts.

Students will

- identify sources of their most common conflicts
- discover what other kids most often get into conflicts over
- reflect on how to be part of the solution to conflicts, especially those caused by teasing, gossip, name-calling, and exclusion

Materials

- chart paper and marker
- handouts: "What Are Your Conflict Starters?" (page 121); "Top 10 Conflict Starters" (page 122)
- student journals

Preparation. On chart paper, write the following: *"You can either be part of the problem or part of the solution."*

Introduction. Distribute copies of the "What Are Your Conflict Starters?" handout and read or have a student read the statistic at the top. Ask: **Does this sound right to you? How often do you see conflicts happening?** Discuss.

Activity and Discussion. Ask students to think about what they get into conflicts about. Pair up students and give them a minute or two to discuss this with their partner and write their ideas in the space provided on the handout. Ask a few students to share their answers with the class.

Now have students circulate around the room, asking three classmates, "What do you get into conflicts over most?" Have students write the answers in the last three blanks on their handouts.

After about five minutes, have students reconvene in a circle. Go around the circle and ask each student to read his or her list. Write the responses on chart paper. For repeat answers, make a tally mark next to the original answer each time it's given. When you have survey responses from all students, rank the top 10 answers in order. At the top of the chart paper, write: "Our Top 10 Conflict Starters."

Now pass out the "Top 10 Conflict Starters" handout. Ask students to compare the results from your classroom to findings from the Survey About Conflicts. Discuss. The survey responses will help your students see how much they have in common with other North American students regarding what

triggers conflicts. Regarding the top three conflict-starters (teasing, name-calling, and gossiping) ask students why all of these so often lead to conflict. Ask: **What do you think it would be like in our school if there wasn't as much teasing, name-calling, and gossip?** Refer to the sign you've created and guide students to understand that they each have the power to be part of the solution rather than part of the problem. Ask: **What does this mean to you?**

Wrap-Up. Ask: **If someone comes to you with gossip, what can you personally do to be part of the solution rather than the problem?** Discuss, then ask: **If someone teases you or calls you a name, is there something you can do to prevent it from turning into a conflict? What?**

Ask: **How about as a class? If we want to have a get-along classroom, what can we each do to be part of the solution?**

Follow-Up. Tell students what you do to be part of the solution. Have them ask a friend or family member this question: "Is there something you do when it comes to conflict so you can be part of the solution instead of being part of the problem?" Have them jot down notes in their journals so they can report back.

Extension. Have students interview older students about conflict starters and ask the older students what they think can be done about teasing, rumors, gossip, exclusion, and other conflict starters. Discuss what your students learned from their older counterparts.

What Are Your Conflict Starters?

In a national survey of more than 2,100 students in grades 3–6:

48% (1,046 students) said they saw conflicts happening often, every day, or all the time.

What do YOU get into conflicts over most?

_____

_____

_____

_____

_____

Ask three classmates, "What do you get into conflicts over most?"
Write the answers here.

1. _____

2. _____

3. _____

Think About It

Conflicts happen all the time! What can you do to be part of the solution instead of being part of the problem when it comes to conflicts?

_____

_____

_____

_____

Top 10 Conflict Starters

In a national survey of more than 2,100 students in grades 3–6, kids wrote about what situations most often lead to conflicts. Here are the Top 10 Conflict Starters reported in the survey:

1. Being teased or made fun of
2. Rumors and gossip
3. Name-calling
4. Being blamed for something
5. Someone being unfair
6. Being left out
7. Being picked on for being different
8. Cheating at games
9. Threats
10. Mean notes or text messages

Lesson 52: Conflict Habits, Part 1

conflict resolution • cooperation • respect • anger management • personal responsibility

Lesson 52 helps students understand that negative conflict habits can be changed.

Students will
- understand that everyone has conflict habits, some that are helpful and others that are harmful
- identify helpful and harmful conflict habits
- reflect on which harmful conflict habits they would like to change

Note: Review Lessons 10 and 11 (pages 40–41) prior to conducting this lesson.

Materials
- handouts: "Scripts About Conflict Habits" (pages 124–125, two copies); "Conflict Habits Self-Test" (page 126)
- student journals

Preparation. Make two copies of the "Scripts About Conflict Habits" handout. Keep one for yourself and cut out the three scripts from the other. Select three students to help lead this lesson. Their roles will be to read their scripts aloud to the class, share their own personal information as indicated, and ask discussion questions. Provide them with copies of their scripts prior to the lesson to help them feel comfortable reading aloud, sharing their stories, and inviting discussion from other students. Talk with them about the information they plan to share, and offer guidance as needed.

Introduction. Lead the class in taking three slow, deep abdominal breaths. Explain that you've asked three students to help lead today's lesson. Introduce the co-leaders and have them sit near you in the circle.

Discussion. Say: **Today we're going to talk about conflict habits and how they affect our lives. Our leaders will tell you some more about this.**

Allow about ten minutes for this student-led presentation and discussion. Begin by having Leader 1 read his or her script. At the discussion points, help student leaders guide brief conversations (one or two minutes) about helpful habits and other habits students would like to change.

Continue with Leader 2's explanation and brief discussion of harmful conflict habits. After Leader 3's reading and short discussion, have the class acknowledge the student leaders and see if anyone has any questions.

Activity. Have students pair up and discuss with a partner one harmful conflict habit they would like to change. Ask them to talk about things they can do to change the habit they've identified. Have them write the following heading on top of a page in their journals: "I have the power to change harmful conflict habits." Below this, tell them to write down the habit they plan to change, along with a few steps they will take to change it.

Wrap-Up. Pass out the "Conflict Habits Self-Test" and ask students to complete it before the next lesson. Have them check off the reactions they commonly have to conflicts and list others that are not included. Note that this handout will be used in Lesson 53.

Extension. Have students share with their parents or another trusted adult what they learned about conflict habits, talking together about conflict habits they each would like to change and thinking of ways to make that happen.

Scripts About Conflict Habits

Script for Leader 1

Habits are things we're used to doing. For example, we might brush our teeth at a set time, study in the same way each night, or even treat people in certain ways. Habits can be harmful or helpful. A helpful habit I have is _____ _____ _____.

What helpful habits do you have? *(Call on students to answer this question.)*

One habit I would like to change is _____.

What habits would you like to change? *(Call on students. Discuss.)*

Script for Leader 2

Helpful habits make life better. Eating healthy foods, getting to bed on time, and finishing homework are helpful habits that improve our lives. Harmful habits make life more difficult. Harmful habits like arguing and fighting, not studying for tests, and being disrespectful can cause problems and make our lives more difficult.

The way we react to conflict is a habit, too. Here's what one fifth grader said about a habit he has when he's angry: "When someone gets me mad, I lose my temper. It's what I've always done. I don't know any other way." How many of you can identify with this? *(Discuss briefly.)*

This boy's habit of losing his temper is a harmful conflict habit. A harmful conflict habit I have is: _____.

What harmful conflict habits do you have? *(Discuss with other students.)*

➡️

Scripts About Conflict Habits (continued)

- -

Script for Leader 3

The good news is that habits can be changed! We can let go of harmful habits, and we can develop new healthy habits. Here's one student's story of success in turning a harmful conflict habit into a helpful one:

"I always used to yell and scream and curse if someone made me mad. I got in trouble a lot, and my friends didn't want to be with me. I decided to change. Now I try to take everything step-by-step. I try to find out the real story instead of flying off the handle. When I control my anger and talk out problems, I feel better inside. It's like I feel stronger."

This student succeeded in turning a harmful conflict habit to a helpful one. Now she feels better about herself. Her confidence is growing. She realizes that she has the power to change a negative conflict habit into a positive one.

Think about what you can do to change a harmful conflict habit into a helpful one. *(Discuss with other students.)*

- -

Conflict Habits Self-Test

Check the things you do **most often** when you have conflicts with people.

_____ 1. I say something mean to hurt the person's feelings.

_____ 2. I try to calm down before I speak.

_____ 3. I hurt the person physically.

_____ 4. I blame the other person.

_____ 5. I blame myself.

_____ 6. I look for ways to solve the conflict rather than just get what I want.

_____ 7. I don't say anything and wish I had.

_____ 8. I avoid using put-downs.

_____ 9. I spread rumors or lies about the person.

_____ 10. I try to understand the person's point of view.

_____ 11. I am willing to forgive the person for mistakes.

_____ 12. I threaten not to be friends with the person.

_____ 13. I send a mean text about the person.

_____ 14. I do something to get even.

_____ 15. I am willing to compromise (give and take) rather than just have my way.

_____ 16. I talk things over with the person and try to work things out fairly.

_____ 17. I talk to an adult for advice (as opposed to tattling).

_____ 18. I apologize if I have done something wrong.

_____ 19. _____

_____ 20. _____

Here are my healthy conflict habits:

_____

_____

Here is a harmful conflict habit I plan to change:

_____

_____

Lesson 53: Conflict Habits, Part 2

conflict resolution • cooperation • respect • anger management

Lesson 53, a follow-up to Lesson 52, helps students further identify the helpful and harmful conflict habits they possess.

Students will
- identify and contrast helpful and harmful conflict habits that people can have
- gain deeper understanding of their own conflict habits and the impact they have
- reflect on why it's important to change harmful conflict habits into helpful ones

Materials
- completed handout: "Conflict Habits Self-Test" (page 126)

Preparation. Make sure students have completed the "Conflict Habits Self-Test" prior to this lesson. Have them bring their sheets to the circle at the start of the lesson.

Introduction. On the board, make two large circles with the following headings: "Helpful Conflict Habits" and "Harmful Conflict Habits."

Ask for volunteers to come up, two at a time, and write in one circle or the other a helpful or harmful conflict habit that someone can have. Ask what happens when people are stuck in the pattern of harmful conflict habits.

Activity. Have students look at their completed "Conflict Habits Self-Test." Ask: **Which conflict habits would you personally like to change? Why?** Share one of your harmful conflict habits and its negative impact; then name a helpful conflict habit you would like to replace it with. Ask your students to name some harmful impacts of harmful conflict habits, followed by helpful conflict habits the harmful ones can be replaced by, and helpful impacts that could result. Remind your students that habits can be changed, and every day is an opportunity to change harmful habits into helpful ones.

Now ask: **What are some helpful conflict habits you already have?** Discuss. **How do your helpful conflict habits help you when you're in a conflict?**

Next put students in pairs and have them circle all of the healthy conflict habits on their sheets. Go over the sheets together afterward and make sure they have circled numbers 2, 6, 8, 10, 11, 15, 16, 17, and 18.

Answer questions and discuss. Have volunteers add any new helpful or harmful conflict habits to the circles on the board.

Wrap-Up. Tell students to underline at least one item on their handouts to work on over the next week. Ask them what they've learned so far that can help them turn their harmful conflict habits into helpful ones (deep breathing, calming statements).

Follow-Up. Check in with students over the next few days to see how they're doing in changing conflict habits. Mark your calendar for a brief check-in discussion in a week or so.

Extension. Conduct a follow-up lesson in which students share and role-play conflict habits they have changed for the better.

Lesson 54: Positive and Negative Choices in Conflicts

Lesson 54 helps students distinguish between positive and negative choices in conflicts, recognizing that they have the power to choose positive responses.

Students will

- understand that negative choices in conflicts generally lead to negative outcomes
- reflect on the positive outcomes that positive choices in conflicts lead to
- understand that their conscience can help them make positive choices in conflict situations

Materials

- chart paper and marker
- handouts: "What Real Kids Have to Say About Making Choices in Conflicts" (page 130); "Conflict Observation Reflection Sheet" (pages 131–132)
- sign from Lesson 31: "Conscience— A feeling or knowledge of right and wrong that guides us to do what is right" (see page 76)

PART TWO
Preventing Conflict

Preparation. Divide a piece of chart paper into two columns. At the top of the left-hand column, write *"Positive Choices in Conflicts."* On the right, write *"Negative Choices in Conflicts."*

Introduction. Say: **Did you know that when we're faced with conflict, we always have a choice in how we're going to handle it? We can make a positive choice that will help resolve the conflict, or we can make a negative choice that ends up making the conflict get worse.**

Distribute the "What Real Kids Have to Say About Making Choices in Conflicts" handout. Ask for volunteers to read aloud the quotes from students on choices they make during conflicts. After each quote, ask: **"Positive choice or negative choice, what do you think?"** Discuss each response.

Referring to the sign, review the meaning of *conscience*. Ask: **Which quotes sounded like the kids were guided by their conscience?** Then say: **Sometimes we know we're making a negative choice, but we do it anyway. Does that ever happen to you? Why do you think people make negative choices?** Discuss.

Discussion and Activity. Ask students to think of a time they handled a conflict in a negative way (hitting, yelling, threatening). Ask how that conflict turned out. Say: **Conflicts often turn out badly when we react without thinking or when we ignore our conscience. When we stop for even a**

few seconds, think about the best thing to do, and choose how we're going to respond, things usually turn out better.

Ask students to think of a time they handled a conflict in a positive way (cooling off, hearing out the other person). Ask how the conflict turned out.

Have students brainstorm negative choices people make in conflicts. List them on the "Negative Choices in Conflicts" side of the chart. Be sure to include making negative faces and using negative body language and tone of voice. Then have students brainstorm positive choices people make in conflicts; list those on the other side of the chart.

Point to the right-hand column and ask: **What generally happens when we make negative choices like these?** (People get suspended, lose a friend, lose the trust of others.)

Ask: **What if someone gets in the habit of making negative choices in conflicts? What might happen as the person grows into adulthood?** (Perpetual trouble, loss of relationships, loss of a job, jail.)

Take a new sheet of chart paper and write at the top "Positive Outcomes of Positive Choices." Ask for examples of positive choices leading to positive results (keeping friends, staying out of trouble, greater self-respect, sense of personal pride). List the positive outcomes students name on the chart. Also discuss future positive outcomes that can result from making positive choices in conflict situations (happier relationships, more success in school and work, respect from others, peace of mind, admirable reputation).

Say: **How we handle conflicts can have a big impact on our lives. That's why learning how to work out conflicts respectfully is so important.** Ask: **If someone has trouble getting along with others right now, is it possible to change?** Discuss.

Wrap-Up. Remind students that they each have the power to respond to conflicts in positive ways. Each time they choose to make positive choices, they are creating a healthy pattern that will support them for the rest of their lives.

Follow-Up. Tell your students they're going to have the opportunity to observe conflicts that happen at school over the next few days. Pass out copies of the "Conflict Observation Reflection Sheet" and have students complete it. Note that this handout will be used in Lesson 55.

What Real Kids Have to Say About
Making Choices in Conflicts

In a national survey of more than 2,100 students in grades 3–6, kids wrote about choices they make during conflicts. Here are some of the things they wrote:

	Positive	Negative
"Sometimes I yell back at people, even though I know I shouldn't."	❏	❏
"I yell and the other person yells and we keep yelling at each other."	❏	❏
"If I'm in a conflict and it's going in the wrong direction, I walk away and ask a fair friend to help."	❏	❏
"If someone starts to get physical with me, I punch them and hit them."	❏	❏
"I usually cry because I'm sensitive."	❏	❏
"I tell the truth about what happened, and I try to be fair."	❏	❏
"I kick the person who is bothering me in the shin."	❏	❏
"If they get mad at me I try to make them jealous."	❏	❏
"I try to talk things out before it can turn into a physical fight."	❏	❏
"I try to prove that I'm the one who's right."	❏	❏
"If I get into a conflict with someone, I usually gossip about them and start rumors."	❏	❏
"I try to compromise."	❏	❏
"I try to ignore the person. Then after a day or two, I go up to them and tell them how I feel."	❏	❏
"One time this girl in my class made up a story and said I punched her in the face on the bus. I didn't know what to do, but I decided to let it go. I thought, she's lying and I don't care. It's not my fault. So I ignored her. I was so happy I ignored her because I felt so good afterwards!"	❏	❏

Conflict Observation Reflection Sheet

Observe conflicts that take place in your school over the next few days. Notice what happens when conflicts arise in the classroom, hall, cafeteria, and gym, and on the playground and bus. Then fill out this form. Be sure not to use people's names when filling out this sheet.

How often did you see conflicts taking place? Circle one.

Hardly ever   Once in a while   Often   All the time

In the following columns, write down some of the choices you saw people make when they got into conflicts. Use an extra sheet if necessary.

Negative choices: **Positive choices:**

_____   _____

_____   _____

_____   _____

_____   _____

_____   _____

What are the top 3 things you noticed kids having conflicts over?

1. _____

2. _____

3. _____

Conflict Observation Reflection Sheet (continued)

In the conflicts you observed, what were some things people did that made conflicts worse?

_____

_____

_____

_____

What positive choices did you observe—things that helped conflicts get worked out?

_____

_____

_____

_____

Were there better ways kids could have handled some of the conflicts you saw? Write about them here.

_____

_____

_____

_____

Lesson 55: Observing Conflict

conflict resolution • decency • fairness

Lesson 55 enables students to gain insights from having observed people in conflict. This lesson is a follow-up to Lesson 54.

Students will
- reflect on and evaluate choices made in conflicts they have observed
- determine which actions made conflicts better or worse
- role-play more positive ways conflicts they observed could have been handled

Materials
- completed handout: "Conflict Observation Reflection Sheet" (pages 131–132)
- student journals
- *optional:* "Our Top 10 Conflict Starters" chart from Lesson 51 (see page 120)

Preparation. Make sure students have completed the "Conflict Observation Reflection Sheet" prior to this lesson. Have them bring their sheets to the circle at the start of the lesson.

Introduction. Tell students they're going to have the opportunity to share things they've learned by observing conflicts. Remind them not to use people's names when sharing about the conflicts they observed, and not to discuss these conflicts after class. Ask: **What were some important things you discovered by observing conflicts?** Briefly discuss.

Discussion and Activity. Refer to the "Conflict Observation Reflection Sheet." Ask students the first question: **How often did you see conflicts taking place?** Ask what negative choices they observed. Discuss.

Put students in pairs and have them discuss negative choices people made that led to conflicts escalating and positive choices that helped conflicts get resolved. After a couple minutes, have students reconvene in the large circle. Discuss the negative and positive choices in the large group.

Cueing off of the last question from the sheet, ask for volunteers to role-play a conflict they observed, replacing negative conflict responses with positive ones. Role-play two or three different situations that were observed, with different volunteers acting in each. After each enactment, refer to the Win/Win Guidelines for Working Out Conflicts and ask: **Which of the guidelines did these people use? How did that help?**

Wrap-Up. Mention one or two of the top three conflict starters that several students noticed—something you consider to be an issue among your students or in your classroom. You may want to refer to your chart, "Our Top 10 Conflict Starters" as well. Say: **Imagine what our class would be like if every time this kind of conflict came up, each person made a positive choice and tried to resolve it in a fair, respectful way. How would that make things different here in our classroom (or school)?**

Follow-Up. Encourage students to write in their journals about a positive way a conflict they observed could have been handled, or a positive way a conflict of their own could have been handled.

Lesson 56: Responsibility vs. Blame, Part 1

personal responsibility • conflict resolution • cooperation

Lesson 56 helps students understand the importance of taking responsibility in conflicts rather than blaming.

Students will

- work in cooperative groups to learn important information about taking responsibility
- understand that in most conflicts, both people are responsible in some way
- understand that blaming causes conflicts to escalate

Materials

- handout: "Group Discussions About Taking Responsibility" (pages 135–137, two copies)
- paper and pencil for Recorders (see Activity and Discussion, below)
- chart paper and marker

Note: Conduct this lesson and Lesson 57 in sequence.

Preparation. Make two copies of the "Group Discussions About Taking Responsibility" handout. Keep one for yourself; cut out the five sections of the other. For this lesson, you'll be giving one section to each of five small groups.

Introduction. Refer to Win/Win Guideline 4: *Take responsibility for your role in the conflict.* Tell students they're going to be working in groups, and each group will be receiving information to read and a question to discuss relating to taking responsibility in conflicts. Let them know that afterward the class will come together and a student from each group will report the key points his or her group discussed. Refer to the "Respectful Listening" chart and remind students to observe respectful listening guidelines as they interact in their groups.

Activity and Discussion. Divide the class into five groups and have each group choose a Leader, a Recorder, and a Reporter. Make sure Recorders have paper and pencils to write down important ideas from their group's discussion.

Pass a section of the handout to each group. Allow five minutes for Leaders to read aloud the information at the top and for the group to discuss the question at the bottom. Remind Recorders to note the main ideas their group talks about so Reporters can present them to the class. Circulate and guide the groups' interactions as needed.

After five minutes, reconvene in a large circle. Beginning with Group 1, have each Reporter take about two minutes to tell the class what his or her group discussed regarding taking responsibility in conflicts. If the class has questions, anyone in the group may respond. On chart paper, list key points from each Reporter as that student speaks. These will be reviewed in Part 2 (Lesson 57).

Wrap-Up. Compliment students for any positives you observed in terms of group interaction and respectful listening. Have Leaders and Reporters put their names on the top of the papers they have. Collect and save these to redistribute during the next lesson. Tell the class they'll be reviewing what they shared in their groups during the next lesson.

Follow-Up. Have students observe themselves in any conflicts they get into between now and the next lesson. Tell them to ask themselves the question, "Is there some way I may be even a little bit responsible for this conflict?" (Do this yourself so you can discuss your own experiences with your class during Part 2.)

Note: If the issue of bullying comes up during this lesson, here's some important information: In bullying situations, all involved do not share responsibility. Make sure students understand that kids who are bullied are not responsible for the bullying. The person who bullies is the responsible party and needs to be held accountable. For more information on bullying, see pages 11–12 and Dealing with Bullying (pages 217–260).

Group Discussions About Taking Responsibility

Group 1: Taking Responsibility

Read to the group:

Did you know that in nearly all conflicts, *both* people are at least a little responsible? Both people usually did something to make the conflict happen, get worse, or keep going. Blaming almost always makes conflicts worse. But when even *one* person takes responsibility, the conflict will usually start to get better. When both people take responsibility, the conflict is likely to get solved. Taking responsibility rather than blaming is one of the most important things you can do.

Talk about it:

Think of a conflict you had. Was there a way you were *even a little bit* responsible? Discuss this in your group.

Group 2: The Problem with Blaming

Read to the group:

What do you think is the number one thing that keeps conflicts from getting worked out?

You're right if you said blaming.

When we blame the other person and don't take responsibility for our part, we make the conflict grow larger. Blaming usually makes the other person madder. Then the person will try to blame us back. Before long, instead of working out the conflict, we end up lost in the blame game. It's not hard to blame, but taking responsibility requires courage. The more you do it, the easier it gets. Next time you're in a conflict, try taking responsibility instead of blaming, and see what happens.

Talk about it:

Think of a conflict you had where you blamed the other person instead of taking responsibility. What ended up happening? Discuss this in your group.

Group Discussions About Taking Responsibility (continued)

Group 3: Benefits of Taking Responsibility

Read to the group:

What positive things can happen when you take responsibility for something you did rather than blaming? What can happen when you really listen to what the other person has to say? Your power to make things better grows. Aside from getting the conflict resolved, many other good things may start to happen. Here are just a few:

- People will respect and admire you more.
- You will respect yourself more.
- You will have healthier relationships.
- You will get along better with your friends, classmates, teachers, and family members.
- People will trust you more.
- You will have fewer conflicts.

Talk about it:

What other benefits are there for taking responsibility? What other good things can happen? Discuss this in your group.

Group 4: Why People Blame Instead of Taking Responsibility

Read to the group:

There is so much to gain from taking responsibility, and so little to gain from blaming! Why do so many people blame instead of taking responsibility? Here's what some kids say:

- "I always feel like I didn't do anything wrong."
- "It's usually the other person's fault."
- "I don't want to admit something and get in trouble."
- "What if the other person doesn't take responsibility, too? Then I look bad."
- "It scares me to admit what I've done."

Talk about it:

Do you ever blame instead of taking responsibility? Why? Discuss in your group. List more reasons people might not want to take responsibility for their role in a conflict.

Group Discussions About Taking Responsibility (continued)

Group 5: Looking at Our Own Conflicts

Read to the group:

Even though taking responsibility for your part in conflicts can be a hard thing to do, people who've learned to do it feel happy they did. Taking responsibility is a sign of strength and maturity. Here's what one person said about taking responsibility rather than blaming:

"I used to blame. But I stopped doing it when I began to see that it just made things worse. When I started taking responsibility, I was able to get along better with people in my life."

What was your last conflict about? Did you take responsibility for your role in it or did you blame? Was there a way you were *even a little bit* responsible?

Talk about it:

Discuss with your group conflicts some of you have had. For each one, talk about what happened. How might each person have been at least a little bit responsible for the conflict happening or for its not getting solved?

Lesson 57: Responsibility vs. Blame, Part 2

personal responsibility • conflict resolution • cooperation

Lesson 57 reinforces the importance of taking responsibility in conflicts rather than blaming. This lesson is a follow-up to Lesson 56.

Students will

- work in cooperative groups to review important information about taking responsibility
- understand that in most conflicts, both people are responsible in some way
- review the concept that blaming causes conflicts to escalate

Materials

- soft globe or ball
- "Group Discussions About Taking Responsibility" sheets and Reporters' notes from Lesson 56 (see pages 135–137)
- chart with key points from Lesson 56 (see page 134)
- handout: "Responsibility vs. Blame" (pages 139–140)
- *optional:* student journals

Preparation. For the first half of this lesson, take down or cover up the chart you wrote in Lesson 56 with key points from the Reporters on taking responsibility. You'll be showing it after a short review.

Introduction. Gather students in a circle and tell them you want to do a quick review of what they learned in the previous lesson about taking responsibility versus blaming. Ask one or two students to state the most important thing they remember from the last lesson.

Discussion. To further review concepts on responsibility versus blame, throw the soft globe or ball to someone and ask the student to share something else she or he remembers from the preceding lesson. Have that student throw the ball to someone else. Continue with a few more students until most major concepts have been covered.

Have students get back into the same cooperative groups they were in during the last lesson. Pass out the sections of the "Group Discussions About Taking Responsibility" and the notes Reporters took. Give each group about three minutes to review what they discussed in the last lesson.

Activity. Have students reconvene in the large circle. Show the chart from the last lesson listing important ideas from each group. Ask students to look over the list and see if there's anything else that should be added to it on taking responsibility versus blaming.

Now ask for a few volunteers to role-play a common conflict (ask the class to suggest one). Have role players blame each other for something that happened rather than take responsibility. Ask for two more volunteers to replay the conflict, this time with each person taking responsibility for something that happened. Afterward, debrief with the class, asking which role play worked better and why.

Wrap-Up. Direct attention to the "Respectful Listening" chart and ask the class how they think they did working in their groups and in the large circle. Have them acknowledge respectful listening they observed. Let students know that listening respectfully is a form of taking responsibility, too. The more we do it, the better everyone gets along.

Distribute the "Responsibility vs. Blame" handout and encourage students to read it and share it with parents and friends.

Extension. Have students keep a responsibility log in their journals. For one week, ask them to note every conflict they have at home and in school, then answer this question for each: "Was there some way I was responsible, too, even if it was something small?"

Responsibility vs. Blame

Taking Responsibility

Did you know that in nearly all conflicts, *both* people are at least a little responsible? Both people usually did something to make the conflict happen, get worse, or keep going. Blaming almost always makes conflicts worse. But when even *one* person takes responsibility, the conflict will usually start to get better. When both people take responsibility, the conflict is likely to get solved. Taking responsibility rather than blaming is one of the most important things you can do.

Think of a conflict you had. Was there a way you were *even a little bit* responsible?

The Problem with Blaming

What do you think is the number one thing that keeps conflicts from getting worked out?

You're right if you said blaming. When we blame the other person and don't take responsibility for our part, we make the conflict grow larger. Blaming usually makes the other person madder. Then the person will try to blame us back. Before long, instead of working out the conflict, we end up lost in the blame game. It's not hard to blame, but taking responsibility requires courage. The more you do it, the easier it gets. Next time you're in a conflict, try taking responsibility instead of blaming, and see what happens.

Think of a conflict you had where you blamed the other person instead of taking responsibility. What ended up happening?

Responsibility vs. Blame (continued)

Benefits of Taking Responsibility

What positive things can happen when you're in a conflict and you take responsibility for something you did rather than blaming? What can happen when you really listen to what the other person has to say? Your power to make things better grows. Aside from getting the conflict resolved, many other good things may start to happen. Here are just a few:

- People will respect and admire you more.
- You will respect yourself more.
- You will have healthier relationships.
- You will get along better with your friends, classmates, teachers, and family members.
- People will trust you more.
- You will have fewer conflicts.

Why People Blame Instead of Taking Responsibility

There is so much to gain from taking responsibility, and so little to gain from blaming! Why do so many people blame instead of taking responsibility? Here's what some kids say:

- "I always feel like I didn't do anything wrong."
- "It's usually the other person's fault."
- "I don't want to admit anything and get in trouble."
- "What if the other person doesn't take responsibility, too? Then I look bad."
- "It scares me to admit what I've done."

Even though taking responsibility for your part in conflicts can be a hard thing to do, people who've learned to do it feel happy they did. Taking responsibility is a sign of strength and maturity. Here's what one person said about taking responsibility rather than blaming:

> "I used to blame. But I stopped doing it when I began to see that it just made things worse. When I started taking responsibility, I was able to get along better with people in my life."

> What was your last conflict about? Did you take responsibility for your role in it or did you blame? Was there a way you were *even a little bit* responsible?

Lesson 58: Willingness to Work Out Conflicts

Lesson 58 focuses on the importance of being willing to resolve conflicts fairly and the impediments to doing so.

Students will

- learn that working out conflicts requires being willing to compromise, to hear the other person out, and to be patient
- understand that without willingness, conflicts can't get resolved
- role-play using compromise, sincere listening, and patience to resolve a conflict

Materials

- chart paper and marker
- student journals

Preparation. Create a sign that says the following:

"Working out conflicts requires WILLINGNESS to:

1. *compromise*

2. *hear out the other person*

3. *be patient"*

Introduction. Compliment students on any progress you've observed in the ways they've been handling conflicts. Ask: **Do you ever find it hard to work out conflicts peacefully? What makes it hard for you?**

Discussion. Ask: **How do you feel when you're involved in a conflict that doesn't get resolved?** Discuss. Then say: **Having conflicts that aren't resolved makes most of us feel really bad. It can affect our mood, our energy, and our concentration. Has that ever happened to you?** Discuss.

Continue: **On the other hand, how do you feel when you've been successful at working out a conflict?** Discuss. Say: **Before any conflict can be worked out, one thing needs to be present: willingness to do so.**

Show the sign you made. Point to the word *willingness* and ask: **What does it mean to be willing to do something?** Ask students the meaning of *compromise.* Discuss, asking for examples. Also give an example of a time you compromised.

Ask: **Do you ever have trouble compromising? Hearing out the other person? Being patient?** Discuss. **Why do you think people sometimes aren't willing to work out conflicts peacefully?** (habit,

wanting power, needing to be right, fear of looking bad)

Referring to the sign, reiterate: **To be willing to work out conflicts, we need to be willing to compromise. We need to be willing to hear out the other person—really listen to what the other person has to say, even if we disagree. And we need to be patient. Working things out can take time. Sometimes, conflicts can get worked out even if only one person is willing. It's important to try to be that person.**

Ask students to think of conflicts they observed (or took part in) that didn't get resolved. Which of the three willingness skills might have been missing? Give a personal example.

Note: Sometimes kids get frustrated when they're willing to work out a conflict and the other person isn't. Let them know that it's still important to be willing to try. In time, the other person may follow suit. If not, at least you know you tried your best.

Activity. Ask for two volunteers to role-play a conflict that didn't get resolved. Use a scenario students suggest or the following conflict reported by a fifth-grade boy:*

Zach plays Ultimate Frisbee every day at school with a bunch of kids. Zach plays on one team and his friends Max and Hector play on the other. Zach is good at intercepting the Frisbee. When Zach's side is winning, Max and Hector get mad and say he's cheating. When the students go back inside after recess, Max and Hector call Zach names and

---

* Quotes and stories attributed to real students and teachers come from author interviews and from responses to the Survey About Conflicts conducted by the author and publisher. See pages 1 and 282–284 for further information.

spread rumors that he cheats. Zach feels hurt and mad, especially because Max used to be his best friend. Today, he tells Max that he's not cheating and Max should quit saying he is. Max says, "Yeah—right!"

Have students take the parts of Zach and Max to role-play the conflict. Ask them to do something to chill out before facing each other. Guide the role players through the Win/Win Guidelines. Encourage them to compromise, really listen, and be patient so they can come to a fair solution. Let the class suggest solutions, too.

Afterward, ask students to assess how the conflict-solving went. Did Zach and Max show willingness to compromise? To hear each other out? Did they stay patient? Did they solve the conflict fairly?

Discuss any problems the two role players had in resolving the conflict. Emphasize that it takes practice to solve conflicts. Each time students practice willingness skills, this will get easier.

Wrap-Up. Acknowledge students for progress they're making in learning to get along and work out conflicts. Ask: **Why is it so important to be willing to work out conflicts? Which willingness skill is most challenging for you? Jot it down in your journal.**

Follow-Up. Ask students to write or draw in their journals about a time their most challenging willingness skill got in the way of working out a conflict. Have them reflect on what they plan to do differently next time.

Extension. Tell students to continue observing themselves when conflicts arise. Encourage them to ask themselves this question each time: "How willing am I to listen, compromise, and be patient?"

Lesson 59: Willingness Blocks

conflict resolution • fairness • compromise

Lesson 59 has students identify their personal willingness blocks—things that stand in their way of working out conflicts.

Materials

- chart paper and marker or "WILLINGNESS" skills sign from Lesson 58 (see page 141)
- handout: "What Are Your Willingness Blocks?" (page 144)
- two large wooden blocks

Preparation. If you have not already done so, create a sign that says the following:

"Working out conflicts requires WILLINGNESS to:

1. *compromise*

2. *hear out the other person*

3. *be patient"*

Introduction. Display the sign and introduce or review the three willingness skills needed to solve conflicts: willingness to listen, compromise, and be patient.

Say: **Today we're going to look at the opposite of willingness, something called** *willingness blocks.* **Willingness blocks are all the things we think, feel, and do that hold us back from working out conflicts.** Pass out the "What Are Your Willingness Blocks?" handout. Ask students to think of some recent conflicts they've had at school or at home, and fill out the quiz as honestly as possible. Let them know you'll be taking the quiz right along with them.

Discussion. After everyone has completed the quiz, ask students which willingness blocks they checked off. Share what yours are. Discuss.

Ask students: **When you hold onto your willingness blocks, are you able to work out conflicts peacefully? Why not?** Discuss.

Then ask: **What happens when people hold onto willingness blocks?** (They keep blaming others, conflicts escalate, they get into more conflicts.) **What other negative things happen when we go around having conflicts all the time?** Discuss outcomes like the following:

- We lose friends.
- We get punished.
- We're stressed out.
- People avoid us.

- We feel bad about ourselves.
- People start thinking we're troublemakers.
- Our health can be affected.
- We can set up a lifetime pattern of dealing with conflicts in negative ways.

Activity. Ask students to think of an unresolved conflict they've had at home or at school. Ask for two volunteers to role-play the conflict. Before they start, have each volunteer hold a block in front of themselves as if literally blocking the other person. Tell them to role-play the conflict with their willingness blocks in place, not listening, not compromising, and not being patient. Caution students not to use real names or physically touch each other.

Next, have the role players put down their blocks and replay the conflict, this time showing willingness to compromise, hear the other person out, and be patient. Guide them through Stop, Breathe, Chill and the Win/Win Guidelines.

Ask the class: **What was different this time? Which worked better—holding onto willingness blocks, or letting them go?** Discuss. **What's to be gained by letting go of our willingness blocks?**

Wrap-Up. Have students look at the handout they completed. Ask them to circle one or two willingness blocks they plan to work on giving up. Follow up with the class in about a week to see how they're doing with this.

Extensions. Have students continue observing themselves in conflicts, taking note of willingness blocks that come up. They can optionally write, draw, or record themselves talking about this, reflecting on what they can do to let go of their willingness blocks.

Start a Willingness Blog in your class where kids can comment on willingness blocks that come up and things they're doing to let go of them.

What Are Your Willingness Blocks?

When you're in a conflict, which willingness blocks apply to you? Check any that do. If you have a different willingness block than those listed, write it down.

- ☐ I want to show I'm "right" and make the other person "wrong."

- ☐ I don't want to look like a wimp.

- ☐ I think people will take advantage of me if I compromise.

- ☐ I like to be on top.

- ☐ I don't want to hear out someone I don't like or someone who did me wrong.

- ☐ Sometimes I'm afraid of looking stupid.

- ☐ Sometimes I feel too angry to work things out.

- ☐ It takes too long to talk things out.

- ☐ Sometimes I want to get even with the other person.

- ☐ I'd rather blame than take responsibility.

- ☐ I've always dealt with conflict one way and I don't know how to change.

- ☐ _____

- ☐ _____

When you hold onto willingness blocks, you can almost *guarantee* that your conflicts aren't going to get worked out. Ask yourself:

"Is it really worth holding onto my willingness block?"

Which willingness blocks are you willing to give up?

_____

_____

_____

Lesson 60: Examining Our Willingness Blocks

conflict resolution • fairness • compromise

Lesson 60 encourages students to reflect on the ramifications of holding onto their willingness blocks when they are faced with conflicts. This lesson is a follow-up to Lesson 59.

Students will

- review what willingness blocks are and the negative outcomes they lead to
- write about a time when a willingness block kept them from working out a conflict
- visualize themselves letting go of a willingness block and resolving a conflict successfully

Materials

- two large wooden blocks
- student journals
- *optional:* completed handout, "What Are Your Willingness Blocks?" (page 144)

Introduction and Discussion. Hold up the blocks and review by asking: **What are willingness blocks? What happens when people hold onto willingness blocks?** (We keep blaming others, conflicts escalate, we get into more conflicts.) **What other negative things happen when we go around having conflicts all the time?** Briefly review ideas discussed in Lesson 59 (loss of friends, punishment, stress, loneliness, negative lifetime pattern).

Ask: **What three things do we need to be willing to do to resolve conflicts?** (Compromise, hear the other person out, be patient.) **Why is willingness so important when it comes to solving conflicts?**

Activity. Holding up the blocks again, ask students to think about how their willingness blocks have gotten in the way when they've had conflicts. Have students pair up and discuss this together briefly.

Have students take out journals and do several minutes of automatic writing on the following topic: "A Time I Was Unwilling to Work Out a Conflict, and Why." Have students write for three to five minutes.

Afterward, ask for volunteers to share what they wrote. Ask each volunteer why he or she held onto the willingness block. What negative results came from holding onto it? Also ask the volunteers what they might have done differently if they were truly willing to work out the conflict.

Tell students they're going to be doing a visualization that will let them replay in their minds the conflict they just wrote about. Have students close their eyes, or cover them and look down, and picture the conflict they had. Say:

Take some slow, deep abdominal breaths. (Breathe with students.) **Feel yourself getting calmer and calmer. Picture yourself putting down your willingness block and leaving it on the floor.**

Picture yourself talking to the person you have your conflict with—the same person you just wrote about. **Picture yourself getting ready to talk out the conflict using the Win/Win Guidelines. Say your calming statement in your head. Take another slow, deep breath. Think about the I-message you want to give. Now hear yourself say it to the other person.** (Pause.)

Picture the person responding to you. See yourself listening to what the person has to say. (Pause.) **See yourself saying back the main idea of what you heard.** (Pause.) **Now see yourself and the other person talking over the problem and coming up with a fair solution.** (Pause.)

Picture yourself shaking hands and walking away satisfied. You've done it! You've resolved your conflict in a mature way, and you feel proud of yourself.

Have students open their eyes. Ask for one or two volunteers to share what they envisioned. Ask how the ending they envisioned differed from what happened in real life.

Wrap-Up. Affirm students for the important work they're doing to become truly willing to work out conflicts. Let students know that letting go of willingness blocks doesn't guarantee that the conflict will work out. But there's a greater chance that it will get resolved. Also, they'll feel better about how they handled themselves knowing they tried to be part of the solution rather than being part of the problem.

Extension. Encourage students to share their "What Are My Willingness Blocks?" handout with a trusted adult or friend. Have them talk with this person about what they're doing to try to let go of a willingness block.

Lesson 61: Let's Compromise
(10-Minute Time Cruncher)

conflict resolution • compromise • fairness • personal responsibility

Lesson 61 helps students open their minds to a variety of possible ways to compromise in a conflict situation.

Students will
- brainstorm ways to compromise in a conflict
- recognize that there are often many possible solutions

Materials
- chart paper and marker

Introduction. Write the word *compromise* on the board. Ask students what it means. Tie the idea of compromise to the concept of fairness.

Activity and Discussion. Ask students to think of conflicts that often come up in the classroom, on the playground, in the cafeteria, or somewhere else at school. Listen to their ideas and choose a conflict to focus on for this lesson—something all students will relate to.

Explain that you want the group to brainstorm all the ways someone could compromise to help work out this conflict. If you're comfortable, have students call out their ideas as they have them, allowing you time to list what they say on chart paper. Otherwise, pass a soft globe or ball to elicit ideas. Include your own ideas for compromising on the chart as well.

After several minutes, look at your list together. Ask: **Which of these ideas would be realistic for you to do in a conflict like this one?**

Wrap-Up. Tell students: **In nearly all conflicts, there's a way for both people to compromise, as long as they are willing to do so.**

Follow-Up. Encourage students to brainstorm in their journals or with a friend ways to compromise in a conflict they've had.

Extensions. Have students look online for quotes about compromise, copy down those they like best, and share them with friends. Students can also create a bulletin board or other class display with the quotes they found.

Lesson 62: Basement or Balcony? Part 1

conflict resolution • compromise • personal responsibility

Lesson 62 introduces the idea of "basement or balcony" as a metaphor for making negative versus positive choices in conflict.

Students will

- understand and develop their power to choose positive over negative responses to conflicts
- recognize that they feel better about themselves when they "go up to the balcony" and make positive choices in the face of conflict
- recognize that choosing the balcony is powerful and can lead to better outcomes for conflicts

Materials

- chart paper and marker
- handouts: "Basement or Balcony?" (page 149); "Basement or Balcony: Which Did You Choose?" (pages 150–151)

Note: Conduct this lesson and Lesson 63 in sequence.

Preparation. On chart paper, write the following: *"Be bigger than the problem."*

Introduction. Read aloud to students the following statement from a teacher:

"I realized that when I'm involved in a conflict and the other person is acting mean or nasty, if I do that, too, it's like I'm going down to the basement inside myself—to the lowest part of me. But if I choose to keep behaving with dignity and respect, then it's like I'm up in the balcony—the highest part of me. I feel better about myself when I choose the balcony."

Ask the class what these words mean to them. You might ask: **Where's the basement? Where's the balcony? What does this teacher mean by the "lowest part" of her? The "highest part"?** Reread the statement and invite any other student responses.

Discussion. Toward the top of the board make a large square, at least 2' x 3'. Above it write "Balcony." Toward the bottom of the board make another large square. Beneath it write "Basement." Ask students to think of negative ways they and others sometimes behave during conflicts—ways that put them in the basement. Write their ideas in the "Basement" box (yelling, blaming, being sarcastic, name-calling, not listening, rolling the eyes, making negative faces, threatening, hitting).

Now ask students: **What are some things people do to get to the balcony during a conflict?** Guide students to include many possible positive choices

(listening, compromising, taking responsibility, cooling off, keeping things in perspective, telling the truth, being respectful, refraining from name-calling, staying patient). List these in the "Balcony" box. Leave the boxes on the board for use in Lesson 63.

One by one, read the following quotes from real students, each time asking: **Did this person choose the basement or the balcony?**

- "I try not to say mean stuff."
- "When I'm in a conflict with people, I either call them names or get revenge."
- "I count backwards from 50 to let my anger out."
- "I do everything in my power not to hurt them or make a scene."
- "It's hard. If it's not my fault, I usually get mad and yell."
- "I try to calmly talk it out."
- "I usually say, 'You know what? I'm not going to argue.' Then I walk away."
- "I do my best to compromise."

Activity. Have students pair up and think of strategies and concepts they've used that have helped them stay in the balcony. After two or three minutes, reconvene in the circle and say: **No matter how much time we may have spent down in the basement, we have the power to go up to the balcony. It's always there for us, and when we choose to go there, we feel better about ourselves, and the conflict usually gets easier to deal with.**

Ask students to think of a time they went to the balcony instead of the basement. Ask how it felt to be up in the balcony, especially if the other person was down in the basement. Share your own example, too.

Distribute the "Basement or Balcony?" handout. Ask for volunteers to read each paragraph. After the second paragraph is read, refer to the sign you have made. Discuss the idea of being bigger than the problem. Then continue going over the handout.

Wrap-Up. Distribute the "Basement or Balcony: Which Did You Choose?" handout. Say: **Pay attention to what you do when you get into conflicts this week. Each time, ask yourself, "Did I go to the basement or balcony?" Don't judge yourself too hard if you found yourself in the basement. We've all gone there many times. Observing your own behavior is a powerful step in making new choices. If you're willing to take responsibility, getting to the balcony will be easier than you think.**

Tell students you'll be filling out the same handout, that learning how to stay in the balcony is something we all need to practice. Note that the handout will be used in Lesson 63 and is briefly discussed in Lesson 64.

PART TWO
Preventing Conflict

Basement or Balcony?

Sometimes when people get us really mad, we automatically go down to the basement. We don't even think about it—we're just there. But the truth is, the balcony is available in every moment, and when we choose to go to the balcony, we feel better about ourselves, and the conflict usually works out a lot better.

Can you remember a conflict where you went up to the balcony instead of going down to the basement? How did it feel to be up in the balcony? For most people, going up to the balcony feels really good. Why? Because when we go to the highest part of ourselves, we feel proud and in control. We know we didn't let something or someone get the best of us. We discover that we can be bigger than the problem.

Now think of a time when you went down to the basement. What did you do? How did you end up feeling?

It's a big difference and an important choice: Basement or balcony? You have the power to choose the balcony each time you have a conflict. When you make this choice, you take a big step forward to becoming a conflict solver who knows how to get along with others. And when you do this, you start creating a pattern of success that can last the rest of your life.

Basement or Balcony: Which Did You Choose?

Observe yourself when you're involved in conflicts. Then fill out the sections below.

Conflict 1

Description of the conflict:

_____

_____

What I did in response to the conflict:

_____

_____

Where did I go—down to the basement or up to the balcony?

_____

_____

If I went down to the basement, what had me end up there?

_____

_____

If I went up to the balcony, how did I manage to stay there?

_____

_____

If the conflict ended in a negative way, what can I do differently next time?

_____

_____

If the conflict got resolved, what did I do that I can do in future conflicts?

_____

_____

Basement or Balcony: Which Did You Choose? (continued)

Conflict 2

Description of the conflict:

_____

_____

What I did in response to the conflict:

_____

_____

Where did I go—down to the basement or up to the balcony?

_____

_____

If I went down to the basement, what had me end up there?

_____

_____

If I went up to the balcony, how did I manage to stay there?

_____

_____

If the conflict ended in a negative way, what can I do differently next time?

_____

_____

If the conflict got resolved, what did I do that I can do in future conflicts?

_____

_____

Lesson 63: Basement or Balcony? Part 2

conflict resolution • compromise • personal responsibility

Lesson 63 guides students to reflect on their own choices in conflicts and take greater responsibility for their behavior. This lesson is a follow-up to Lesson 62.

Students will

- reflect on their "basement" or "balcony" reactions to conflict
- explore ideas for staying in the balcony during conflict
- understand that patience and practice can help them stay in the balcony more often

Materials

- completed handout: "Basement or Balcony: Which Did You Choose?" (pages 150–151)
- "Basement" and "Balcony" boxes (written on the board in Lesson 62—see page 147)
- "Ways to Chill" chart from Lesson 40 (see pages 100–101)
- student journals
- "Be bigger than the problem" sign from Lesson 62 (see page 147)

Introduction. Have students bring their completed "Basement or Balcony: Which Did You Choose?" handouts to the circle. Ask: **What did you notice when you observed yourself during conflicts? Did you spend more time down in the basement or up in the balcony? Why? What made it hard to go up to the balcony and stay there?**

Point out that going down to the basement is a conflict habit; we each have the power to change our conflict habits, even if it's hard at first. Give a personal example. Discuss.

Activity and Discussion. Ask: What "basement" kinds of things did you observe yourself doing? Discuss. Share your experiences, too. Then ask: **What "balcony" kinds of things did you do? What are some examples of how people were able to get themselves up to the balcony when there's been a conflict?** Affirm students for whatever they did to get to the balcony.

One at a time, share and discuss these examples of how two real students described how they get to the balcony:

- "I take time to cool off. Then I let the other person tell their side of the story."

- "I think about what happened and try to understand why the other person is reacting to it."

Ask students if they've tried doing these things. Continue the discussion, eliciting other things students do, or can do, to stay up in the balcony more often. Remind them to Stop, Breathe, Chill and to use calming statements, ideas from the "Ways to Chill" chart, or the temper tamers they listed in their journals (see page 112).

Ask students what they learned about themselves through this activity. Referring to the sign, ask if anyone did something that enabled him or her to experience being bigger than the problem. What was that like?

Wrap-Up. Remind students that we each have the power to go up to the balcony during conflict. It takes practice, patience, and willingness to try again when we fall short. Acknowledge students for the progress they are making. Be sure to acknowledge small steps, especially with students who've had difficulty getting to the balcony.

Lesson 64: Staying in the Balcony

conflict resolution • compromise • personal responsibility • fairness

Lesson 64 lets students explore a variety of positive ways to deal with conflict—to stay in the balcony. This is a follow-up to Lesson 62.

Students will

- explore a variety of ways to "stay up in the balcony" when faced with conflict
- role-play staying in the balcony by using a Peace Shield, calming statement, and I-messages

Materials

- "Be bigger than the problem" sign from Lesson 62 (see page 147)
- handout: "What Real Kids Have to Say About Staying in the Balcony" (page 154)

Note: The Peace Shield is introduced and explained in Lesson 47.

Introduction. Check in with students about how they're doing using Stop, Breathe, Chill and the Win/Win Guidelines in real conflicts to help them stay up in the balcony. Discuss progress and challenges. Share your own challenges and successes. The more authentic experiences you share, especially in terms of how you deal with challenges to peacefully working out conflicts, the more your kids are likely to buy in to doing so themselves.

Discussion. Refer to the "Be bigger than the problem" sign. Ask for examples of conflicts where students managed to stay in the balcony and be bigger than the problem when the other person was in the basement. Ask how they helped themselves stay up in the balcony.

Activity. Pass out copies of "What Real Kids Have to Say About Staying in the Balcony." Ask for volunteers to read aloud the quotes from real kids. After the quotes have been read, ask students to share what they found most helpful in hearing the experiences of other kids. Discuss.

Have students read the quotes again and circle one they find most useful, especially when dealing with someone who is down in the basement. Discuss.

Ask for volunteers to role-play the following scenario, shared by a fourth-grade girl (or use a scenario students suggest):

"This kid seems to have a problem with me. When I first moved here, I know I acted kind of annoying, but other kids get along with me, even the kid's friends. But sometimes he acts like he hates me. I mean there are times he hits me, or he calls me terrible names. Other times we get along, and then I like him, but when he's mean I just want him to leave me alone."

Ask: **What can this girl do to solve the problem? Is there a way she can go up to the balcony as she stands up for herself?** Discuss, encouraging students to consider strategies they've learned that could be helpful (put on her Peace Shield, breathe deeply, use a calming statement). Remind students that they should never open themselves to abusive comments or physical harm from anyone. If that happens, they should walk away and seek the help of an adult.

Now ask for volunteers to role-play addressing the problem at a neutral time, like when the two students are getting along. Before the role play begins, coach the student who is being picked on to put on her Peace Shield, use a calming statement, and think about an I-message to deliver. When she feels fully prepared, have her approach the other role player and talk about the problem.

Wrap-Up. After the role play, ask for responses from the class, including other I-messages or approaches that could be helpful.

Extension. Have students work in pairs or small groups to come up with conflict scenarios and practice different ways to get to the balcony instead of the basement.

What Real Kids Have to Say About
Staying in the Balcony

In a national survey of more than 2,100 students in grades 3–6, kids wrote about positive choices they make in conflict situations. Here are some things they wrote:

"When I'm involved in a conflict, I tell the truth, try to calm down, and think about ways to handle it without hurting anyone. I try not to let my anger get to my head and cause me to say or do mean things."

"I try to figure out the problem and fix it in a fair and equal way."

"If I did something that bothered the other person, I say, 'Sorry I did that. I hope we can leave this behind and become friends again.' It works almost every time."

"I think about what happened and try to understand why the other person is reacting to it."

"I tell myself to back off and cool down."

"I try to calm the other person down, then tell myself not to get too involved. Later I write it out to vent my feelings."

"I walk away and try to clear my mind, and think about the good things in my life."

"When I'm in a conflict, one thing that really helps is I pretend my cat is next to me, and I feel better. Sometimes I talk to her in my imagination. It helps me come up with solutions."

"Sometimes I go in my room and find a little space where I just curl up in a ball. I'll read a book, and that really calms me down. Reading helps me think of solutions, too."

"I could have ended up in a fight with one of my friends when I tagged him during a game and he said, 'At least I'm not the one with bad eyes.' Instead of fighting, I decided to leave the park and ignore him. I decided to focus on how I feel about myself, which is good. I find if I take a break and talk to the person later, it works out. That's what I did with him."

Lesson 65: Introducing Assertiveness

conflict resolution • compromise • fairness • personal responsibility • assertiveness

Lesson 65 introduces the concept of assertiveness and helps students see the link between assertiveness and preventing and effectively solving conflicts.

Students will

- understand what it means to be assertive
- recognize the difference between being assertive and being aggressive
- role-play handling a conflict assertively

Materials

- chart paper and marker
- student journals
- handout: "Conflict Solver Interview" (page 156)

Preparation. On chart paper, write the following: *"Assertive—Strong and honest, yet respectful, saying what you need to say with confidence."*

Introduction. Say: **Today we're going to talk about being assertive. Does anyone know what** *assertive* **means?** Discuss briefly.

Say: **Here's an example of an assertive person I know: She gets along really well with others and always manages to say what's on her mind in a respectful way when she's in a conflict. Even when people try to argue or start a fight, she keeps a** *neutral* **facial expression and speaks in a firm but calm voice. She comes across as strong without being mean.**

Discussion and Activity. Ask students to describe what a neutral facial expression is. Discuss the importance of keeping a neutral facial expression and tone of voice, along with neutral body language that shows pride without being threatening. Ask for two volunteers to demonstrate neutral and non-neutral facial expressions, tone of voice, and body language.

Ask students: **What word describes people who can be strong and honest, stay respectful, and get their point across without bossing or threatening?**

Show the definition of *assertive*. Have students copy the definition into their journals. Lead a brief discussion of the difference between being assertive and being aggressive, making sure that students understand *assertive* means speaking our minds with

strength and respect, while *aggressive* means being ready to argue, threaten, or fight. Say: **Think of someone you know who is good at solving conflicts. Is the person assertive or aggressive?** Discuss.

Ask for two volunteers to role-play the following conflict, or another one students suggest, using the Win/Win Guidelines. Have both role players act assertively, not aggressively:

T.J. lent his friend Maya a book that needed to be returned to the library on Monday. Maya didn't return it on time and T.J. ended up having to pay a fine. T.J. is really annoyed.

Afterward, debrief with the class. Were role players assertive, not aggressive? Did they resolve the conflict in a fair way? Did they both manage to stay up in the balcony? (See Lesson 62.) If so, how?

Wrap-Up. Pass out the "Conflict Solver Interview" handout and go over it with students. Make sure students know that adults as well as kids can be interviewed. Note that the completed handout will be used in Lesson 66.

Follow-Up. Check in with students to make sure they know who they can interview. As needed, help them figure out who this could be and how they can conduct their interview. (Some students may wish to record their interviews—this is fine as long as the interviewee agrees. They may also ask the person being interviewed to help complete the form as they talk.)

Conflict Solver Interview

Choose someone who you think is good at preventing or solving conflicts. This person should be someone you respect who gets along well with others, works out problems fairly, and speaks his or her mind assertively, without becoming aggressive.

Ask your conflict solver the following questions. Write the answers below:

1. What do you do to keep your cool when someone gets you mad?

    _____

    _____

2. How do you stay calm during conflict?

    _____

    _____

3. What do you do to avoid using put-downs when you're in a conflict?

    _____

    _____

    _____

4. Is there something you say to yourself that helps you keep your cool in conflict situations?

    _____

    _____

    _____

5. What advice do you have for other people when it comes to handling conflict?

    _____

    _____

Lesson 66: Conflict Solver Interviews

conflict resolution • compromise • fairness • courage • personal responsibility

Lesson 66 asks students to share what they learned from conflict solvers they interviewed and reflect on how to apply any new understandings in their own lives. This lesson is a follow-up to Lesson 65.

Students will

- discuss ideas they have learned from interviewing effective conflict solvers
- recognize skills effective conflict solvers use to stay calm and handle conflicts assertively and fairly
- role-play assertive, respectful approaches to handling a typical classroom conflict

Materials

- completed handout: "Conflict Solver Interview" (page 156)
- sign with definition of *assertive* from Lesson 65 (see page 155)
- chart paper and marker
- student journals

Preparation. Prior to this lesson, pass out copies of the "Conflict Solver Interview" handout. Have students use it to interview someone they know who gets along well with others and is good at preventing and resolving conflicts. Post the sign that defines *assertive* to refer to as needed.

Introduction and Discussion. Have students bring their "Conflict Solver Interview" sheets to the circle. Put students in pairs. Give them five minutes to share the most important things they learned from the conflict solver they interviewed.

Afterward, ask students to share with the large group some of the most helpful things they learned from their conflict solvers. List key points on chart paper.

Go over the questions on the handout one by one, sharing and discussing interviewees' ideas and responses:

- What do you do to keep your cool when someone gets you mad?
- How do you stay calm during conflict?
- What do you do to avoid using put-downs when you're in a conflict?
- Is there something you say to yourself that helps you keep your cool in conflict situations?
- What advice do you have for other people when it comes to handling conflict?

Ask students if they have had the chance to apply anything they learned from the conflict solvers they interviewed. Discuss.

Activity. Ask for two volunteers to pretend they are the conflict solvers they interviewed. Have the students role-play a typical conflict that goes on in your room, but have them do so in a way their conflict solvers would likely resolve it. Guide role players to use the Win/Win Guidelines as they enact the scene.

Briefly discuss the role play; conduct additional role plays if time permits.

Wrap-Up. Remind students to keep applying what they're learning to real-life situations. Tell them you'll check in with them to hear how things are going.

Follow-Up. In their journals, have students reflect on what they learned from the conflict solver they interviewed. Have them include changes they want to make in the way they handle real-life conflicts, and how insights from these interviews can be applied.

Lesson 67: Staying Respectful with Someone You Don't Like

respect • tolerance • self-control • compassion • fairness • courage • personal responsibility

Lesson 67 guides students to choose to remain respectful even when dealing with people they don't especially like.

Students will
- understand why it's important to be respectful toward someone they don't wish to be friends with
- recognize behaviors to avoid in order to remain respectful
- learn and practice ways to stay respectful even when it's hard to do

Materials
- chart paper and marker

Preparation. On chart paper, write the following: *"We agreed we didn't need to be friends, we just needed to respect each other."*

Introduction. Say: Sometimes it can be hard to be respectful to someone we don't like. Have you ever had that problem? Briefly discuss. Say: Here's something a real student wrote about handling the challenge of being around someone she didn't like:

"I used to have a problem with this girl named Lanny. She wasn't a true friend. She would threaten that she wouldn't be my friend if I didn't do what she wanted to do. She would act mean to me. My mom said there will always be a Lanny in every grade you go into. She asked, 'What can you do to handle the one you're dealing with now?'

"I decided to talk to Lanny. We agreed we didn't need to be friends, we just needed to respect each other."

Ask: What do you think is the most important lesson the girl who told this story learned from her experience?

Discussion. Display the sign you prepared and have the class read it aloud together: "We agreed we didn't need to be friends, we just needed to respect each other." Ask: Have you ever managed to treat someone you don't like with respect? Discuss. Give a personal example.

Then ask: What do you think people can do if they're in the same class, or on the same team, with someone they're no longer friends with? Or with someone they might not like? Think about how you would want to be treated by someone who may not like you. Discuss and list students' ideas on chart paper.

Ask: Even though you might not want to be friends with someone, what can you do to show basic respect? What things should you avoid doing? Add responses to the list. Guide students to understand that there are minimum basic things we need to do to survive together in the same room or school, or on the same team, with someone we might not like. Add the following to the chart if they have not been mentioned:

- Avoid using negative face or body language.
- Refrain from whispering about the person when you see him or her.
- Resist talking behind the person's back.
- Refrain from texting or passing notes about the person.
- Be polite, and if you can, say hello (in a courteous, non-sarcastic way).

Activity. Say: There are certain kinds of body language we need to avoid when we see someone we don't like. One at a time, ask for several volunteers to model different kinds of negative body language. After each demonstration, say: This is what we need to avoid doing. It's not respectful.

Continue, asking for volunteers to model the following:

- giving a negative look or gesture
- leaning in toward each other and starting to whisper as a third role player walks by
- saying hello sarcastically

After each demonstration, repeat the line: **This is what we need to avoid doing. It's not respectful.**

Next, ask volunteers to model passing each other in the hall and being respectful even though they don't like each other. Invite at least three more sets of volunteers to model it as well.

Reiterate to students that, hard as it might be to do what was just modeled, it's critical that they do. Ask why this is so important. (It shows integrity, it helps us avoid starting conflicts, it's never cool to be cruel, it's a way to stay up in the balcony.)

Ask students: **What can you do if someone is going out of their way to be mean to you and you are doing all the things talked about today?**

Discuss, making sure to include these ideas as part of your conversation:

- Try talking to the person directly and privately to find out why she or he is acting that way. (Plan out what you're going to say first, and rehearse it.)

If you feel like you can't do this alone, ask your school counselor, teacher, or another trusted adult to help the two of you talk it out.

- If nothing you've tried works, seek the help of a trusted adult.

Wrap-Up. Ask if students have any questions. Reassure students that it isn't always easy to stay respectful, and it takes courage to commit to doing so. Emphasize that this is something they can get in the habit of doing through practice. Acknowledge students for the work they are doing to take responsibility for their behavior in challenging situations.

Follow-Up. To give students further help dealing respectfully with someone who isn't willing to cooperate or stay respectful, conduct Lesson 71 (pages 167–168).

Extension. Have students write skits or create additional role plays showing ways to handle being with someone they don't typically get along with at school, on the bus, at lunch, and in extracurricular activities. Encourage students to demonstrate a variety of ways to stay respectful.

Lesson 68: The Dignity Stance

courage • self-worth • calmness • assertiveness • self-control

Lesson 68 introduces the Dignity Stance, an effective assertiveness tool students can use when they are involved in conflicts or mistreated by others.

Students will
- learn to use the Dignity Stance in conflict situations
- understand how to act assertively rather than aggressively or passively

Materials
- chart paper and marker
- handout: "The Dignity Stance" (page 162)

PART TWO Preventing Conflict

Preparation. On chart paper, write the steps for the Dignity Stance (see page 162).

Introduction. Tell students that today they're going to learn about an important way to stand up for themselves when they're involved in a conflict, or when they want to prevent a conflict or stop one from getting worse: the Dignity Stance.

Review with students what it means to be assertive (strong and honest, yet respectful, saying what you need to say with confidence).

Say: **You can show *assertiveness* in the way you hold your body and how you speak. The Dignity Stance is one way to do this.**

Activity. Tell students that starting with deep breaths and a calming statement will make it easier for them to use the Dignity Stance. Spend a few moments taking deep, abdominal breaths together; remind students to say a calming statement to themselves as they breathe.

Direct students' attention to the chart you have created. Go through each of the steps of the Dignity Stance with the group.

Stand tall with your head held high, feet apart, shoulders back. Demonstrate the Dignity Stance. Ask students to stand and also take the stance. Scan the class for kids who may need coaching. Some students might stiffen their bodies while others may take an aggressive stance, maybe even balling up their fists. Others will stand tall with head down, shoulders hunched. Give coaching where needed.

Take slow, deep breaths to keep your cool. Have students join you in taking three slow, deep abdominal breaths. Remind them that they can do this "invisibly" (in a non-exaggerated way) and no one else will know they're doing it. Demonstrate how.

Keep your body language and facial expression neutral but strong. Emphasize that it's important to keep a *neutral* (nonemotional) expression that is strong but respectful. Demonstrate this for students. Then say: **Sometimes we have to act "as if." We need to act *as if* we are feeling brave, even if we're really scared. The more we act like we feel brave, the braver we will actually begin to feel. Our body language can help us look and *feel* brave and strong.**

Make direct eye contact. Demonstrate looking someone in the eye with confidence, not aggression.

Note: In some cultures, children are taught that looking someone in the eye is disrespectful. If you have students who have been raised to look downward or avert their eyes, let them know that, with many people, making direct eye contact is an important way to communicate respect and confidence. Help students identify when and how to do this comfortably.

Speak in a firm, steady tone of voice. Model this with the following statement that can be used when facing an angry person: **"I know you're mad, but let's see if we can talk this out."** Have students turn to one another and make this statement standing tall, speaking in a steady, neutral tone of voice.

Select one student to join you before the group. Face your partner and say: **Now let's pretend you've just said something hurtful to me. First I'm going to take a deep breath and make my calming statement. Then I'm going to stand tall, look directly in your eyes, and in a firm, level voice I'm going to say how I feel.**

Still facing your partner, say: **"I find that insulting."** Now ask students to practice doing the same with the person next to them.

Walk away tall and strong. Demonstrate walking away tall and strong. Tell students that breathing deeply and repeating their calming statements will help them walk away with poise and dignity. Now have them practice walking away tall and proud. Give coaching where needed, and help students modify any aggressive or passive postures or gestures.

Remind your students of the way Martin Luther King Jr. carried himself during civil rights marches. Even when people were yelling racist words and threats, he would consistently stand tall, walk strong and proud, and maintain a neutral facial expression. This is the finest example of the Dignity Stance that exists for all of us.

Discussion. Have students sit back down in the circle. Ask for two volunteers to come to the center. Ask one student to imagine the other has just called him or her a name. Have the recipient of the put-down assume the Dignity Stance, give an assertive I-message, then walk away tall and strong.

Ask students to give feedback. Did the person stand and speak assertively, not aggressively? Did the person walk away tall and strong (not wimpy or aggressive)?

Ask students to come up with other assertive statements that can be used in similar situations. They might be I-messages or simple statements, but they should always be firm and respectful. Some examples:

- "That wasn't funny."
- "Not cool."
- "I don't need to listen to this."
- "You're wasting your time."

Ask for more volunteers to come to the center of the circle, stand in the Dignity Stance, look the person in the eye, deliver a firm, steady response, and then walk away tall and strong.

Say: **If someone calls you a name or puts you down, the Dignity Stance is a way you can be strong and assertive without having to name-call back. You can walk away strong and brave, the way Martin Luther King Jr. did, not scared and weak.**

Wrap-Up. Entertain questions and comments. Give students the "Dignity Stance" handout and suggest they tape it into their journal or onto a wall at home.

Extension. Suggest that students do the following visualization activity at home: **Tonight, while you're lying in bed before falling asleep, practice some deep breathing and picture yourself using the Dignity Stance. See yourself standing tall and brave, looking someone who has insulted you in the eye, and speaking assertively. See yourself walking away tall and strong.**

The Dignity Stance

Stand tall with your head held high, feet apart, shoulders back.

Take slow, deep breaths to keep your cool.

Keep your body language and facial expression neutral but strong.

Make direct eye contact.

Speak in a firm, steady tone of voice.

Walk away tall and strong.

Lesson 69: Staying Out of Physical Fights

Lesson 69 introduces a practical, real-life approach students can use to stay out of physical fights. This lesson is a follow-up to Lesson 68.

Students will

- understand the importance of avoiding physical fights
- learn a realistic tool for staying out of fights
- come up with statements to use when faced with the possibility of a fight

Materials

- handout: "Staying Out of Fights" (page 164)
- "Dignity Stance" chart from Lesson 68 (see page 162)
- chart paper and marker

Introduction and Discussion. Say: Today we're going to talk about ways to stay out of physical fights. Here's some advice from a middle schooler who figured out a way to successfully do this. Distribute the handouts and invite a student or students to read the story from a real middle school student.

After the story has been read, ask: **Why does it take courage to walk away when someone's trying to pick a fight?** Discuss, and encourage students to be frank. For some kids, fighting is a way of life and a tool for proving one's worth.

Make it clear to students that avoiding physical fights doesn't mean letting people harm them. What it does mean is using every other option available. If students are in danger and need to defend themselves against oncoming violence, a physical response may be the only option, but that's the exception. Strongly emphasize the need to stay away from groups and places where fighting is likely. Say: **If you need to walk down another street on the way home from school to avoid a possible fight, do it. What else can you do?** Discuss.

Ask: **What happened to the boy in the story when he fought in sixth grade?** (He got suspended.) Ask students what the rules at school are regarding fighting. What are the consequences? Discuss. Also ask what would happen if they were adults and they got into a fight. Talk about adult consequences of fighting. Remind students that by learning how to resist fighting now, they're setting a pattern that can support them for the rest of their lives.

Ask students what technique the boy in the story came up with to keep himself from fighting when others were egging him on (Stop, Drop, Roll). Ask students: **What do you do to resist fighting? What else can you do?** Remind students of Stop, Breathe, Chill and the Dignity Stance.

Activity. Draw students' attention to the "Dignity Stance" sign, particularly "Speak in a firm, steady tone of voice." Put students in pairs and have them come up with statements that can be used if someone's trying to draw them into a fight. Give the following example that many kids use: "This isn't worth fighting over." After a few minutes, bring the class back together and ask for their ideas, listing them on chart paper.

Wrap-Up. Acknowledge students for their efforts to stay out of physical fights and get along better with others. Affirm them for honesty, respect, and respectful listening you've observed during the lesson.

Extensions. The middle school boy came up with his own unique strategy to stay out of fights: Stop, Drop, Roll. Students may want to come up with their own individual strategies to stay brave, respectful, and safe. Have students share their ideas through a classroom display.

If physical fighting is common in your school, introduce the following sometime after you've completed this lesson:

Tips for Staying Out of Physical Fights

- Don't provoke people.
- Resist hanging out with kids who get into physical fights.
- Find healthy ways to express anger; never go on the attack.
- Avoid places where fighting is likely to occur.
- Be willing to apologize if you've offended someone.
- Be guided by what you know is right, not your reactions.
- Remember the consequences of fighting and how that can affect your life.

Staying Out of Fights

A middle school boy discovered that he could keep himself out of fights by using the same saying that's used in fire prevention: "Stop, Drop, and Roll." This is what the boy recommends:

> Here's what I realized after I got suspended for fighting: If someone tries to tempt you to fight, don't do it. There's no realistic point to fighting. If somebody's picking on you, that person might have a troubled life. Their problems might lead them to act differently than they should. What I like to do when someone tries to get me to fight is stop, drop, and roll.
>
> **STOP to think about it.**
>
> **DROP whatever you want to say or do that's not respectful.**
>
> **ROLL on over to what you're going to do next.**
>
> Instead of getting pulled into fights, focus on your schoolwork. That's what I do. Many a day, people try to get me involved in fights. If someone intentionally throws things at me, I don't let it get to me. People will egg me on and try to get me to hit the other person. I just try to let their words go and do what I know is right.
>
> I learned my lesson when I was in sixth grade. This kid was throwing things at me. We just came back from an assembly. So I pushed him and he pushed me back. We got sent to the office and we started kicking each other. It was a mistake. I could have just let it go, something stupid like that, but I didn't. We both ended up getting suspended. Now I know better.

Think About It

Is there a place in your life where you can Stop, Drop, and Roll to stay out of an argument or a fight?

_____

_____

_____

Responding to Conflict

The more your students are able and willing to work out conflicts, the less likely they will be to bully or stand by passively (or aggressively) and watch bullying happen. This section will help you teach kids how to resolve different kinds of common conflicts using the Win/Win Guidelines. The lessons will enable your students to role-play and resolve conflicts brought on by gossip, exclusion, hurt feelings, negative group dynamics, and other familiar conflict triggers. The activities in the Preventing Conflict lessons on pages 119–164 lay the groundwork for the Responding to Conflict activities in this section. Conduct at least some of those lessons before doing these.

Be sure to have these charts displayed: "Respectful Listening," "The Win/Win Guidelines for Working Out Conflicts," and "Stop, Breathe, Chill" (introduced in Lessons 2, 8, and 9), and "Ways to Chill" (see Lesson 40, pages 100–101).

Lesson 70: Win/Win Guidelines for Working Out Conflicts (Review)

respect • personal responsibility • conflict resolution

Lesson 70 offers a refresher on the Win/Win Guidelines and gives students the opportunity to practice using all the guidelines together through role play.

Students will
- review how they've been using the Win/Win Guidelines to resolve conflicts
- address challenges they've encountered using the Win/Win Guidelines
- role-play conflicts using the Win/Win Guidelines and evaluate how effectively the guidelines were applied

Materials
- chart paper and marker
- *optional handout:* "Win/Win Guidelines for Working Out Conflicts" (page 36)

PART TWO
Responding to Conflict

Introduction and Discussion. Ask students how they've been using the Win/Win Guidelines to prevent or resolve conflicts. Refer to the "Win/Win Guidelines for Working Out Conflicts" chart and ask about different parts of the process: **What are you doing to cool off? Have you run into any challenges using I-messages? Which steps are most helpful? Most challenging?**

Refer to the Rules for Using the Win/Win Guidelines. Ask: **Are you remembering to use these rules? Are there any that are hard to stick to?** Discuss. Affirm students for progress they're making. Assure them that challenges are normal. With more practice and roleplay, the guidelines will become easier and more natural to use.

Activity. Ask for two volunteers to role-play a conflict. You can have students choose a conflict that's fairly common and role-play that one, or use this idea: **Person A spread a mean rumor about Person B. Person B retaliated by gossiping about Person A.**

Have volunteers role-play the conflict, using the guidelines and rules. Allow the role players to work their way through without interruption, unless they get stuck and need help.

After they finish, ask the class if they noticed each guideline being used. Ask for specific examples. Ask if the role play went well. Why or why not? What improvements could have been made?

Give the role players a chance to replay the scene, incorporating ideas that came up in the discussion.

As time permits, invite other volunteers to role-play one or two more scenarios. Choose common conflicts that happen in your class, or ask students to suggest conflicts to enact. Each time, offer support only when role players seem stuck. After each role play, ask the class to evaluate how the Win/Win Guidelines helped students solve the conflict, suggesting ideas that might have made the process go smoother. Discuss.

Wrap-Up. End the lesson by affirming students for their continued efforts toward resolving conflicts peacefully and respectfully. You may want to distribute fresh copies of the handout for students to keep in their journals or tape inside their notebooks, desks, or lockers.

Follow-Up. Continue to check in with students on how they're doing as they use the Win/Win Guidelines. Provide refresher lessons on the guidelines, referring back to Lessons 9–14 as needed. You may want to provide fresh copies of the Win/Win Guidelines handout for students as well.

Extension. Have students develop conflict-solving skits to perform for younger students.

Lesson 71: Working Out Conflicts with Someone Who Is Unwilling

conflict resolution • compromise • fairness • respect

Lesson 71 explores how to talk out a conflict with a resistant person.

Students will
- recognize that it can be possible to resolve a conflict even when only one person is willing
- role-play resolving a conflict with an unwilling partner
- see the relationship between misunderstandings and willingness blocks

Materials
- chart paper and marker or "WILLINGNESS" skills sign from Lesson 58 (see page 141)
- large wooden block (to represent a "willingness block")

Note: If you have not conducted Lessons 58 and 59 (pages 141–144), read through them prior to conducting this one.

Preparation. If you have not done so before, create a sign that says the following:

"Working out conflicts requires WILLINGNESS to:
- *compromise*
- *hear out the other person*
- *be patient"*

Introduction. Display the sign and review or introduce the three willingness skills, making sure students understand that working on these will help them become better and better at working out conflicts with other people.

Discussion. If you've done Lesson 59, Willingness Blocks, ask students what willingness blocks are (things we think and feel that hold us back from working out problems). Otherwise give them the definition. Ask: **What are some examples of willingness blocks?** (Wanting to be right, not liking the other person, wanting to blame someone, not wanting to look like a wimp.)

Ask students: **Have you ever been willing to work out a conflict with someone, but the person seemed unwilling to work it out with you?** Discuss, sharing your own story as well.

Activity. Say, **Let's see if we can work out a real conflict where one person was really holding on to her willingness block.**

Read the following real conflict shared by a real student. The boy who wrote this story expressed deep frustration at the other person's unwillingness to work things out.*

"I was in a conflict where someone blamed me for something I didn't do. It started at recess when we were playing a game called four square. Someone threw a ball at my shoe. It flew up and hit a girl on the nose. The next day I tried to talk to her but she told me that she hates me because I hit her with the ball on purpose. Now you can see how much pressure I have! She doesn't want to be my friend anymore and she hates me for something I never actually did."

Ask for volunteers to role-play the conflict. Have one student be the boy who wrote the story. Have the other be the girl who's angry with him. Before attempting to resolve the conflict, have the boy rehearse in his mind what he's going to say, then steady his nerves by taking deep breaths and silently repeating his calming statement. Have him approach the girl at a neutral time, and then use the Win/Win Guidelines to try to talk out the conflict. Remind him to keep using deep breathing and his calming statement while he talks with the other student. Have the girl hold onto her willingness blocks (anger and blame). Ask her, at first, to actually hold a block in front of her to represent her unwillingness, then put it aside if and when her resistance starts to dissolve.

Note: If at any point during the role play either student gets overwhelmed, step in as mediator to help the two work out the conflict. Let your kids know

* Stories and quotes attributed to real students and teachers come from author interviews and from responses to the Survey About Conflicts conducted by the author and publisher. See pages 1 and 282–284 for further information.

No Kidding About Bullying   **167**

that the option of asking a trusted adult to mediate is a good one if they need the help.

Afterward, debrief. Did the conflict get worked out? Did the girl let go of her willingness blocks? Why or why not? Is there something that could have been done differently?

Point out that this conflict was caused by a misunderstanding. Ask: **What was the misunderstanding?** Explain that the majority of all conflicts are caused by misunderstandings. Say: **Misunderstandings and willingness blocks go hand in hand.**

Ask students to think about a time they were involved in a conflict over a misunderstanding. Ask: **Did you hold onto a willingness block? Did the other person? What happened?**

Wrap-Up. End by reminding students that sometimes even if only one person is willing to talk things out, conflicts can be resolved. Ask students to notice times when they find themselves holding onto a willingness block. Have them ask themselves the following: "Why am I holding onto this willingness block? Could there be a misunderstanding here?"

Lesson 72: Using I-Messages and Reflective Listening in Conflicts

conflict resolution • fairness • compromise • respect • personal responsibility

Lesson 72 gives students practice using the Win/Win Guidelines for Working Out Conflicts with an emphasis on I-messages and reflective listening.

Students will
- review how to use I-messages and reflective listening

- observe and discuss a role play using the Win/Win Guidelines
- role-play using I-messages and reflective listening in conflict situations

Introduction and Discussion. Take three to five minutes to review I-messages and reflective listening. Ask students: **How do you feel when you're in a conflict and someone keeps saying "you" this and "you" that?** (Hearing things like "You started it" or "You're wrong" causes people to feel defensive, angry, blamed, or hurt.) **Why is it important to start from the word "I" when you're trying to work out a conflict?** (Doing so makes people feel less angry and defensive.) Point to Guideline 2: *Talk it over starting from "I," not "you."* Ask for a couple examples of I-messages. Remind students that using I-messages is not just about the words you speak, but also how your face and body look when you say them.

Next, ask students how they feel when someone truly listens to them. As they share, reflect back what was said. ("So you feel like someone really cares when that person truly listens to you?" Or, "I hear you saying that you feel respected when someone sincerely listens to what you have to say.") Emphasize

that when we have conflicts, truly listening to the other person can be really hard, but when we do so, we're much more likely to work things out. Ask why this is often the case. Briefly discuss.

Refer to the Win/Win Guidelines and tell students they are going to get extra practice with the guidelines today, with some special focus on I-messages and reflective listening (saying back what you heard).

Activity. Ask for a volunteer to come to the center of the circle and demonstrate the following conflict-solving scenario with you. The student will play Person A and you will play Person B. Spend five to ten minutes role-playing. As you do, point out to students each stage of the Win/Win Guidelines.

- Person A lent his kneepads to Person B, and Person B lost one of them. Now Person A is angry.

Have Person A take a few breaths to cool off, then give an I-message expressing his displeasure about what happened (Guidelines 1 and 2).

In your role as Person B, take some deep breaths as you hear his words, then paraphrase what he said (Guideline 3). Don't offer excuses or apologies at this time. Just listen and say back what was said. ("So you're really annoyed because you can't use your skateboard without your kneepads, and now one is gone. You were counting on me to take care of your things, and you feel let down.")

If Person A has more to say, continue to listen and say back.

Now deliver your I-message to Person A (Guideline 2). Example: "I feel really bad about losing the kneepad. Sometimes I get really disorganized. I should have been more careful (Guideline 4), and I wish you wouldn't be angry with me."

Have Person A say back what you just said (Guideline 3).

Discuss possible solutions together and have the class help think of some, too (Guideline 5). Choose a solution with Person A.

Now go to Guideline 6: *Affirm, forgive, thank, or apologize.*

Next, have students get into pairs, choose a Person A and Person B, and role-play one of the following scenarios, or other scenarios students suggest, using the Win/Win Guidelines. Remind students to make sure to start from "I" and to say back what they hear the other person saying. Tell them to see if they can get to a resolution.

- Person A got a bad grade on a math quiz. Person B says sarcastically, "Way to go, genius."
- Person A gave Person B a look in the lunchroom, and Person B is offended.

Circulate as students role-play and offer guidance where needed.

Wrap-Up. Take a minute or two to debrief in the large circle. Ask students how it went in terms of taking deep breaths before speaking, using I-messages, and truly listening. Affirm students for whatever positives you observed.

Follow-Up. If time permits, invite some partners to reenact their role plays for the large group. Then discuss with the group how the role players used the skills and what other things they could have said or done.

Lesson 73: Gossip and Conflict

conflict resolution • personal responsibility • fairness • courage • compassion • respect

Lesson 73 guides students to consider the damage done by gossip and to see the link between gossip and conflict.

Students will
- role-play working out a conflict resulting from gossip
- understand the role gossip plays in creating and fueling conflicts
- recognize their responsibility for being part of the solution when it comes to gossip

Materials
- handout: "What Real Kids Have to Say About Gossip and Conflict" (page 171)
- chart paper and marker
- student journals
- *optional: Sixth Grade Secrets* by Louis Sachar

Introduction. Distribute handouts and read or have a student read the statistic at the top. Ask: **Does this sound right to you? Is gossip a big problem in our school? Do you think it leads to a lot of conflicts?**

Read or have a student read the quoted story from the handout. Invite responses from students. Ask: **Has anything like this ever happened to you? How does gossip affect the atmosphere in a class or school?**

Have students take a couple of minutes to complete the bottom of the handout. Invite a few volunteers to share their experiences with the class, either reading what they wrote or talking about it. Caution students not to use real names. Ask students: **Why do people gossip? Is it easy to do it without thinking? Is it hard not to gossip?** Discuss briefly.

Discussion. Write the word *conscience* on the board. Review its meaning—a feeling or knowledge of right and wrong that guides us to do what is right. Ask students: **When gossip is being spread, what does your conscience guide you to do?** Discuss, sharing these words from a fourth-grade student: "If people are talking about someone, I walk away if I can. And I never say anything when kids ask, 'What do you think of So-and-So?' "

Ask students to respond. Then ask: **What are some ways you can stop gossip in its tracks?** List students' ideas on chart paper under the heading "No More Gossip."

Activity. Using the Win/Win Guidelines, have a few students role-play the gossip scenario from the handout. Ask them to role-play it in two different ways: The first role play should show what happens when gossip is spread. The second should show what happens when someone takes a step to stop the spread of gossip.

Debrief with students after the role plays. Ask why it's so important to stop the spread of gossip.

Wrap-Up. Affirm students for the measure of personal responsibility they exhibited in coming up with solutions to gossip. Remind them that their task is to put these solutions into action in real life. Post the "No More Gossip" chart as a reminder of how to be part of the solution when it comes to the spread of gossip.

Follow-Up. Encourage students to write in their journals about how gossip has affected them, what they can do to avoid gossiping, or how they can help stop gossip when it's happening.

Extensions. Have students read *Sixth Grade Secrets* by Louis Sachar. Afterward, talk together about the negative results of secrets and gossip.

Discuss examples from books, movies, or TV shows that depict people gossiping. What often happens when gossip is spread? What could the characters have done to stop the spread of gossip and the conflicts that ensued as a result?

What Real Kids Have to Say About
Gossip and Conflict

In a national survey of more than 2,100 students in grades 3–6:

64% (1,394 students) said that rumors and gossip are a top cause of conflict in their lives.

Here's what one student wrote:

"Last year I got into a huge fight with four other girls. It all started with gossip. That is probably the #1 thing that starts fights in our school. One of the girls said something incredibly mean about another girl. The girl that she told it to, Corinna, was not very trustworthy, and she told the girl who the gossip was about! I was with Corinna so I got blamed, too, even though I never said anything. It was *not* fun.

"The girl who was gossiped about was so mad she told on both of us to the principal! I knew that I didn't do what she accused me of so I got extremely angry. Then I blurted out something that I was trying to hold in: 'If it wasn't for Corinna we wouldn't be in this mess!' I was ashamed of myself. Corinna started to cry. I apologized very sincerely but everyone was still mad. It was a mess.

"After a few days we ended up talking it over. Finally we all ended up forgiving each other."

What do YOU have to say about gossip and conflict?

Do you gossip? How do you feel when someone gossips about you? What can we do to stop gossip from happening?

_____

_____

_____

_____

Lesson 74: Conflicts with Friends

personal responsibility • conflict resolution • compassion • respect • forgiveness

Lesson 74 helps students understand the value of taking responsibility, apologizing, forgiving, and working things out through compromise when conflicts come up between friends.

Students will

- reflect on what gets in the way of resolving conflicts with friends
- role-play working out conflicts with friends
- recognize that taking responsibility, compromising, and forgiving are essential for working out conflicts

Materials

- handout: "Being Willing to Stay Friends" (page 173)
- student journals

Introduction. Distribute the handouts and read or have a student read the quote from a student who responded to the Survey About Conflicts. Invite comments from students about the quote. Ask if they ever find themselves waiting for an apology and then watching the conflict drag on and on. Discuss.

Ask: **In situations like this, what keeps you from being willing to apologize or talk things out? What willingness blocks get in your way?** (Wanting to be right, not wanting to take any responsibility, stubbornness, feeling too hurt to want to talk things out.) Discuss.

Activity and Discussion. Ask for two volunteers to role-play working out the following conflict, or another one students suggest, using the Win/Win Guidelines:

There's a boy in the class Mahli has a crush on. Mahli's friend Audra mentions it in passing to the boy's friend, and now the boy knows. When Mahli finds this out, she tells people in the class that she hates her friend Audra because she has a big mouth.

Afterward, debrief with the class. **Were Mahli and Audra willing to hear each other out? Did they try to understand each other's point of view? Were they willing to take responsibility, compromise, apologize, and forgive each other? Did the conflict get resolved? How? Did either girl do anything that worked against solving it? What helped them work things out? What else might have helped?** Discuss what students observed and other ideas they offer.

Have two different volunteers role-play working out the following conflict, or another one students suggest, using the Win/Win Guidelines:

Henry fumbled the ball during touch football, causing his team to lose the game. His friend screamed at him and called him a name for doing it. Henry got mad, pushed his friend down, and called him a name back. Now neither friend is talking to the other.

Again, debrief with the class. **Were Henry and his friend willing to hear each other out? Did they try to understand each other's point of view? Were they willing to take responsibility, compromise, apologize, and forgive each other? Did the conflict get resolved? How? Did either of the boys do anything that made it harder to resolve the conflict? What helped them work things out? What else might have helped?** Discuss what students observed and other ideas they offer.

Wrap-Up. Tell students to silently ask themselves if they have any ongoing conflicts with friends where they need to compromise and work something out. Ask them to think about things they learned in this lesson that could help them do so. Remind students to keep applying what they are learning to real-life situations. Affirm them for acts of compassion, insights given, and helpful solutions.

Follow-Up. Have students write in their journals about any ongoing or repeated conflicts they have with friends. Is there something they need to take responsibility for? Is there a way they can see themselves compromising? Is there something they need to apologize for?

Being Willing to Stay Friends
Advice from a Fifth Grader

In a national survey of more than 2,100 students in grades 3–6, kids wrote about conflicts they had with friends. Here's what one fifth grader wrote:

"The most important thing to remember when you get into a conflict with a good friend is this: If you're really good friends, there's nothing you *can't* work out. Sometimes you have to be willing to say 'I'm sorry' first. Some kids make the mistake of waiting for the other person to apologize first. That's the biggest mistake you could possibly make, because the conflict keeps going. Letting things go on too long can destroy the friendship."

Write about a conflict you had with a friend where **neither of you was willing** to say "I'm sorry." What happened?

_____

_____

_____

_____

_____

Write about a conflict you had with a friend where **one of you was willing** to say "I'm sorry." What happened?

_____

_____

_____

_____

_____

Lesson 75: Brainstorming Solutions
(10-Minute Time Cruncher)

conflict resolution • compromise • fairness • personal responsibility

Lesson 75 has students look at their own personal conflicts and brainstorm a variety of possible compromise solutions.

Students will
- brainstorm in journals possible solutions to an unresolved or ongoing conflict they have
- identify one or two solutions they can use to resolve their real-life conflicts

Materials
- student journals

Introduction. Read aloud the following words from a fourth-grade student: **"Sometimes I write about conflicts in my journal. It really helps. I number the solutions I come up with. I memorize them and try to use them when the conflict happens again, or if it hasn't been solved."**

Ask students to each think of a conflict they've had that either isn't resolved or is likely to occur again. Give your own example. Ask for one or two examples from students.

Have students open their journals and briefly write a description of the conflict.

Activity. At the board, demonstrate doing a quick brainstorming of solutions to the conflict you described in your example. Come up with five to ten solutions, and don't censor any of your ideas. Explain that brainstorming is a creative act. Something that might seem like a silly idea at first can actually hold the key to a solution.

In their journals, have students brainstorm a numbered list of possible solutions to the conflict they just wrote about. Tell them to let their ideas flow freely and without judgment. Encourage them to come up with five to ten solutions, and to write down all ideas that pop up.

Wrap-Up. When their brainstorming lists are completed, ask students to circle one or two solutions they like best. Tell them to try using one of the solutions to work out their conflict during the coming week. Let them know you'll check back in with them about how it went.

Follow-Up. Check in with students to hear if and how their solutions worked. Encourage them to continue looking for solutions to conflicts. If any students are having serious difficulty working out a conflict, remind them to talk to a trusted person to get some help with it.

Lesson 76: Group Conflicts: Talking Someone Down

conflict resolution • anger management • self-control • personal responsibility • integrity

Lesson 76 looks at a conflict on the verge of getting physical that was sparked by mean text messages. It helps students consider ways to be part of the solution, not part of the problem, when tempers flare.

Students will
- identify actions that cause a conflict to escalate
- consider the harmful and pernicious effects of nasty text messages
- come up with ideas to help de-escalate a conflict
- learn that "talking someone down" can help prevent some conflicts from getting physical

Materials
- chart paper and marker
- handout: "Tom's Story: Mean Texting Leads to a Fight" (page 177)
- *optional: Eagle Song* by Joseph Bruchac

Preparation. On chart paper, write: *"You can either be part of the problem or part of the solution."*

Introduction. Lead students in taking three slow, deep abdominal breaths. Remind them that deep breathing will help them calm down and stay in better control whenever there's a conflict.

Say: **Today we're going to look at a conflict that took place among a group of boys: Tom, Logan, and Jack. (These aren't their real names.) After the story, I'm going to ask you to think of ways Tom and Logan could have been part of the solution, rather than being part of the problem.**

Activity and Discussion. Distribute the handout. Ask for a volunteer to read Tom's story aloud to the class.

After the story has been read, ask students if mean texting is a problem in your school. Discuss briefly.

Ask students: **What started the conflict on the playground? What did Logan do to escalate the conflict—to make it grow? Remind students that in nearly all conflicts, both people are responsible in some way.**

Say: **What about Tom? He wrote that Jack threw the icicle at both Logan and him. What might Tom have done to provoke this?**

Ask: **Does it sound like Tom was part of the solution or part of the problem? Why? What might Tom have done to be part of the solution? Is there a way he could have helped prevent the conflict from getting out of hand? Discuss.**

At the top of a piece of chart paper, write *"Talking Someone Down."* Ask students: **What does it mean to talk someone down? Have you ever tried to talk down someone who was angry?** Ask for examples and give one yourself. Ask how the conflict that Tom wrote about could have been less serious if he or someone else had tried to talk Logan down. Or perhaps someone could have tried to talk Tom down when he started fueling the fire. Have students look back at the story and identify places where someone could have helped de-escalate things. Discuss.

Ask what tools students can use to calm themselves and the other person if a conflict is escalating. (Walk away together, take deep breaths, lower your voice if the other person's gets louder, use things on the "Ways to Chill" list, remind the other person that it's not worth getting into a physical fight.) Ask what else they might say to someone on the verge of losing his or her temper. List ideas on the "Talking Someone Down" chart.

Ask for two volunteers to play the roles of Tom and Logan. Have the student playing Tom role-play using some of the things that were just discussed to help Logan calm down. Invite other ideas from students.

Wrap-Up. Refer to the sign, "You can either be part of the problem or part of the solution." Invite someone to read it. Reiterate that in every conflict, each person has the choice of being part of the solution or part of the problem.

Reiterate that spreading rumors via texting or other means, threatening, or putting someone down is cruel and inevitably leads to conflict.

Follow-Up. Encourage students to keep making efforts to prevent and resolve conflicts in their lives at home and at school. Remind them to turn to a trusted adult if things get physical or they don't know what to do.

Extension. Have students read *Eagle Song* by Joseph Bruchac to find out how one boy turned an enemy into an ally.

Tom's Story

Mean Texting Leads to a Fight

My best friend, who I'll call Logan, started getting all these bad texts from a kid I'll call Jack. When some of the texts came, Logan's cell phone was in his mom's pocket, so she saw them. She told Logan she was going to talk to Jack's mom about the texts after school the next day.

But during recess the next day, things got physical. Logan and I were with a couple other friends, and Jack was with a bunch of his. Jack said something mean to Logan, and Logan swore at Jack. People started saying things, then yelling. A kid from Jack's group got chased by someone in ours and ran away. Everybody was all riled up. I was about to charge in because of lies Jack told. A kid had to hold me back. Logan just kept yelling at Jack, and Jack ended up throwing a huge icicle at Logan's head and at mine. The bell rang and we had to go in, but we were all really mad!

Everyone at school was talking about what happened. The news got around and the principal heard about it. Eventually Jack got suspended and Logan was held in the principal's office till his mom came to school.

Think About It

When he got really mad Tom said he "was about to charge in." What would have happened if he had actually done that?

_____

_____

_____

When things started getting out of hand, how could Tom have talked himself down? How could he have talked Logan down and prevented the conflict from getting worse?

_____

_____

_____

Lesson 77: Group Conflicts: Check In with Your Conscience

conflict resolution • compassion • fairness • personal responsibility • respect • integrity • forgiveness

Lesson 77 has students evaluate an incident involving gossip and shunning through the lens of conscience.

Students will

- understand how gossip hurts friendships and leads to conflict
- reflect on the understanding that excluding others is cruel and unfair
- recognize the role each person can play in stopping the practice of shunning
- come up with solutions to a conflict involving gossip and shunning

Materials

- sign from Lesson 31: *"Conscience—A feeling or knowledge of right and wrong that guides us to do what is right"* (see page 76)
- handout: *"Josie's Story: 'She Thinks She's So Great!'"* (page 179)
- chart paper and marker
- paper and pencil for each group of four

PART TWO
Responding to Conflict

Introduction. Say: Today we're going to look at a conflict that took place when a group of kids turned against another girl we'll call Josie. Distribute the handout. Ask for a volunteer to read the conflict aloud to the class.

Discussion. Ask students: **Have you ever had the experience of being shunned by a group— purposely left out and ignored? Do you know anyone this has happened to? How does it feel to be cast out in this way?**

Ask students if they've ever shunned someone else. Refer to the definition and say: **If you're shunning someone, check in with your conscience. Sometimes people excuse this kind of behavior by saying the other person deserves it. Is that true? Is it ever right to shun someone?** Discuss. Some students may have justified this kind of behavior to themselves. Guide them to think about how they would feel if they were the person who was cast aside. Point out that even if they're mad at someone, shunning is never okay.

Activity. Tell students they're going to work in groups to come up with solutions to the conflict in the story.

Put students into groups of four. Have each group choose a Leader, a Recorder, an Announcer, and an Encourager. Say: **Each group's goal is to come up with ways the kids in the story could have prevented this conflict from starting or escalating.**

What could Josie have done? What about Sasha and Kasi? Explain that the role of the Leader is to keep the group focused on the goal. The Encourager's job is to affirm people when they share ideas and to encourage those who are quiet to take part. Recorders should list ideas. Everyone in the group can contribute ideas. At the end of the discussion time, the Announcers will share their groups' ideas with the class.

Allow about five minutes for groups to discuss solutions. Then have students reconvene in the large circle. Ask the Announcer from each group to share ideas their group came up with. List the ideas on a chart labeled "Troubleshooting Group Conflicts."

Ask students if there are any group conflicts that exist now that could be put to an end with some of the solutions on the chart. Discuss without using real names.

Wrap-Up. Remind students that you'll be checking in with them to see how they're implementing the things they came up with.

Follow-Up. Continue to check in with students about ways they're preventing and resolving conflicts. Ask how they're doing in regard to excluding others. Checking in often is the key to holding students accountable. It also affords you opportunities to affirm progress and learn what help students might need with specific issues, skills, and questions.

Josie's Story

"She Thinks She's So Great!"

A conflict happened when these rumors were being spread about me. People started saying that I thought I was really popular and I was too good for my friends. Even Sasha, my best friend in the world, was acting mad toward me. After a while none of my friends were talking to me anymore.

I tried to convince them that it wasn't true. Some people wouldn't even listen. Sasha said she didn't know who to believe and told me to leave her alone. I felt sick inside. I confronted Kasi, the girl who started the rumors, and we talked about it. She said that she wouldn't spread rumors about me anymore. I didn't really believe her, even though I wanted to.

Since then people have been a little nicer to me, but not like before. Sometimes I still cry because I wonder if I can ever really trust my friends anymore.

Think About It

Has something like this ever happened to you or someone you know? How did it make you feel? What could you have done to make things better?

_____

_____

_____

_____

_____

_____

_____

_____

Lesson 78: Confronting Someone Who Has Hurt You

courage • conflict resolution • integrity • personal responsibility • respect • compassion • assertiveness

Lesson 78 gives students strategies for talking assertively and respectfully to another person when a conflict isn't sufficiently resolved. This lesson is a follow-up to Lesson 77.

Students will
- understand how to use a "think-aloud" to rehearse talking to someone they've been hurt by
- role-play working out a conflict involving hurt feelings
- gain a deeper sense of empathy regarding the impact of shunning and excluding

Materials
- computer or overhead projector
- handout: "Josie's Story: 'She Thinks She's So Great!'" (page 179)
- "Dignity Stance" chart from Lesson 68 (see page 162)

Note: Before conducting this lesson, read or review Lesson 49 (Using Think-Alouds) and Lesson 68 (The Dignity Stance).

Preparation. Bring up the reproducible handout from the digital content on a laptop, or make an overhead transparency so you can project the story for all students to read without having to use individual copies. You may wish to have students refer to their copies of the handout, which was used in Lesson 77, as well.

Introduction. Project the handout on your screen or wall and read or have a student read the story aloud. Tell students: **At our last lesson, we talked about ways this conflict could have been prevented or stopped. Today we're going to role-play ways Josie, the girl who was shunned, can stick up for herself and talk through the conflict with Kasi, the girl at the core of it.**

Ask a volunteer to play Josie. Say: **Although this conflict appears to be over, Josie still feels she can't trust her friends, particularly Kasi, who started the whole thing. Josie has decided that she needs to speak to Kasi.**

Activity. Have Josie start by doing a think-aloud, rehearsing what she's going to say. Refer to the "Dignity Stance" chart. Tell Josie to stand tall before a pretend mirror (or a pretend trusted person), take some deep breaths, and speak her words aloud, holding her head high, and making eye contact. Invite ideas from students about what Josie can say. Have them give help on body language and tone of voice if needed.

Ask a second volunteer to take the part of Kasi. After Josie is mentally prepared, have her role-play

approaching Kasi to talk things over using the Win/Win Guidelines. Have Josie start by taking some deep breaths, silently making her calming statement, and beginning with an I-message such as: "I have something on my mind that I'd like to talk with you about." As the students role-play, coach and invite input from the class as needed.

After the role play, debrief and have the class give feedback: **What worked? What didn't work? What else might Josie have said or done? Did Josie and Kasi come to an understanding? In real life, do you think you could stick up for yourself and talk things through like Josie did? Why or why not?**

If time permits, invite another set of role players to reenact Josie working out the conflict with Kasi.

Wrap-Up. Affirm the role players and the class for the work they're doing to solve conflicts peacefully, fairly, and respectfully. Ask if students would like to affirm someone in the class. Acknowledge that it takes courage to speak up for yourself, and doing it with dignity shows respect for both yourself and the other person.

Extensions. Tell students that Josie is still hurt because Sasha, her very best friend, let her down. Have students work in pairs to role-play Josie preparing to talk to Sasha, then using the Win/Win Guidelines to work out this conflict.

Have students think about characters from literature who were shunned by others. What helped them make things better?

Lesson 79: Dealing with Exclusion and Rejection

compassion • kindness • respect • conflict resolution • fairness

Lesson 79 builds empathy and fosters problem solving in conflicts that involve exclusion and rejection.

Students will

- see exclusion and rejection through the eyes of different people involved in a conflict sparked by being left out
- brainstorm and role-play solutions to a conflict where someone is excluded and rejected
- learn ways to be respectful, assertive, and realistic in working out conflicts

Materials

- handout: "Anna's Story: Feeling Rejected" (page 182)
- chart paper and marker
- student journals

Introduction. Say: Today we're going to look at a conflict that happened among three kids we'll call Anna, Sophia, and Carl. After we hear their story I'm going to ask you to think of ways each of them could have been part of the solution, rather than part of the problem.

Activity and Discussion. Distribute the handout. Ask for a volunteer to read Anna's story aloud to the class.

After the story has been read, ask students if they've ever been in a situation similar to Anna's. Ask: **Why might Sophia have left out Anna? What did Carl do that was hurtful? Why do you think he did that?** Discuss.

Have three volunteers role-play the conflict as described in the story. At the end of the role play refer to Win/Win Guideline 5: *Come up with a solution that's fair to each of you.*

Put students in pairs and have them brainstorm at least three more compromise solutions for the conflict. Have them list solutions on the handout or in their journals.

Have students share solutions they came up with. List these on chart paper under the title "Solutions to a Conflict Where Someone Is Left Out."

Now ask for three volunteers to replay the conflict using a new solution from the list.

Caution role players not to be "fake nice" but to act out the conflict taking into consideration real feelings that could contribute to a situation like this one. For example, Anna's cousin may have needed a break from playing with her and might have wanted time with her new friend; Carl may have feared that if he let Anna be included, *he* would be the one left out. Encourage role players to be real yet respectful, assertive yet kind. Guide them to come up with realistic solutions, not solutions that sound good but that they wouldn't actually use in real life.

Wrap-Up. When the role play is complete, remind students to use what they're learning when real-life conflicts come up. Tell students you'll be checking in with them about how they're applying what they've learned. Be sure to check in a few days from now.

Follow-Up. Have students write in their journals about a time they were excluded or a time they excluded someone else. Tell them to write about the feelings they experienced and the feelings the other person may have experienced. What can they do differently next time?

Extension. Discuss some of the reasons kids treat each other in mean ways. Review healthy strategies they can use to deal with strong feelings instead of hurting others or continuing to feel hurt and angry.

Anna's Story

Feeling Rejected

I got into a conflict when I was at my cousin Sophia's birthday party. Sophia was playing with this boy she never met named Carl. They were playing for about half of the party. I couldn't even find her, and when I did Sophia and Carl ran away from me.

I felt bad and asked my cousin, "Why aren't you playing with me?" That's when Carl said, "Sophia can do whatever she wants! You're not the boss of her!" I got mad and said some things back to Carl. Then he called me short and ugly. I started to cry.

Sophia *never* said a word to help. I couldn't believe my cousin was on Carl's side. I said to Sophia, "Why are you playing with him? He's calling me names!" My cousin said nothing. Then Carl said *they* were cousins! I knew it wasn't true, because if it was, he would be *my* cousin, too. I said to Sophia, "You should think about what you're doing. You don't even know this kid. I've known you ever since we were little babies!" She said nothing. Then I walked away heartbroken.

Think About It

What are some ways this conflict could have been prevented?
What can be done to resolve it?

_____

_____

_____

_____

_____

_____

_____

_____

Lesson 80: The Problem with Fighting

conflict resolution • fairness • courage • self-control • personal responsibility • integrity

Lesson 80 takes another look at a conflict that's in danger of becoming physical. It highlights the consequences of physical fighting.

Students will

- examine what to do when there's an escalating conflict that's about to get physical
- understand that intervening in a physical fight is not safe
- consider the long-term consequences of physical fighting

Materials

- handout: "Jason's Story: 'It's Worthless to Fight'" (page 185)
- *optional handout:* "Tips for Staying Out of Physical Fights" (page 186)

Note: Before conducting this activity, you may find it helpful to review Lessons 46 (Don't Get Physical) and 67 (Staying Out of Physical Fights).

Introduction. Lead students in taking three slow, deep abdominal breaths. Remind them that deep breathing will help them calm down, gain greater self-control, and think more clearly whenever they are faced with a conflict.

Discussion. Distribute the handout. Ask for a volunteer to read Jason's story aloud to the class. Then ask students for responses. Also ask: **What might have happened if the argument kept going?**

Then ask: **What if people had started punching and kicking? Would it have been safe for Jason to try to stop a physical fight? What could happen?** Make it clear to students that it is never safe to step in and try to stop a physical fight.

Ask students: **What should you do if friends get into a physical fight?** (Get an adult.)

Refer back to the story and ask students: **What if kids who were watching—bystanders—decided to get involved? What are some things they might have done that could have *escalated* the conflict?** (Take sides, get physical, egg people on, gossip about what happened after it ended.)

Write the word *neutral* on the board. Ask students if they know what it means. Define neutral as not taking sides. Ask: **Was Jason neutral?** (He was: He addressed the problem, not taking sides.) **Why is it important to stay neutral when trying to help friends work out a conflict? What are some ways you can help yourself stay calm and neutral if you** want to step in when friends are in a conflict? (Use Stop, Breathe, Chill; calming statements; Peace Shield; Dignity Stance; Win/Win Guidelines.)

Activity. Have groups role-play the conflict in the story with the players trying not to let the argument grow. What can they do to prevent its escalation?

Ask students what the consequences of fighting are in your school. Discuss. Help students understand that if they get in the habit of yelling and fighting when they're in elementary or middle school, they'll have a hard habit to break when they get older.

Ask students to name some of the many consequences for adults who get into physical fights or shouting matches (physical harm to people, broken relationships, trouble with the law, bad reputation, low self-esteem, etc.). Discuss.

Reread Jason's statement. "It's worthless to fight." Ask students: **Is it worthless to fight? Why?** Help students recognize that fighting actually *is* worthless because it does not lead to a solution, it hurts people, and it escalates conflicts.

Wrap-Up. Acknowledge students for any acts of respect and good listening you have observed. See if any students want to acknowledge peers.

Extension. If fighting is a problem in your school, review and discuss the "Tips for Staying Out of Physical Fights" handout.

Avoiding Physical Fights: Students' Real Concerns

When you tell students to get an adult when friends get in a physical fight, they may raise concerns such as:

"What if there's no adult around?" If students ask this question, talk about realistic options such as running to get help, calling for help on a cell phone, taking themselves out of the fray so they don't get drawn into it, and imploring the kids to stop fighting like Jason did and, at the very least, not egging on people who are fighting or threatening to fight.

"I won't stand there and watch somebody beat up my friend." Reiterate to students that if they, or someone they know, are being physically attacked and there's *no one* around to help, this is the only time a physical response might be needed. Emphatically stress how critical it is to stay out of situations that can lead to a physical fight, and to avoid places where fights are likely to happen. Bring up the fact that physical fighting can lead to escalating forms of violence. Someone could have a weapon in a pocket or could decide to have several people help him or her retaliate after school or at another time. Tell students, "If you want to help your friend (or yourself), sometimes running as fast as you both can is the best option."

"I don't want to look weak." Remind students that it takes more courage to resist fighting than to give in to it. As one middle school student said, "Sometimes the brave kids just walk away. Sometimes the unbrave kids fight and try to show off." Remind them of the example set by Martin Luther King Jr.

"My mom/dad told me to hit back." In response to this, say, "When you're here you need to obey the school rules. Physical fighting is against the rules of our school and our country." Remind students that adults who fight are often arrested and sent to jail, and kids who fight in school are suspended. Is it really worth it to fight?

"Going to an adult is snitching." Make it clear to kids that snitching is telling on someone for the express purpose of getting the person in trouble. Seeking the help of an adult if someone's safety is in jeopardy is the responsible thing to do. Everyone has the right to be safe.

Jason's Story
"It's Worthless to Fight"

A conflict I was involved in was when some of my friends got into a big argument. We were all in the middle of a ball game. I didn't know what to do. So, I went up to them and said, "What's wrong, guys?"

They just ignored me, so I asked again, and they ignored me some more. I tried to calm them down, but they didn't listen. So I said, "Stop!" in the firmest voice I could, and finally they backed up. But they just looked at me and said, "Bug off, buddy." Then I started reminding them about their friendship, and how we all have great times together. But, they were still really mad and kept arguing. They were shouting and calling each other names. One guy threatened another one. Nobody was hitting yet, but I was afraid they would start to. That's when I yelled, "STOP FIGHTING! IT'S WORTHLESS TO FIGHT!"

They all stopped and looked at me. And then they *did* stop. They must have realized it really *was* worthless to fight. After that, they were finally able to let go of what was bothering them and get back to playing the game.

Think About It

What helped stop this conflict from turning into a fight?
What could have made it worse?

_____

_____

_____

What can you do if your friends are about to fight?

_____

_____

_____

Tips for Staying Out of Physical Fights

- Don't provoke people.

- Resist hanging out with kids who get into physical fights.

- Find healthy ways to express anger. Never go on the attack.

- Avoid places where fighting is likely to occur.

- Be willing to apologize if you've offended someone.

- Be guided by what you know is right, not your reactions.

- Remember the consequences of fighting and how they can affect your life.

Lesson 81: Mediating a Friend's Conflict

conflict resolution • compassion • fairness • integrity • kindness • forgiveness

Lesson 81 addresses how and when to help friends resolve a conflict.

Students will

- recognize that there are times when they might be able to help friends resolve a conflict
- role-play a situation where an unbiased friend mediates a conflict for two friends using the Win/Win Guidelines
- understand the importance of remaining neutral and maintaining confidentiality when helping friends resolve a conflict

Materials

- chart paper and marker
- handout: "Bob's Story: Best Friends Since Kindergarten" (page 188)

Preparation. On chart paper, write:
"Mediate—To help settle a disagreement between two other people
Neutral—Not taking sides"

Introduction. Tell students that sometimes it's possible for friends to help other friends mediate a conflict, and that it's critical to remain neutral if they try this. Refer to the chart paper and clarify the definitions of the words *mediate* and *neutral* with students.

Say: **Today we're going to hear a real story of how a boy named Bob helped mediate a conflict that threatened to destroy the long-term friendship between Pennie and Maria. (These aren't their real names.)**

Activity and Discussion. Distribute the handout. Ask for volunteers to read each paragraph.

At the end ask: **How did Bob know Maria and Pennie had a conflict? What did he do to help?** (He suggested going to the Peace Place to work out the conflict, he reminded the girls of their friendship, he listened as both girls told their side of the story, he remained neutral, he didn't talk about who was wrong and who was right.)

Ask for three volunteers to role-play the scenario that took place in the Peace Place, following the Win/Win Guidelines.

Afterward, ask the class: **Did Bob stay neutral? Why is staying neutral important when you're helping friends work out a conflict?** Discuss.

Tell students: **When you're helping friends solve a conflict, the things they say to each other are personal. They need to trust that you won't tell anyone else what they said. Keeping a personal conversation confidential shows respect, integrity, and maturity.**

Discuss, making sure students understand how important it is to honor confidentiality between friends.

Note: An exception is if a student needs adult help. Occasionally in the process of mediating a conflict, a student may hear something that makes him or her uncomfortable or seems dangerous. Make sure students understand that maintaining confidentiality among peers is not the same as keeping secret something that needs to be addressed with a trusted adult.

Ask: **Can you think of a conflict friends might have where it would be a good idea to try to mediate? Are there ever times it might *not* be wise to mediate friends' conflicts?** Discuss, making sure students understand that it's not appropriate to mediate when friends don't want the help. Make it clear that students should never try to mediate in the middle of physical fighting.

Wrap-Up. Draw students' attention to the Peace Table or Peace Corner in your room and remind them to use it when they need to work out a conflict or unhook from anger.

Follow-Up. Have students suggest some other scenarios where friends could help mediate a conflict. Have them role-play a few using the Win/Win Guidelines, in small groups or in front of the class.

Extension. Discuss how the conflict between Pennie and Maria could have been stopped earlier or avoided altogether. Have students role-play scenarios at the dance class and in the lunchroom in which Maria and Pennie find a way to resolve their conflict rather than say mean things about each other.

Bob's Story

Best Friends Since Kindergarten

Pennie and I were really good friends, and her closest friend in the world was Maria. They'd been best friends since kindergarten. But one day everything changed and I didn't know why.

They started saying bad things about each other. It really got to me when we were in the lunchroom. Pennie and I were at one table, and Maria was at the other. They were making fun of each other and trying to get the kids at their tables to join in. It made me sad to see them treating each other that way.

It bothered me so much I was ready to leave the table. But then I thought about the Peace Place, this corner in our room where you can go to work out conflicts. I decided to ask the teacher if we could all go there. I asked Pennie and Maria, and they agreed.

When we got there I said, "You guys are such good friends. Why are you fighting?" At first they just kept arguing. They kept blaming each other. So I decided to ask each of them to think of something good about each other. That kind of changed the mood between them.

Then the whole story came out. Maria said it all started in dance class the day before. Pennie was supposed to hold onto her hand while they were spinning around. But Pennie let go, and Maria ended up falling down and spraining her wrist. Maria thought Pennie did it on purpose, and she was really hurt and mad.

Pennie said the reason she let go of Maria's hand was because she got dizzy. In no way had she done it on purpose, and she was mad that Maria thought she would do something so mean. She actually felt bad Maria had gotten hurt.

Once Maria understood that it really was an accident, she let go of her anger. She and Pennie both started talking about how bad they felt that it all had gotten so out of hand. They ended up hugging and apologizing.

I was so happy they made up! They'd been best friends for so long, and they almost lost their friendship over this conflict. By talking out the problem, they were able to work things out and stay best friends. They thanked me over and over again for helping them. I felt really good that I was able to help them work things out.

Addressing Name-Calling and Teasing

Name-calling, put-downs, and teasing can be precursors to bullying and, if the intent is to do deliberate harm, can qualify as actual bullying. This section of *No Kidding About Bullying* emphasizes the critical understanding that mean words, names, and gestures have no place in our schools or in our lives. The lessons give students strategies for responding to teasing, name-calling, put-downs, cruel words, and other forms of meanness. These strategies form a fundamental foundation for helping students deal with cruel behavior of any kind. (More on this is addressed in Dealing with Bullying, pages 217–260.)

In the Survey About Conflicts, girls and boys alike reported name-calling and teasing as two of the top three causes of conflicts. Sixty-eight percent of respondents (1,485 participants) reported that being teased or made fun of was a major source of conflict; sixty-four percent (1,389 participants) cited name-calling.

Many lessons from Fostering Kindness and Compassion (pages 51–81) introduce concepts revisited here, so it's suggested that you conduct some of those lessons prior to introducing these. Also familiarize yourself with Lessons 38 (Calming Statements), 47 (Peace Shield), 65 (Introducing Assertiveness), and 68 (The Dignity Stance).

Be sure to have these charts displayed: "The Win/Win Guidelines for Working Out Conflicts" and "Stop, Breathe, Chill" (introduced in Lessons 8 and 9), "No More Hurtful Words" (Lesson 22), and "Dignity Stance" (Lesson 68).

82. Taking Responsibility for Mean Words
83. Effects of Name-Calling, Put-Downs, and Meanness
84. Dignity Stance Review (10-Minute Time Cruncher)
85. Assertive Responses to Mean Words, Part 1
86. Assertive Responses to Mean Words, Part 2
87. Mean Comments, Gestures, and Laughter
88. Unhooking from Mean Words and Actions
89. Tools for Unhooking
90. Learning to Detach
91. "I Was Just Kidding"
92. Don't Get Stung by Zingers
93. Becoming Zinger-Proof
94. Being an Upstander for Someone Who's Being Teased

Lesson 82: Taking Responsibility for Mean Words

personal responsibility • conscience • compassion • respect

Lesson 82 guides students to take responsibility for hurtful words they might have spoken to another person.

Students will

- understand how mean words hurt and lead to conflict
- reflect on how they want to be regarded by others
- take greater responsibility for their words and actions and refrain from treating others in mean ways

Materials

- chart paper and marker or sign from Lesson 16 (see page 52 and Preparation, below)
- handout: "Jenna's Story: 'I Said Something Really Mean'" (page 192)

Preparation. If you haven't done so before, on chart paper write: *"Our words and actions today create memories that will fill others' memory banks tomorrow."*

Introduction. Ask for a volunteer to read the sign. Ask students what these words mean to them. Briefly discuss, emphasizing that when we're hurtful to another person, we risk creating in him or her a negative memory of us that can last forever. Say: **Today you'll be hearing a real story from a girl named Jenna whose mean words deeply hurt a classmate named Renee. (These aren't the girls' real names.)**

Discussion and Activity. Distribute the handout. Ask for a volunteer to read Jenna's story aloud to the class.

Afterward, ask students if they've ever been in a situation similar to Jenna's. Discuss briefly.

Ask: **Have you ever said something mean that ended up hurting someone? Why did you say what you said? Discuss briefly. Can you remember ever having someone say mean things about you? How did it make you feel? Briefly share responses.**

Then ask: **What important insight did Jenna gain from this experience? What did she learn?**

Emphasize that Jenna ended up taking responsibility for what she did. Ask why this is so important.

Refer to Win/Win Guideline 4: *Take responsibility for your role in the conflict.* Say: **By taking responsibility, Jenna was able to make things better. If she had denied what she'd done, what might have happened? How might she have felt inside?**

Ask students to turn to a partner and share about a time they said or did something hurtful that they still

need to take responsibility for. Let students know this might relate to a conflict with a friend, a sibling, a family adult, or someone else.

After several minutes, ask students what they might say to the person they hurt if that person were here right now. Some examples are: "It was wrong of me to say what I did. I'm really sorry and I hope you'll forgive me." Or, "I feel really bad that I hurt your feelings before. I was having a stressful day, but it was still wrong for me to take it out on you." The latter is an excellent example of truly taking responsibility without trying to excuse one's bad behavior. (In contrast, the following attempt at self-justification cancels out any good done by the apology: "I feel really bad that I hurt your feelings before. I was having a stressful day, and you should have known better than to annoy me.")

Encourage students to seek out the person later and make amends. Have them practice doing this with their partners. Circulate and give help where needed.

Reconvene in the circle and say: **Jenna realized that she didn't want to say mean things about people behind their backs. How else could she have handled the resentment she felt toward Renee? What can she do differently if a situation like this comes up again?** Discuss. Remind students that I-messages are an ideal alternative to hurtful words. Say: **If you have an issue with someone, try speaking to the person directly, starting from "I,"** *instead* **of resorting to name-calling, sarcasm, put-downs, or talking behind the person's back.**

Ask students to think of an I-message Jenna could have used had she chosen to talk directly to Renee about how she felt.

Wrap-Up. Refer back to the sign: *"Our words and actions today create memories that will fill others' memory banks tomorrow."* Ask: **How do you want to be remembered by others?** Discuss.

Affirm students for their willingness to take responsibility, and for any acts or words of kindness, insight, and integrity during this lesson.

Follow-Up. Have students observe themselves as they go through their day, taking note of how they speak to others at school and at home. If someone gets on their nerves, do they react with a mean comment? If they do, are they willing to take responsibility afterward without making excuses for themselves?

Jenna's Story

"I Said Something Really Mean"

At the beginning of the year, I said something really mean about Stacy, this girl in my class who used to be my friend. I was mad at her because it seemed like she was the teacher's favorite kid. The mean thing I said got back to her during recess.

When we got inside I started crying because I knew I had done something really wrong. I found Stacy and told her I was sorry. I told her about 1 million times, but she was still mad (I know I would be, too).

Later I started crying again and went to the girls' bathroom. There was Stacy. She was crying, too.

When she saw me crying, she realized how bad I really felt. She finally accepted my apology. Now she and I are good friends again.

The lesson I learned is that it's bad to talk about people behind their backs, because then you're just being like a bully. It is so true that no one is perfect. And it really hurts people when they find out you were talking about them. So why do it?

Think About It

How would you answer the question Jenna posed at the end of the story?

_____

_____

_____

If you have the urge to talk behind someone's back, what can you do instead?

_____

_____

_____

Lesson 83: Effects of Name-Calling, Put-Downs, and Meanness

compassion • kindness • respect • personal responsibility

Lesson 83 fosters empathy in students regarding the impact of name-calling, teasing, and mean words. It also clarifies the differences between teasing and bullying.

Students will
- understand that teasing is never okay to do if it makes the other person uncomfortable
- gain greater awareness of the hurt teasing and name-calling can cause
- gain empathy for people who are teased or put down
- resist engaging in hurtful teasing and name-calling

Materials
- handout: "Bullying vs. Teasing: What's the Difference?" (page 195)
- student journals
- chart paper and marker or "No More Hurtful Words" pledge from Lesson 22 (see page 62)

Preparation. If you have not conducted Lesson 22, write the pledge on chart paper as directed on page 62.

Introduction. Tell students that today they're going to be looking at how name-calling, put-downs, and mean words affect all of us. Say: **First let's take a few minutes to think about the differences between teasing and bullying. How are they different?** Invite a few responses. Then distribute the "Bullying vs. Teasing: What's the Difference?" handout and ask for volunteers to read it aloud. Discuss it briefly.

Tell students that hurtful teasing almost always involves name-calling, put-downs, and mean words. Cruel words of any kind create conflicts and hurt feelings, even if the other person seems to be going along with it. Discuss this briefly.

Discussion. Say: **Here's how some real kids feel about name-calling and put-downs.** Read the following student quotes* one at a time, inviting brief responses:

- "One time I decided to play basketball, but I took a shot and missed. Everyone started calling me names and scolding me. I hated it. One kid said, 'At least my only friend isn't my dad, unlike *you*.' It was very hurtful. I thought I would start to cry, so I left."

- "It makes me really mad when kids talk and look at me in mean ways and say mean things about people I like, like my friends and family."

- "People say how ugly our clothes are and how cute theirs are. It really hurts. Not every kid can afford fancy clothes."

Ask students if name-calling, put-downs, and other forms of meanness have decreased since you've started doing the activities in *No Kidding About Bullying*. Say: **Since we've been working on creating a get-along classroom, are you getting better at treating people with kindness and respect, even when you're annoyed?** Encourage them to be honest. Discuss.

Ask if there are times or places where name-calling, put-downs, and meanness are still a big problem. Ask: **How do you feel when you see these things taking place?** Discuss.

Note: If you encounter any cavalier attitudes, like "I don't really care how other people feel. I like to make them feel bad," clearly voice how you feel when you see mean behavior.

Activity. Put students in pairs and have them briefly discuss how they are personally affected by name-calling, put-downs, and meanness, including as observers.

Now have students take out their journals to do automatic writing about the following question: **"How do name-calling, meanness, and put-downs affect you and the people you know?"** After about three minutes, ask if anyone would like to share what they wrote. (Be sure to write yourself, and consider sharing what you wrote, too.)

---

* Stories and quotes attributed to real students and teachers come from author interviews and from responses to the Survey About Conflicts conducted by the author and publisher. See pages 1 and 282–284 for further information.

Ask students to think of ways they might need to improve when it comes to using name-calling, put-downs, and other forms of meanness, including at home. Discuss.

Ask students if they need to get better at handling name-calling, put-downs, and other forms of meanness directed at them. Caution them not to use real names.

Ask: **What do you need help with when it comes to name-calling, put-downs, and other forms of meanness? Are there any important questions you need answered?** List what students say on chart paper, letting students know you will talk together about the questions in the near future.

Wrap-Up. Refer to the "No More Hurtful Words" pledge. End by saying the pledge together. Remind students to live the words of the pledge outside of school, too.

Follow-Up. Plan to follow up by addressing with the class concerns and questions listed on the chart. Engage students in brainstorming some answers to these questions. Help them become part of the solution.

Let students know they can also come to you privately to discuss their questions.

Bullying vs. Teasing: What's the Difference?

Bullying is when a person or group repeatedly picks on someone in order to purposely hurt and gain power over the person.

Teasing is a different story. Teasing can be annoying and upsetting, but it's generally not intended to gain power over another person or do serious harm. If teasing is done in an aggressive or unkind way, with the intent of gaining power over someone else, that's bullying. This includes when the teaser says she or he was "just kidding."

Sometimes teasing is meant to be light and playful without hurting the person's feelings. If it's fun for *both* people involved, and it truly *stays* playful for each of them, it can be okay to do. But if either person finds the teasing hurtful or uncomfortable, it's *not* okay to do.

Cruel teasing hurts many kids and creates lots of conflicts in their lives. In a national survey of more than 2,100 students in grades 3–6:

> **68% (1,485 students)** said that **being teased or made fun of are top causes of conflicts** in their lives.

Think About It

Is there someone you like to tease? Is there someone who likes teasing you? Have you ever been in a situation where teasing hurt? Write about it.

_____

_____

_____

_____

_____

_____

Lesson 84: Dignity Stance Review
(10-Minute Time Cruncher)

courage • personal responsibility • respect

Lesson 84 provides a review of the Dignity Stance, introduced in Lesson 68, which helps students deliver assertive responses.

Students will

- review and practice how to use the Dignity Stance in situations involving name-calling and meanness
- understand how to respond assertively and bravely without being aggressive

Materials

- "Dignity Stance" chart from Lesson 68 (see page 160)
- *optional handout:* "The Dignity Stance" (page 162)

Note: You may want to review Lesson 68 for background on helping students use the Dignity Stance.

Introduction. Post the chart and remind students that the Dignity Stance will help them stand up for themselves when they're involved in conflict or faced with name-calling or bullying. Say: **Today we're going to review how to use the Dignity Stance so you can respond to name-calling with both courage and respect.**

Activity. Have students take three slow, deep abdominal breaths to get to a calm place.

Ask students to stand. Take them through each step of the Dignity Stance, doing each step with them:

- Stand tall with your head held high, feet apart, shoulders back.
- Take slow, deep breaths to keep your cool.
- Keep your body language and facial expression neutral but strong.
- Make direct eye contact.
- Speak in a firm, steady tone of voice.
- Walk away tall and strong.

When you get to "Speak in a firm, steady tone of voice," have students imagine they are facing someone who just called them a name. Have them look at this imagined person and say, "I find that disrespectful," then turn and walk away.

Next, put students in pairs to practice the Dignity Stance with their partner. Have them say, "I find that disrespectful" (or something else you agree would work) and practice walking away with head held high.

Wrap-Up. Briefly review what it means to be assertive: strong and honest, yet respectful, saying what you need to say with confidence. Say: **Remember, the Dignity Stance will help you be strong and assertive without having to engage in name-calling or put-downs.**

If you wish, distribute copies of the "Dignity Stance" handout for students to keep.

Lesson 85: Assertive Responses to Mean Words, Part 1

respect • courage • personal responsibility • self-control

Lesson 85 helps students come up with assertive responses to teasing, put-downs, and insults.

Note: Conduct Lesson 68, The Dignity Stance, prior to this one. You will also find it helpful to read through Lesson 65.

Students will

- more fully understand the distinction between being assertive and being aggressive
- come up with assertive comebacks they can use in response to put-downs
- practice using assertive comebacks in conjunction with the Dignity Stance

Materials

- sign with definition of *assertive* from Lesson 65 (see page 155)
- chart paper and marker
- "Dignity Stance" chart from Lesson 68 (see page 160)

Preparation. If you haven't done so before, write the following on chart paper: *"Assertive—Strong and honest, yet respectful, saying what you need to say with confidence."*

Introduction and Discussion. Start by leading students in taking three slow, deep abdominal breaths. Tell them that today's lesson will help them find the right words when someone picks on or teases them or someone they know.

Remind students that even though they may feel very angry or upset if they're picked on, or if they witness a friend being picked on, it's still important to be respectful (stay "up in the balcony"*) and respond assertively, not aggressively.

Display the definition of *assertive* and ask for a volunteer to read it aloud.

Ask students: **What's the difference between being *assertive* and being *aggressive*?** Make sure students understand that being *assertive* means speaking one's mind with directness and strength while remaining respectful. Being *aggressive* means responding by arguing, threatening, fighting, or hurting someone with name-calling or put-downs.

Activity. Share with students this story from a third grader named Mia (not her real name):

"On my bus there are two boys who are really mean to me. They make fun of me and they say things like, 'You don't know anything 'cause you're just a girl. You'll never be as smart as we are!' Most

of the time I just ignore them, but that doesn't always work. Sometimes you have to speak up for yourself. One day I decided to outsmart them. I said, 'I bet you don't know how much 12 times 13 is.' They just looked the other way and got quiet, so I knew they didn't know the answer. I told them what the answer was and walked away, proud of myself. After that, they left me alone."

Ask students: **What did Mia do to respond to the kids who were teasing her?**

Ask students to think of some other assertive comebacks Mia could have given. Ask: **What I-messages could she have used?** Give the following examples: "I have no interest in listening to this." "I'm not interested in something this silly. Girls are smart, capable, and cool."

List students' responses on chart paper entitled "Assertive Comebacks."

Ask students to think of other common put-downs kids use. Now have them suggest assertive comebacks they can respond with. Add them to the chart.

Caution students against using sarcasm or veiled put-downs. Emphasize that how they deliver the comeback is just as important as the words they speak. Say: **Stopping and breathing first is critical. This will calm you down so you can think clearly and speak in a way you're proud of.**

Demonstrate delivering an assertive comeback. Stop and breathe first, assume the Dignity Stance, and use a firm, confident voice. Then walk away tall and strong. Remind students: **Do this even if the**

---

* This refers to the concept "Basement or Balcony?" addressed in Lessons 62 and 63. See pages 147–152.

other person tries to draw you back in. Repeat your calming statement in your head, ignore what the other person is saying, and remind yourself to be the bigger person.

Put students in pairs and have them practice some of the assertive comebacks they came up with, standing and delivering the comebacks using the Dignity Stance. Circulate to make sure students are on the right track.

After about five minutes, ask a few pairs to demonstrate in front of the group. Have the class take note of tone of voice, eye contact, body language, and posture. Point out or have students point out any hints of sarcasm or aggressiveness.

Wrap-Up. Acknowledge students for working on something that even adults find hard to do. Remind them that learning how to act assertively now will help them for the rest of their lives.

Follow-Up. Conduct Lesson 86, which gives students practice incorporating calming strategies into their assertive comebacks, or Lessons 88 and 89, Unhooking from Mean Words and Actions, and Tools for Unhooking.

Lesson 86: Assertive Responses to Mean Words, Part 2

self-control • calming • personal responsibility • courage • anger management

Lesson 86 helps students integrate calming strategies and manage anger when delivering assertive comebacks. This lesson is a follow-up to Lesson 85.

Note: Complete Lessons 38, Calming Statements, and 47, Peace Shield, prior to this one.

Students will
- review the difference between being assertive and being aggressive
- practice delivering assertive comebacks
- practice using calming statements, deep breathing, and the Peace Shield when someone treats them meanly

Materials
- "Assertiveness" sign and "Assertive Comebacks" chart from Lesson 85 (see page 197)
- "Dignity Stance" chart from Lesson 68 (see page 160)
- *optional:* student journals

Introduction. Review with students what it means to be assertive (strong and honest, yet respectful, saying what you need to say with confidence). Also review the distinction between being assertive and being aggressive (*aggressive* means being argumentative, demeaning, threatening, or hurtful).

Ask students what were the most important things they learned in the last lesson about body language, tone of voice, and facial expressions when delivering assertive comebacks.

Activity and Discussion. Say: **Three things that will help you assertively deal with name-calling, put-downs, and teasing are your calming statement, deep breathing, and your Peace Shield. Think about your calming statement now.** (Students wrote these in their journals during Lesson 38.) Guide students in taking several slow, deep abdominal breaths and silently saying their calming statements. Have them visualize putting on their Peace Shields. Say: **Picture yourself surrounded by your Peace Shield. See it protecting you from all mean words.**

Now ask for volunteers to role-play the following scenarios, or others students suggest, using assertive comebacks.

- **You just got a haircut. The kid who sits next to you keeps making fun of it and tries to get others to join in.**

- **This kid in your class keeps putting down the shoes you're wearing today. Then she starts putting down your family, too.**

- **Your friend always does well on tests. Two kids in the class start calling him a nerd and try to get others to join in. You decide to say something to the kids who are teasing.**

Remind role players: **Before you speak, stop and breathe. Silently repeat your calming statement, put on your Peace Shield, and get into the Dignity Stance. Then, deliver your assertive comeback. When the words are out, turn and walk away with your head held high. Do this even if the other person keeps trying to draw you back in. If you feel angry as you walk away, continue breathing deeply, and silently repeat your calming statement to yourself.** Ask students: **What else can you remind yourself of as you walk away?** (For example, "I can be the bigger person.")

After each role play, ask the class to evaluate the comebacks that were used. Were they truly assertive? Were they delivered in an assertive way? Did the person use a firm, strong voice without yelling? How was the person's body language? Was the student able to walk away tall and strong without getting drawn back in? As you discuss these things, add any new assertive comebacks to your chart.

Wrap-Up. Acknowledge students for their hard work in learning how to manage anger and be assertive. Remind them that knowing how to assertively handle disrespect and meanness will help them in situations they encounter for the rest of their lives.

Follow-Up. Tell students to rehearse using assertive comebacks at home (in the mirror or with a family member or trusted friend). Practice will build their confidence in real-life situations. Be sure to check in with students about how they're doing; address challenges they encounter.

Lesson 87: Mean Comments, Gestures, and Laughter

compassion • respect • kindness • personal responsibility • acceptance

Lesson 87 further sensitizes students to the impact of mean or critical comments and gestures and mocking laughter.

Note: Conduct Lesson 22, Words That Hurt, prior to this lesson.

Students will
- reflect on ways they can respond if they see someone being demeaned or ridiculed
- role-play responding to situations where someone is being mocked
- compose songs, raps, or poems that take a stand against cruelty toward others

Materials
- "No More Hurtful Words" pledge from Lesson 22 (see page 62)

Introduction. Ask a student to lead in the reading of the "No More Hurtful Words" pledge. Ask students how they're doing honoring the agreements from the pledge inside and outside of class. Discuss, affirming them for progress.

Discussion and Activity. Ask: **Aside from mean teasing and name-calling, how else do kids put each other down?** Guide students to think about mocking gestures, faces, negative body language, and laughter at someone else's expense. Discuss briefly. Share what you've observed.

Read aloud the following scenario:

Marina just moved here from another country. The lunch she brings to school today is totally different from what kids in her class are accustomed to. Some kids find it gross and make faces when they see it. Other kids start to join in, laughing and pointing at Marina's lunch.

Ask for a volunteer to play the role of Marina. Have several volunteers pretend to be kids sitting near Marina in the cafeteria responding in mean ways to the food she has (mocking faces, hostile laughter, pejorative remarks and gestures).

At the end of the role play, ask the student playing Marina how the comments and gestures made her feel. Ask students to think about how they would feel if they were in her shoes. Tell them how you would feel, and how you feel when you see such things happen. Ask students to specifically identify which gestures and actions were hurtful, negative, or demeaning.

Ask: **If you were watching something like this really happen, what could you do to help?**

Read aloud another scenario:

Lee often has trouble understanding things that are taught in class. Today he gives a wrong answer in front everyone. Kids start to laugh and do other hurtful things. Lee is clearly embarrassed.

Ask for a volunteer to play Lee and for other kids to play the part of students making fun of him. After the role play, ask the student playing Lee how the other students' behavior made him feel. Ask the class how they would feel in his place. As before, have students specifically identify the gestures and actions that were hurtful. Ask students how they felt observing this. Ask: **What could you do or say if you saw this happening in real life? If you want to help, what might stand in your way?** Reiterate that it takes courage to speak up on someone else's behalf.

Wrap-Up. Acknowledge students for the important work they're doing to create a kinder more compassionate climate in the classroom, school, and world.

Close by repeating the "No More Hurtful Words" pledge together.

Follow-Up. Put students in groups of three or four. Ask each group to compose a short poem, rap, or song taking a stand against cruelty in the classroom and school. Allow students time to complete and share their poems, raps, and songs with the class.

Extensions. Have students visit other classes to share what they wrote and to introduce the "No More Hurtful Words" pledge to the school at large.

Ask your principal if your students can share the poems, raps, and songs they created over your school's public address system or during an assembly.

Lesson 88: Unhooking from Mean Words and Actions

calming • courage • self-control • anger management • respect

Lesson 88 gives students a mindset for "unhooking" from mean words and actions and provides specific strategies to help them do this. This lesson is a follow-up to Lesson 85 and a lead-in to Lesson 89.

Note: Complete Lessons 38, Calming Statements, and 47, Peace Shield, prior to this one. Also review Lesson 48, Using Think-Alouds.

Students will

- review assertive comebacks they can use when someone is mean to them
- understand what it means to "unhook" from someone else's mean words or put-downs, and learn how to do it
- role-play unhooking from mean comments and gestures

Materials

- "Assertive Comebacks" chart from Lesson 85 (see page 197)
- "Dignity Stance" chart from Lesson 68 (see page 160)
- handout: "Don't Get Hooked" (pages 203–204)
- *optional:* student journals

Introduction and Discussion. Refer to the "Assertive Comebacks" chart. Ask students: **Have you had an opportunity to use assertive comebacks in real life yet? How did it go?** Discuss.

Remind students that even if the other person continues using put-downs or mean words after they've given their comeback, it's important to walk away and not get "hooked" back in. Say: **The other person may want to have the last word, and might continue saying mean things. If you react, you're just giving the person more power. By ignoring what's being said and walking away with your head held high (as opposed to weak and defeated), you keep your power where it belongs—***inside of yourself.* **That's more important than having the last word.**

Stress that retaliating with more put-downs just adds fuel to the fire and leads to escalation. Ask if this has happened to any of them. Discuss.

Refer to the "Dignity Stance" chart. Tell students that even if they feel shaky inside, it's important to stand tall and speak assertively. Discuss.

Activity. Read aloud the following examples of unhooking, shared by real students.

- Ava's story: **"One time this girl in my class made up a story that I punched her on the bus. I knew she was lying and I didn't know what to do. After I thought about it, I realized that I really didn't care what she said. I decided to ignore her and I was happy I did. It made me feel good not to let her words get to me."**

- Kyle's story: **"There was this kid who was very mean to me. At first, he was my friend. Then he just turned on me. He called me names and put me down. He started making fun of other people I know, too. I told him to stop and he got mad at me. He started yelling more bad things at me and other people I know. It made some of us really upset. I decided to just try and stay away from him. He's still mean, but I've learned not to let it get to me. I don't need to act like him."**

Ask for students' responses to Ava's and Kyle's (not their real names) stories. Say: **When Ava and Kyle decided to ignore or stay away from the person who was being mean, they decided not to get "hooked." What can you do to keep from being hooked?**

Ask for volunteers to role-play the first scenario. Then have the student playing Ava face the class and do a think-aloud that expresses her decision to let things go and unhook from the lie that was being spread about her. If necessary, model doing the think-aloud first.

If time permits, have volunteers role-play Kyle's scenario, then have the student playing Kyle do a think-aloud in front of the class.

Wrap-Up. Many kids are afraid of looking weak if they don't respond with an aggressive comeback. Address this real concern. Remind students of Martin

Luther King Jr. and others who rose above insults without stooping to the level of their aggressors. Say: **Real strength is being able to walk away as though the other person's words have no power over you.**

Follow-Up. Pass out the "Don't Get Hooked" handouts. Tell students to read the information, fill out "My Tools for Unhooking" on the back, and bring their sheets to the next lesson. Tell them to jot down any questions or comments they have in the margins or in their journals. Follow up by conducting Lesson 89.

Note: The handout includes a recommendation to write about angry feelings. Make sure students know that they should *never* write angry feelings on social networking sites or in texts or emails. Angry words written on the computer or cell phone can be transmitted to other people with a single click. Emphasize that the writing is intended for their eyes only.

Don't Get Hooked

Do you ever walk around with somebody's put-down taking up space in your brain? Do you ever spend time focusing on getting even?

Walking around with your head full of angry thoughts about getting even can drain your energy and make you feel worse. It's like walking around covered with a glob of slime. But you don't have to stay hooked that way. Here are four things to help you unhook and release the angry thoughts and feelings. They will enable you to leave that glob of slime on the ground where it belongs, and walk away with your own power in place:

1. Give yourself 30 minutes to stew. Take some time alone and be as mad as you want for those 30 minutes. On paper, write down what you're mad about. This is just for you, so don't show what you wrote to anyone else. When you're done, tear up the paper and throw it away. Once the feelings are out on paper, they won't clog up your brain as much.

2. Keep repeating your calming statement silently and do something that helps you chill out. If you're at school, wash your face and get a drink. If you're home, try exercising or listening to music. When angry thoughts pop back up, replace them with your calming statement so your mind doesn't get trapped in bad thoughts.

3. Talk to a trusted person. Make this confidential. Do this to get bad feelings out of your system—not to get even or get the person in trouble. It won't help to start gossiping about the person who made you mad—that will only make things worse. Come up with a plan of action. For example, you might plan to talk directly to the person who upset you, or to ignore the person. You might decide to ask for more help from a counselor, a teacher, or another adult for help.

4. Do something *constructive* (something useful and healthy). Help someone else, or get involved in a project. Helping others is one of the best ways to help yourself feel better. It turns the energy of anger and hurt feelings into something useful. This is a good step to take any time you feel sad, mad, or worried.

Make a conscious choice *not* to get hooked by someone else's negative words. Hold onto your power instead of giving it away. As one student said, "I refuse to let *their* words ruin *my* day."

Don't Get Hooked (continued)

My Tools for Unhooking

My calming statement is: _____

_____

My Peace Shield looks like this: (Draw and describe it here):

Three things on my list of ways to chill out are:

1._____

2._____

3._____

Two assertive comebacks I can use are:

1._____

2._____

A trusted person I can talk to is:

_____

If that person is not available, another trusted person is:

_____

Lesson 89: Tools for Unhooking

> **calming • courage • self-control • anger management • respect**
>
> Lesson 89 gives students more ways to "unhook" from mean words and actions and provides specific strategies to help them do so. This lesson is a follow-up to Lesson 88.
>
> **Note:** Complete Lessons 38, Calming Statements, and 47, Peace Shield, prior to this one.
>
> **Students will**
> - understand how to "unhook" from someone else's mean words or put-downs
> - learn how to use specific strategies for unhooking from mean actions
> - raise real questions that come up for them about applying unhooking strategies in their lives
>
> **Materials**
> - "Assertive Comebacks" chart from Lesson 85 (see page 197)
> - "Dignity Stance" chart from Lesson 68 (see page 160)
> - completed handouts: "Don't Get Hooked" (pages 203–204)

Preparation. Make sure students have read their handouts and filled in "My Tools for Unhooking" on the back of the sheet. Do the same yourself. Have on hand some extra copies of the handout so students who forgot to bring theirs or have not yet completed it will have a personal copy.

Introduction. Have students take out their "Don't Get Hooked" handouts. Choose a few volunteers to share the most important insights they gained from reading the information and listing their tools for unhooking.

Activity and Discussion. Ask for seven volunteers to read aloud each of the seven paragraphs. Discuss.

Ask students to share questions and comments they've jotted down. Encourage them to be as honest as possible. Remind them that you don't want them to just say the "right thing" when they're in class and then do the "wrong thing" (act aggressively or passively) when they're confronted with real-life situations.

Ask: **How many of you would rather just get even if someone puts you down?** Guide them to understand that it's normal to feel that way sometimes, but taking revenge almost always makes things worse. It leads to escalating conflicts that inevitably end badly.

A student may say, "Sometimes you have to show you're stronger, so the other person doesn't keep trying to push you around." Respond by saying, "You can be strong without being mean. Saying something assertive, then walking away with courage and dignity, is what real strength is all about."

Remind students that the tools for unhooking will help them hold onto their strength and power and build it up. Put students in pairs and have them talk with partners about their tools for unhooking.

Afterward, ask a few students to share what they wrote. Share what you wrote, too.

Wrap-Up. Tell students to put their "My Tools for Unhooking" sheets in a place where they can refer to them often (such as taped to the front of their journal or hung on a wall at home). Say: **Remember to use everything we've talked about in real life.** Tell students you'll be checking in with them to hear how they're applying what they've learned.

Follow-Up. Continue to check back with students about the progress they're making in keeping from getting hooked by mean words and actions. Discuss difficulties that arise, and address students' questions and challenges. Affirm them for progress they make.

Lesson 90: Learning to Detach

self-control • self-respect • self-worth • anger management • courage

Lesson 90 teaches students how to create an attitude of detachment when they are teased or picked on.

Students will

- understand that they do not have to engage with people who are treating them unkindly
- learn about positive self-talk that can help them detach from people's mean words and actions
- reflect on other things they can do to help themselves unhook and detach

Materials

- handout: "What Real Kids Have to Say About Detaching from Name-Calling and Teasing" (page 207)
- a yellow marker or crayon for each student
- journals

Introduction. On the board, write the word *detach*. Ask if anyone knows what it means to *detach* from someone else's mean words. Guide students to understand that detaching from someone's mean words means unhooking and deciding not to let what was said get the best of you or make you feel bad about yourself. Say: **What we tell ourselves in the moment can really help us detach.** Give an example of something you tell yourself that helps you detach from rude comments, such as, **"**This isn't worth getting upset over." Say: **Statements we tell ourselves that help us feel better are called** *positive self-talk.*

Ask students if they have any statements that help them detach from someone's mean words. Also ask what else they do to help themselves detach. Say: **Even though you may still feel the sting of someone's mean words, by using positive self-talk, deep breathing, and your calming statement you'll gain greater control over your reactions. Then you can either choose a response or walk away with your head held high.**

Ask students: **Can you think of a time you detached when someone called you a name or put you down? What helped you detach?** (Students might have said something to themselves, such as "I'm not going to take this personally," or they may have taken an action that helped.)

Activity and Discussion. Distribute the handout and say: **Here are some ideas from middle schoolers who've learned how to detach from mean words and put-downs. The first quote is from a girl who used to react all the time and ended up in lots of conflicts.** Ask a student to read the first quote from the handout.

Ask: **What did this student tell herself that helped her detach?** Discuss, emphasizing the idea of positive self-talk.

Now ask for volunteers, one at a time, to read aloud the rest of the quotes from real kids. Tell students to follow along and highlight in yellow the parts that can help them in their own lives.

Ask: **Why is it important to unhook, detach, and keep from investing your energy reacting to someone's rudeness?**

Refer to the bulleted "Positive 'Self-Talk'" quotes at the bottom of the handout. Ask students: **Which of these quotes would best help you detach next time someone says something mean to you?** Have them highlight the one they choose in yellow.

Review other things students can do to help themselves detach (deep breathing, calming statements, Peace Shield, one of their chill-out strategies).

Wrap-Up. Have students jot down in their journals the positive self-talk quote they chose. Ask them to jot down something else they can do to help themselves detach. Remind students that detaching will help them keep their power rather than give it away.

What Real Kids Have to Say About
Detaching from Name-Calling and Teasing
Tips from Middle Schoolers

Here's how some middle school students detach when someone teases them or calls them names (you can use these ideas, too):

"Here's how I look at it: If they're spending their time trying to get a reaction out of you, it's just not worth giving them the satisfaction. There's no point in talking back. It's better to just ignore what they're saying."

"It's not worth getting into a fight over this stuff. I know I'm a different kind of person than they are, and that's okay. It's good just to be your own self and let their words slide off your back."

"Sometimes classmates call people names just to be cool. They're trying to make you feel powerless and themselves powerful. Try to ignore it. Normally if I just walk away and ignore them they'll just forget about it. Sometimes I ask myself if I did something wrong. If I did I try to fix it. Other times I just realize that it's their loss. If it keeps on happening, I find an adult to talk to about it."

"If someone's name-calling I try to ignore them. If you're with people who are disrespectful, you need to hang around with the right people."

"My advice if they say things you don't like is to let it go. Don't even worry about it. They can talk all they want, but they can't hurt you if you don't let them. If it really bothers you, talk to the school counselor or someone who can keep it private."

Positive "Self-Talk" for Detaching from Mean Words

- "It's not worth getting into a fight over this stuff."
- "I know I'm a different kind of person than they are, and that's okay."
- "It's good just to be your own self and let their words slide off your back."
- "I just realize that it's their loss."
- "If people you're with are disrespectful, you need to hang around with different people."
- "They can talk all they want, but they can't hurt you if you don't let them."

Lesson 91: "I Was Just Kidding"

self-control • courage • compassion • respect • personal responsibility

Lesson 91 helps students respond assertively to mean joking or hostile comments masked in humor.

Students will
- understand that if something said in jest upsets another person, then it's not funny and not okay to say
- role-play and discuss assertive responses to sarcastic or hurtful joking
- strengthen their assertiveness skills

Materials
- "Dignity Stance" chart from Lesson 68
- "Assertive Comebacks" chart from Lesson 85
- handout: "'That's Not Funny'" (page 210, four copies)

Introduction and Discussion. Ask students if they've ever experienced someone saying something hurtful or aggressive, and then saying, "just kidding." Ask: **If something hurts or angers another person, does saying "just kidding" make it okay? Why or why not?** Discuss, emphasizing that it's never okay to cover up a mean remark by saying you were just kidding, nor is it okay to make a joke at someone else's expense.

Read aloud this statement made by a third-grade student:

"It makes me really mad when kids tease me and say they're just kidding, but they really weren't kidding at all."

Ask students to respond. Say: **How about if someone says something mean, sarcastic, or hurtful and then says, "I was only joking around"—is that ever okay to do?** Guide students to understand that it's never okay to mask hostility with humor. Say: Remarks like this are called zingers. If someone says something that hurts your feelings, you don't have to smile and go along with it. If it hurts, it hurts. You have a right to feel how you feel.

Activity. Tell students that today they're going to role-play using the assertiveness skills they've been learning to handle situations where someone tries to mask meanness and sarcasm with humor. Briefly review the skills you've worked on with students (Dignity Stance, I-messages, assertive comebacks, calming statements, deep breathing, positive self-talk).

Put students in pairs and have them come up with assertive comebacks or I-messages they can use if someone makes a mean comment and then says, "I was just kidding."

While pairs are working together, have three volunteers look over the dialogue on the "'That's Not Funny'" handout. Give them each a copy and keep one for yourself.

After a few minutes, have the class reconvene in a circle. Ask the three volunteers to act out the scenario from the handout in front of the class, reading aloud the dialogue. Have the student playing Amy assume the Dignity Stance when responding to Juan. Give her a quick prompt for each step (body tall, head high, feet apart, deep breaths).

After the role play, ask the class how they think it went. Ask "Amy" how she felt using assertiveness to respond to Juan. Ask "Juan" what effect Amy's assertive response had on him. Ask "Ken" the same question. Discuss. Ask the class: **Is there anything else Amy could have said or done to handle the situation more assertively? What could Ken have done differently so he could have been part of the solution rather than part of the problem?**

Remind students: If the person giving the put-downs laughs or makes comments as you walk away, keep walking with your head held high. Having the last word isn't important. Removing yourself from the person who's trying to hook you in is. It takes the wind out of whatever he or she is trying to say. Acting as if you don't care what the person says gives the impression that you're not hooked in (even if you still are on the inside). This helps you detach and take back your power.

Ask: **Do you think there's a way Amy could have responded with humor? What could she have said?** (For example, when Juan said, "Nice shirt. Where'd you get it? From your little sister?" Amy might have responded, "You like it? I'll ask my sister if she can give you one, too.") Tell students that responding with humor can often be effective if they're comfortable doing this. Sometimes a humorous comment can take away the impact of the put-down. Remind students to make sure their humorous comment isn't said with sarcasm or meanness.

Wrap-Up. Say: **Giving an assertive comeback and walking away with your head held high shows self-respect and confidence. Can you think of someone who's assertive, confident, and respected?** (Invite a few responses, and give an example of someone you know.) Say: **Next time someone tries to hook you in with mean words, ask yourself how that person might respond. Following that person's example can help strengthen your confidence.**

Follow-Up. Have students role-play other scenarios they suggest, focusing on how students targeted by mean joking can respond assertively.

"That's Not Funny"

This is a script to be enacted by three students playing the roles of Juan, Amy, and Ken.

Juan: *(laughing)* Nice shirt, Amy. Where'd you get it? From your little sister?

Amy: *(serious)* That's not funny, Juan. I like this shirt.

Juan: *(chuckling)* Hey, stop being so serious. I was just joking.

Amy: *(calm and direct)* I don't find your humor entertaining.

Juan: Oh, stop being so sensitive.

Amy: *(calm and direct)* Your joke just wasn't funny.

Juan: *(leaning in toward Ken and getting him to snicker)* Hey, Ken, have you noticed how Amy can't take a joke? She's soooo serious. *(makes a mocking face)*

Amy: *(in a grown-up voice)* That's not funny either. I'm finding your humor a little immature and I have other things I need to do right now. *(walks away confidently with head held high)*

Lesson 92: Don't Get Stung by Zingers

courage • self-control • self-respect • self-affirmation

Lesson 92 helps students strengthen their internal resources and confidence to deflect "zingers"—sarcastic remarks and put-downs.

Students will

- recognize how zingers lead to a cycle of conflict
- learn ways to become zinger-proof
- begin to create a personal insurance policy against zingers

Materials

- chart paper and marker
- handouts: "Don't Get Stung by Zingers" and "Become Zinger-Proof" (pages 212–213, copied back-to-back); "Zinger Insurance Policy" (page 214)
- yellow marker or crayon for each student

Preparation. On chart paper, write: *"No one can make you feel inferior without your consent." —Eleanor Roosevelt*

Introduction. Display the quote and ask a student to read it aloud. Ask students what the quote means; make sure they understand the meaning of *inferior*. Ask students: **What does this quote mean to *you?***

Activity and Discussion. Pass out the "Don't Get Stung by Zingers" and "Become Zinger-Proof" handouts, copied back-to-back. Refer to the title "Don't Get Stung by Zingers" and go over what zingers are. Discuss briefly.

Tell students you'll be asking volunteers to read the handout aloud. Tell them that as the handout is being read, they should highlight anything that seems especially important or that they have questions about.

Choose three volunteers to read the first three paragraphs of "Don't Get Stung by Zingers." Ask students: **What do you think of Gus's ideas about zingers? Do you have the power to keep yourself out of a zinger match?** Discuss.

Choose other volunteers to read the last four paragraphs on the page. Pause for brief responses, then turn the handout over and have volunteers read the paragraphs in "Become Zinger-Proof." Remind students who are following along to underline anything they want to know more about.

Afterward, have students look at the passages they highlighted. Address their questions and comments. Encourage them to speak honestly.

Next, have students pair up and talk with partners about at least one thing they can put on each of the three lists:

- **List 1:** All the things you're good at, even little things
- **List 2:** All the people in your life who care about you, adults as well as kids
- **List 3:** Happy memories, from as far back as you can remember to the present

Wrap-Up. Bring the circle back together and distribute the "Zinger Insurance Policy" handout. Ask students to fill in the lists on the handout after class or later in the day. Let them know they can refer to their lists when they need a reminder of good things in their lives that help them feel strong on the inside. Have them bring completed handouts to the next lesson (Lesson 93).

Follow-Up. Conduct Lesson 93, "Becoming Zinger-Proof."

Don't Get Stung by Zingers

Zingers are sarcastic comments and put-downs. On TV and in videos, we hear zingers all the time—and people usually laugh at them. But when zingers are directed at us in real life, it can be a different story. If someone insults you with a zinger, you have the right to feel mad. You might feel as if you need to throw a zinger right back at the person. But that's not necessarily the case.

A boy we'll call Gus said this about zingers: "The kids in my class use zingers all the time. Every minute, someone's trying to outdo the next person with sarcastic remarks and put-downs. I refuse to get involved. I don't need to build my self-esteem by making someone else feel bad. I either walk away or think about something else."

Makes sense, doesn't it? Why let someone's put-downs ruin your day? And why be a part of ruining someone else's day? Sure, it can be hard to pull back from a zinger match, or to let harsh words bounce off you, but you have the *power* to do this.

If zingers are directed at you and you feel yourself reacting, remember to Stop, Breathe, Chill. Use your calming statement and some positive self-talk to activate the strength you have inside. Try telling yourself: "I don't need their approval," or "Their words are meaningless."

Some kids feel like they can't survive without returning zingers. It's normal to want to protect yourself. But sending zingers back usually makes things worse, and it won't make you feel better about yourself. The truth is, it's often better to let the zingers fly right past you. That's what Gus does. And since he doesn't take part, people are less likely to send zingers his way. He has plenty of things in his life that make him feel good about who he is, so he doesn't need to build himself up by throwing zingers at people.

If zingers are flying at you, and you don't want to just walk away, you can say something assertive like, "It's too bad you have to build yourself up by trying to put someone else down." Say this in a neutral, matter-of-fact way—not sarcastic or mean. Then, walk away with your head held high and focus on things that give you strength and confidence.

Remember the words of former First Lady Eleanor Roosevelt:

"No one can make you feel inferior without your consent."

Become Zinger-Proof

Do you want to become zinger-proof? Make your own personal insurance policy against zingers. Start by writing these three lists:

List 1: All the things you're good at, even little things

List 2: All the people in your life who care about you, adults as well as kids

List 3: Happy memories, from as far back as you can remember to the present

These lists are your Zinger Insurance Policy. When someone says something that gets you down, don't let it take up space in your brain. Instead, think about all the things you're good at, or all the people who care about you, or a happy memory. Direct your focus to stuff that makes you feel better, not worse.

Whenever someone sends a zinger your way, remember this insurance policy. Then remember to breathe, stay calm, and stand tall. Say something assertive back if you want to, or ignore the person. Then walk away strong and tall. All these things will help you look confident and in control, even if you don't feel that way in the moment.

Over time, kids who want to throw zingers will see that they're not getting the result they're looking for. Remember this: The more you react, the more it encourages them. The less you react, the less likely they'll be to keep throwing zingers. You have the power to break this cycle!

Zinger Insurance Policy

For each list, write as many things as you can think of. You can add to these lists each day.

List 1: All the Things I'm Good At

List 2: All the People Who Care About Me

List 3: Happy Memories

On the back of this sheet, draw yourself wearing your Peace Shield as a protection against zingers.

Lesson 93: Becoming Zinger-Proof

courage • self-control • self-respect • self-affirmation • personal responsibility

Lesson 93 helps students strengthen their internal resources and confidence to deflect "zingers"— sarcastic remarks and put-downs. This lesson is a follow-up to Lesson 92.

Note: Complete Lessons 38, Calming Statements, and 47, Peace Shield, prior to this one.

Students will

- understand how zingers lead to conflict
- reflect on their personal insurance policies against zingers
- become more zinger-proof

Materials

- sign with Eleanor Roosevelt quote from Lesson 92 (see page 211)
- handouts: "Don't Get Stung by Zingers" and "Become Zinger-Proof" from Lesson 92 (pages 212–213, copied back-to-back)
- completed handout: "Zinger Insurance Policy" (page 214; see "Preparation," below)

Preparation. Have students complete the "Zinger Insurance Policy" handout prior to this lesson.

Introduction. Refer to the quote and ask students how Eleanor Roosevelt's words relate to their lives. Briefly discuss.

Discussion. Refer students to the "Don't Get Stung by Zingers" handout and ask the following questions:

- **Does anyone feel like Gus—not affected by zingers? What helps you feel that way?**

- **Does anyone like to throw zingers at others? Why? How do you suppose the person receiving zingers feels?**

- **What kinds of zingers do kids use on each other? How do you feel when zingers are flying toward you? Toward other kids?**

- **How do you respond to zingers that come your way? Is there a better way you could be responding?**

Activity. Have students take out their "Zinger Insurance Policies." Put students in pairs and have them share the lists they made.

After about five minutes, ask for a volunteer to act out the following (a student who is the target of zingers) as you read it aloud:

You are at home thinking about what will happen at school tomorrow. Two kids who sit next to you always toss zingers at you and everyone else. Tonight you decide to prepare yourself. Look over your "Zinger Insurance Policy" and zero in

on some things that make you feel good about yourself. Put on your Peace Shield for protection. Take some deep breaths and practice your calming statement. Think about whether you want to just ignore the zingers or respond. In case you decide to respond, think of an assertive comeback you might use. Rehearse it in the mirror.

Ask for two volunteers to join the first one and role-play what happens at school the next day. Tell the central role player: **When the kids start throwing zingers, you feel ready and confident. When they try to draw you in, you know just what to do.**

Coach the central role player along, and invite feedback from the class.

Afterward, debrief. Ask the central role player how it felt to try to detach from the zingers. Ask the other players how it felt when someone didn't respond to sarcasm and put-downs. Ask the class to comment on what they observed.

Wrap-Up. Let students know that you'll be observing how they apply the strategies and understandings of zinger-proofing. Remind them that zingers have no place in a get-along classroom.

Follow-Up. Suggest that students team up with a friend to help stop zingers and put-downs. Say: **Talk together about ways you can help each other stay zinger-proof. Agree on a plan of action. You might use a signal like putting your hands in your pockets. Or maybe you can agree to say something like "This is probably making _____ uncomfortable." Or you can walk away together.**

Lesson 94: Being an Upstander for Someone Who's Being Teased

compassion • courage • respect • integrity • personal responsibility

Lesson 94 fosters in students the willingness to stand up for someone who's being teased or put down.

Students will
- understand the importance of being an upstander, even when it's hard to do
- visualize themselves supporting someone who's being put down and role-play doing so
- create drawings of themselves as upstanders

Materials
- chart paper and marker
- student journals
- large sheets of drawing paper, markers, other art materials for creating posters
- *optional handout:* "8 Ways to Be an Upstander" (page 65)

Preparation. Make the following sign to post prominently in your room: *"If you have a chance to accomplish something that will make things better for people . . . and you don't do that, you are wasting your time on this Earth." —baseball great Roberto Clemente*

Introduction. Say: **We all know how much it hurts to be picked on and put down. How do you feel when you see this happening to someone else?** Discuss.

Continue: **We've talked about how hard it can be to stand up for someone, especially if you're the only one. Have you ever done this? What happened?** Accept responses. Then say: **Here's a story from a fourth-grade student who became an upstander:**

"I knew someone with special needs. She was being made fun of by one of my friends. It really bothered me. I tried to get him to stop, but he wouldn't listen to me. Finally I told the teacher what was going on. I ended up losing this friend, but I helped someone who really needed it. I'm glad I did it." Discuss.

Activity. Say: **Sometimes** *how* **we help depends on** *who's* **doing the teasing. If it's a close friend, we might be able to help by saying something like, "I'm uncomfortable with what you're doing." But with kids you don't know well, or don't know at all, it's more helpful to support the person who's being teased.**

Have students look at their "8 Ways to Be an Upstander" handouts. Say: **Rather than saying something to the kids who are teasing, you can do any of the things on your handout.** With the group, brainstorm specific actions they can take as upstanders, and invite volunteers to role-play several of these ideas. Be sure not to have students act out the teasing. Instead, have them role-play only the intervention. Also, make a point of having students role-play at least one scenario in which multiple students work together to be upstanders.

Tell students that all of these actions will help them be upstanders for students who are teased, picked on, or bullied.

Display the Roberto Clemente quote and ask students to read it aloud in unison. Ask: **What does Roberto Clemente mean when he says "you are wasting your time on this Earth" if you could help someone but don't?** Discuss, then ask students to write the quote in their journals.

Now lead students in a short visualization that will help them find the courage to become upstanders. Take two or three minutes to have students close their eyes, breathe deeply, and look into the highest, bravest part of themselves. Have them picture themselves breathing deep, standing tall, and supporting someone who is being picked on. Have them picture the person thanking them. Have them picture themselves feeling full of strength, courage, and pride.

Wrap-Up. Have students open their eyes. Ask: **What strategies can help you find the courage to be an upstander for someone who needs your support?** Review willingness skills, Peace Shield, deep breathing, calming statements, Dignity Stance, and rehearsing ahead of time.

Follow-Up. Give students drawing paper and have them create posters entitled "Be an Upstander." They can include Clemente's words along with pictures of themselves, or use other ideas about being an upstander that are meaningful to them. When the posters are complete, have students display them throughout the school.

Dealing with Bullying

What can you do when bullying takes place? This section gives you ways to help students recognize bullying and respond to it in healthy, assertive ways. It defines bullying as when a person or group purposely engages in actions, usually repeated over time, intended to harm someone else emotionally or physically and show power over the person. The lessons include a range of strategies to help kids who are bullied, a key strategy being to develop a culture of upstanders.

Lessons in this section help students define and recognize bullying, respond to bullying if they are targeted, become upstanders if they witness bullying, and discuss and role-play real "bullying stories" from the perspective of all students involved. You will also find support for helping kids who are bullying to stop doing so, and for fostering and reinforcing empathy and a strong conscience in all students.

Note: Often the terms *bully* and *victim* are used to define the roles that occur in bullying situations. Because these terms label students, I prefer to use terms that emphasize the behavior that occurs: *the person who is bullying* and *the person who is being bullied*. While using this language can feel awkward, it makes the important point that people should not be defined by their behavior or role during a given moment in time.

Key tools for this group of lessons include the informational handouts introduced in Lessons 95, 96, 98, and 99. Many skills introduced in Managing Anger (pages 83–118) and Preventing Conflict (pages 119–164) will be helpful for students as they take part in these lessons, particularly those from Lessons 38 (Calming Statements), 65 (Introducing Assertiveness), 68 (The Dignity Stance), and 85 and 86 (Assertive Responses to Mean Words, Parts 1 and 2).

Your Role When Bullying Happens

If you are aware of someone in your class who's bullying a friend or classmate, speak first to the child who's being bullied. Students who have been bullied need to know that they have a right to be safe and that you want to help. If a friend has done the bullying, remind them that kids who hurt their friends are not true friends, and that the wise choice might be to hang out with someone else—someone who treats them with respect. Help a student in this situation make a new friend.

Then speak to the child who is bullying. Let this student know you're aware of what's been happening, and that no one ever has the right to harm other people, even if the student is hurt or angry. Give a consequence if there's been physical aggression in your classroom, and follow through with other school staff about consequences for bullying outside of your classroom. Offer to help the student stop bullying and find ways to get along better with other students. Alert other school personnel who are generally present during lunch, recess, or other out-of-class times at school.

Be sure to inform your principal or other designated school official about the situation so all students involved can get appropriate intervention and support. If you think the child who's bullying is experiencing physical aggression at home, follow your school's procedures for mandatory reporting and student support.

Lesson 95: What Is Bullying?

> **self-respect · courage · compassion · kindness · personal responsibility**
>
> Lesson 95 defines bullying and helps students understand that bullying is harmful to everyone involved, including those who witness it.
>
> **Students will**
> - learn the meaning of bullying
> - learn about the three roles involved in the bullying cycle
> - reflect on the harmful impact of bullying on all involved
>
> **Materials**
> - chart paper and marker
> - handout: "The Real Deal About Bullying" (pages 221–222)
> - blank sheet of paper for each student
> - small box (or other container) with a lid labeled "Question Box"

Preparation. On chart paper, write the title *"If You Are Bullied: Do's and Don'ts."* List these key points from the handout:

DO
- Get away if you don't feel safe.
- Tell an adult about it.
- Buddy up.
- Be an upstander for yourself.

DON'T
- Get physical.
- Threaten or call the person names.
- Cry in front of the person who is bullying you.
- Ignore bullying and hope it stops.

Introduction. Ask students if they think bullying happens much in their school or neighborhood.

Ask students how they've been personally affected by bullying. Discuss, but don't push students to reveal if they have been or are being bullied. Kids who are bullied sometimes feel ashamed about it, so ease into this slowly. Let them know that bullying is always harmful and is never okay to do.

Tell students they're going to be learning ways to handle bullying, but first you'll share some facts about it.

Activity and Discussion. Pass out the "Real Deal About Bullying" handout. Explain that you will ask some questions and that they can find answers on the handout. Refer to your own copy of the handout as you ask and discuss the following:

What is bullying? Have someone share the definition from the handout. Briefly discuss examples of bullying.

Reiterate the difference between teasing and bullying. Teasing is usually not done to have power over another person. It can be annoying and upsetting, but can also be playful at times. Bullying is never playful and always does harm.

Ask: **What percentage of kids from the Survey About Conflicts say bullying goes on often, all the time, or every day? How often do you see bullying going on?**

What are the three roles in bullying? Ask students if they know what a bystander is (someone who stands by and watches bullying happen). Bystanders observe and don't try to help. Bystanders can actually make bullying worse just by providing an audience, even if it's just an audience of one.

Note: Sometimes students will rush to label less aggressive acts as bullying. Clarify that if someone leaves you out from time to time or calls you a name, that doesn't qualify as bullying. But if someone is truly cruel to you, and treats you this way often, that's bullying. If your students use labels like *bully* and *victim*, model the nonlabeling way *(person who bullies, person who's bullied)* and have them rephrase.

Who does bullying harm? The answer is everyone—the person who is bullied, the one who does the bullying, and the bystanders. Ask students why they think this is the case. You might ask: **How does bullying hurt those who are bullied? How does it hurt the people who watch it happening? How does it hurt those who do the bullying?** Help students understand that bullying creates an atmosphere of fear, danger, and "un-safety."

Ask students how they feel when they see someone being bullied. Mention that bystanders often feel guilty and afraid.

What often happens to 25 percent of kids who bully? Explain that kids who develop a pattern of bullying often find it hard to break this pattern as they get older. The result can be law-breaking behaviors like harassment, assault, and vandalism.

Ask students what is the most important role they can play if they see bullying taking place (the role of an upstander). Also ask what an upstander can do for kids who are bullied (intervene to help stop the bullying). Let students know you'll be going over strategies in future lessons to help them be upstanders.

Ask students: **What do you think you can do to help end the cycle of bullying?** (Don't bully others, be an upstander for kids who are bullied, get help if you or others are being bullied.)

Briefly go over the chart: "If You Are Bullied: Do's and Don'ts," referring to the handout for elaboration and clarification. Let students know that in upcoming lessons they'll be learning more about how to be an upstander for themselves and others when bullying takes place. (Note that assertive comebacks are introduced in Lesson 85.)

Wrap-Up. Pass out paper and have students write "Question/Comments About Bullying" at the top of their sheet. Tell them to take their papers home and write down any questions or comments they have about bullying.

Show students the Question Box. Explain that they are to bring their questions and comments back to school and place them, folded, in the Question Box. Tell them you're going to read everything and emphasize that they don't have to put their names on their papers; however, if they want an individual answer from you, they should include their name.

Follow-Up. On an ongoing basis, read through the questions in the Question Box and select some that you can address with the class. Also follow up with students who want personal help. This lesson may bring out painful feelings for some of them. If this is the case, follow up confidentially. If you come across any questions or situations you need help addressing, discuss them with the school counselor, psychologist, social worker, principal, or students' parents. You are welcome to email me about any questions at help4kids@freespirit.com. Keep the Question Box available as you conduct other lessons and encourage students to add questions to the box whenever they have them.

The Real Deal About Bullying

In a national survey of more than 2,100 students in grades 3–6, **44% (963 students)** said that bullying happens often, every day, or all the time (in school or other places).

What Is Bullying?

Bullying: When a person or group purposely engages in actions intended to harm someone else emotionally or physically and show power over the person. Bullying often consists of a series of cruel acts repeated over time. It may include any of the following:

- hurting someone physically
- cruel teasing
- harmful threats
- spreading nasty rumors
- mean phone calls, texts, notes, and emails
- cruel name-calling, put-downs, and gestures
- excluding someone repeatedly and getting others to do it, too

Three Roles in Bullying

- the person who bullies
- the person who is bullied
- the bystander(s)—the person or people who watch acts of bullying

Bullying Harms Everyone

Bullying harms not only the person who's being bullied, but also those who watch it happen (bystanders) and even those who do the bullying. In fact, 25% of kids who bully over and over again eventually end up in trouble with the law.

The Real Deal About Bullying (continued)

If You Are Bullied: Do's and Don'ts

What If Someone Is Bullying You?

DO

- **Get away if you don't feel safe.** Walk (or run) away as fast as you can.

- **Tell an adult about it.** Telling isn't tattling—it helps you stay safe. Tell the adult where and when the bullying took place, what happened, and who did it.

- **Buddy up.** People who bully like to pick on kids who are alone, so stick with other kids.

- **Be an upstander for yourself.** If you feel safe, tell the person to stop bullying you. Use an I-message or another assertive comeback.

DON'T

- **Get physical.** Fighting might make the bullying worse. If someone physically threatens you, don't fight: Instead, get away as fast as you can. The *only* exception is if you are in immediate physical danger and have no other possible choice but to defend yourself.

- **Threaten or call the persons names.** This can cause the bullying to escalate—get worse.

- **Cry in front of the person who's bullying you.** Someone who is bullying might like to see you cry. Take deep breaths and try to stay calm. You can cry in private after you walk away and find someone to help.

- **Ignore bullying and hope it stops.** People who keep bullying aren't likely to stop or go away by simply being ignored. Decide whether to stand up for yourself or get help from a grown-up.

Lesson 96: Questions About Bullying

compassion · personal responsibility · integrity

Lesson 96 reviews the bullying information introduced in the previous lesson and addresses students' questions and comments about bullying. It also reinforces the concept that bullying harms everyone and that, by working together, we all have the power to stop it. This lesson is a follow-up to Lesson 95.

Students will

- discuss and respond to questions and comments about bullying from the Question Box
- reflect on the impact of bullying described in two stories from real kids
- understand the critical need to be an upstander rather than a bystander

Materials

- Question Box from Lesson 95 (see page 220) with students' questions
- handouts: "The Real Deal About Bullying" from Lesson 95 (pages 221–222) and "If You're Being Bullied" (page 225)

Preparation. Have students bring their "Real Deal About Bullying" handouts, distributed in Lesson 95. Have on hand some extra copies of the handout so students who forgot to bring theirs or were absent during Lesson 95 will have a personal copy.

Prior to this lesson go through the questions in the Question Box. Choose a few to discuss now.

Introduction. Have students put any remaining questions and comments in the box if they haven't already done so.

Gather in the circle and review information from "The Real Deal About Bullying" handouts, focusing on the definition of bullying, the bullying cycle, and the fact that bullying harms everyone involved.

Discussion and Activity. Choose a question you have preselected from the Question Box. Read it aloud and ask for student responses to it. Provide any information that's needed.

Discuss several more questions and comments.

Next, read aloud the following story, shared by a fourth-grade student:*

"My friends didn't like this one girl, so they made a club against her. They asked me to join. I didn't really know the girl, so I decided to go along with my friends. When the girl found out about the club, she was so upset she told the principal. We had to sit down with her and have a talk. The girl was so hurt by what we did she was crying. I never meant to hurt her and I didn't know what to say.

"After the talk, she ended up forgiving us. She and I ended up becoming good friends. Sometimes you might not know that what you're doing is bullying. I learned how important it is to be nice to everyone even if you don't know them, and to not always go along with your friends."

Ask students: **Why might the friends have started a club like this? Why do you think this student joined the club against the girl?** Review the student's statement: "Sometimes you might not know that what you're doing is bullying." Ask: **How was joining the club an act of bullying? What important lesson did this girl learn?** Discuss, emphasizing issues like peer pressure, thinking about how other people might feel, and checking in with one's conscience.

Read aloud another story, this one from a fifth-grade student:

"There is a boy at school who gets bullied all the time. It started last year and still goes on. Everyone I know, except me and my best friends, tease him. I feel so bad for him. I think he should learn better comebacks.

"Last year I was hoping they'd forget about him over the summer, but right after summer break was over, they kept bullying him. I wish it could stop, but it doesn't. I feel so bad for him."

Discuss, particularly the following, "They kept bullying him. I wish it could stop. But it doesn't. I feel so bad for him." Ask students: **Will bullying stop if no one says or does anything about it? What could this boy and his friends have done to be upstanders for this boy?**

Say: **The boy who told this story was being *passive*. He cared, but was afraid to help, so he did**

---

*Stories and quotes attributed to real students and teachers come from author interviews and from responses to the Survey About Conflicts conducted by the author and publisher. See pages 1 and 282–284 for further information.

nothing. Review what it means to respond assertively, as opposed to being aggressive or passive. Tell students that upstanders are always assertive, not mean. They respond to what's going on with directness and strength rather than getting down to the level of the person who's bullying.

Wrap-Up. Let students know that it's possible to put an end to bullying in a school. It can happen when *everyone* makes up their mind *not* to bully, and to be upstanders for kids who are being bullied, and for themselves, if they're bullied. Say: **This includes adults in the school, too. That's why it's important to let them know when bullying takes place. If they don't know about it, they can't help. We're doing** these lessons so we can have a school without bullying.

Pass out "If You're Being Bullied." Tell students to be sure to read it, highlight any parts they have questions about, and write comments in the margins. Let them know you'll discuss it with them during the next few days.

Follow-Up. Continue to discuss with students ways to recognize and stop bullying. Note that Lesson 97 addresses how students who are being bullied can respond to it.

Also continue to invite questions for the Question Box and to discuss these as a group or individually.

PART TWO
Dealing with Bullying

If You're Being Bullied

If you're being bullied, remember your own worth and value.

Kids who are bullied often think they're being picked on because there's something wrong with them. *This is absolutely not true.* If you're feeling that the bullying is your fault, let go of that idea. It's not your fault. No one deserves to be bullied. Period.

Too often kids who are bullied keep the problem inside because they feel embarrassed, ashamed, or scared. Doing this only makes it worse. Shame and silence can make you forget who you really are. Never forget the personal power you have inside yourself.

Some kids think everyone has to dress, talk, eat, think, act, and look alike. You don't have to be like everybody else to be worthy of respect. Your individuality is what makes you special. Don't let anyone else's words or actions make you feel "less" than anybody else. Always remember that you are a valuable person worthy of respect.

Lesson 97: What to Do If Someone Bullies You

courage · personal responsibility · self-respect · assertiveness

Lesson 97 provides skills and strategies students can use if they are being bullied. This lesson is a follow-up to Lesson 96.

Students will

- understand that the words of someone who bullies them should never be taken personally
- review what they can do if they are bullied
- understand that they don't have to shoulder bullying alone
- reflect on the fact that bystanders can become upstanders who help

Materials

- handouts: "If You're Being Bullied" from Lesson 96 (page 225) and "The Real Deal About Bullying" from Lesson 95 (pages 221–222)
- "If You Are Bullied: Do's and Don'ts" chart from Lesson 95 (see page 219)
- *optional:* student journals

Preparation. Have on hand some extra copies of the handouts so students who forgot to bring theirs or were absent during Lessons 95 or 96 will have personal copies.

Introduction and Discussion. Have students bring their "If You're Being Bullied" handouts to the circle. Ask: **What questions came up for you as you read through this?** Respond to questions and comments kids had about what they read.

Remind students that if they've ever been bullied, they're not alone. At least 50 percent of kids in all age groups are bullied.* Consider sharing your own story if you've ever been bullied, too. Doing so will help kids who've been bullied feel less alone and safer about opening up.

If anyone reveals having been bullied, allow time for discussion. Refer to both handouts and to the chart. Say: **If you're being bullied, it's really important to remember that you have worth and value just as you are, no matter what the other person says or does.** Discuss.

Say: **Let's take another look at the story from a real student you heard in the last lesson. I'm going to be asking several of you to play the roles of the kids in this story. Then we're going to think about what the boy who was being bullied might have done to help himself.** Read the story aloud to your class:

"There is a boy at school who gets bullied all the time. It started last year and still goes on. Everyone I know, except me and my best friends, tease him. I feel so bad for him. I think he should learn better comebacks.

"Last year I was hoping they'd forget about him over the summer, but right after summer break was over, they kept bullying him. I wish it could stop, but it doesn't. I feel so bad for him."

Ask for a volunteer to play the role of the boy who was being bullied. Have two groups play the roles of the kids who bullied and the bystanders. Afterward, ask students: **What assertive comeback could this boy use to be an upstander for himself?** ("I don't deserve to be treated this way." "I'm not listening to you anymore.") Have the boy choose a comeback and speak up assertively. Then ask the class: **What other things could he do to deal with the bullying?** Discuss students' ideas, focusing on the "Do's and Don'ts."

Note: Lessons 107, Bullied on the Playground, and 109, Physically Bullied by a Group, address physical bullying in more depth and include a handout, "Keep Yourself Safe from Physical Harm" (see page 250).

Ask the bystanders to face the class next, and ask: **What could these students have done to help instead of remaining silent?** Finally, ask the kids who bullied to face the class. Have the class suggest what these students should or could have done differently, especially those in the group who had guilty feelings about contributing to the bullying. Discuss, addressing students' fears about speaking out and their concerns about not going along with the crowd.

---

* New York University Child Study Center, January 2010.

Wrap-up. Stress that in all three roles—the person who's bullied, the bystanders, or the student or students who are bullying—there are positive choices everyone can make. Reiterate that students who are being bullied do not ever deserve to be bullied.

Follow-up. Have students review with a trusted friend or family member things they can do to help themselves if they are ever bullied, and what might stand in the way of advocating for themselves. Suggest that they write about this in their journals, too.

"What If?" Questions About Getting Help from Adults

Students are likely to have concerns about telling an adult about bullying. Here are some questions they may ask and responses you can give:

"What if someone hurts me and they threaten to do it again if I tell?" Tell students: People threaten because they're afraid of getting in trouble. If someone threatens your physical or emotional safety in any way, don't remain silent. Talk to a trusted adult as quickly as you can.

"What if they tell me they're going to wait for me off the school grounds?" Tell students: This is all the more reason to talk to an adult, like the teacher or guidance counselor. The school has rules that are meant to protect you in school and on the way home. If you remain silent, you put yourself at greater risk.

"What if telling makes it worse?" Tell students: If this happens, it's time for a family grown-up (a parent or guardian) to meet with the principal. Adults at school and at home have an obligation to keep you safe. Don't let yourself be defeated by someone else's cruelty.

"What if it's someone from my group of friends who is threatening me? I feel like I need to be loyal." Tell students to think about this: If your best friend was being threatened, what advice would you give? Wouldn't you want to make sure your best friend was safe? So if the same thing is happening to you, you need to treat yourself like you would a good friend. Another thing to think about: If someone in your group is threatening or hurting you, do you really want to be loyal to this person?

"What if I'm too scared to tell anyone?" Tell students: By going to an adult, you can help yourself stop feeling scared. Plus, if you get help, you may help other kids find the courage to get help, too. One thing you might do is talk to an adult about how you can deal with the person who's picking on you. You can decide what to say and role-play it first for practice. If this assertive approach doesn't work, the adult can talk to the person who's bullying you.

Lesson 98: Help Yourself Deal with Bullying

personal responsibility · courage · compassion · assertiveness

Lesson 98 gives students strategies for dealing with people who bully them and for building confidence and assertiveness.

Note: Prior to conducting this lesson, it would be helpful to review Lessons 85 and 86, which focus on assertive comebacks students can use when dealing with mean words and put-downs.

Students will
- reflect on things they can do to prevent themselves from being bullied
- know what to do to deflect bullying if it should happen (or is happening) to them
- be empowered to be their own advocate if bullying takes place

Materials
- chart paper and marker
- handouts: "8 Keys to Putting on Your Anti-Bullying Armor" (page 230)
- "Dignity Stance" chart from Lesson 68 (see page 162)
- student journals

Preparation. On chart paper, write the title *"8 Keys to Putting on Your Anti-Bullying Armor."* List these key points from the handout:

1. *Don't believe a word they say.*
2. *Fake it till you make it.*
3. *Claim your dignity.*
4. *Use an assertive comeback.*
5. *Talk to a trusted adult.*
6. *Stick around other kids and adults.*
7. *Build yourself up from the inside out.*
8. *Reprogram your brain.*

Introduction. Pass out the "8 Keys to Putting on Your Anti-Bullying Armor" handout. Let students know that these keys can do two important things: First, they can help students build the confidence and courage to handle bullying. Second, the eight keys can also help them send the message that they are not an easy target.

Activity and Discussion. Referring to the chart and the handout, go over the eight keys, discussing the following:

1. **Don't believe a word they say.** Ask a volunteer to read aloud this first key. Tell students that one of the biggest problems with bullying is when we believe the things the person says about us. Say: **Anyone who bullies is doing it to have power over another person. Even if the person has picked you to bully, they could just as easily bully someone else. If you're being bullied, it's** very important to remember that there's nothing wrong with you, no matter what the other person says. Discuss.

If you have conducted Lesson 47, Peace Shield (page 114), remind students about it and ask how their Peace Shield could help keep out the hurtful words.

2. **Fake it till you make it.** Ask someone to read this key aloud. Ask: **What does it mean to "fake it till you make it"? How can pretending to feel strong and brave help you?** Help students understand that even if they feel upset, it's critical to act as if they don't when in the presence of kids who are bullying. Make sure students know they can let out the feelings when they get home or privately at school with a trusted person.

3. **Claim your dignity.** Have a volunteer read this key aloud. Ask what students have learned that can help them do this. Briefly review the Dignity Stance, having everyone stand and go through each step.

4. **Use an assertive comeback.** Invite someone to read this key aloud, and briefly discuss assertive comebacks students might use if they are bullied.

5. **Talk to a trusted adult.** After having a student read this key aloud, ask: **Who are some adults that can help you?** (Examples include a teacher, guidance counselor, principal, parent or guardian, youth leader, and others.) Remind students that talking to a trusted person is critical; emphasize that they have the right to ask for help. The adult can either help solve the problem or find

someone else who is better able to. Acknowledge that even if it's hard to get help, it's important not to stop trying.

If students say, "Asking an adult for help will make the bullying worse," tell them that if it does get worse, they need to go back for more help. Reiterate that bullying is against the law in many states and against the rules of your school.

Note: Lesson 50, Getting Help with Anger, is a ten-minute time cruncher that helps kids figure out which adults they can go to for help.

6. **Stick around other kids and adults.** Have a student read this key aloud, then ask: **How can this help you protect yourself?** Briefly discuss situations where kids might be alone, and help them strategize ways they could buddy up or stay closer to other people. You might give this example: **Maybe you feel like hanging out by yourself during recess rather than play. Instead of sitting somewhere alone, see if you can get a friend to join you. If there's no one to do that, sit somewhere within the sight of a teacher or an aide.**

7. **Build yourself up from the inside out.** Have a student read this key aloud. Then ask: **What can you do to build your confidence? How can building yourself up inside help you protect yourself from bullying?** If you conducted Lesson 92, refer back to the "Zinger Insurance Policy" (page 214) and review it with students.

8. **Reprogram your brain.** Discuss how visualization—picturing yourself handling a situation in a strong, confident way—can help you become more strong and confident.

Note: Lessons 100 and 101 focus on keys 7 and 8 in more depth and detail.

Wrap-Up. Reiterate that bullying has no place in your school and that you are someone students can come to for help. If they do, let them know things will be handled with confidentiality and care.

Follow-Up. Conduct Lesson 100, Build Yourself Up from the Inside Out, and Lesson 101, Reprogram Your Brain.

8 Keys to Putting on Your Anti-Bullying Armor

What does it mean to wear anti-bullying armor? It means you think and act in ways that show you won't let others have power over you. Here are 8 important steps you can take to help protect yourself from bullying:

1. When people try to bully you with words, don't believe a word they say. It's more about them than you.

2. Don't let them see you sweat. "Fake it till you make it."

3. Claim your dignity. Stand tall and walk proud.

4. Use an assertive comeback like, "I don't have time for this stuff." Then walk away with your head held high.

5. Talk to a trusted adult. Report who bullied you, what happened, and where it happened. If it happened online, show the adult the email, text, or Web page.

6. Stick around other kids and adults. People who bully look for kids who are on their own.

7. Build yourself up from the inside out. Remind yourself of your own worth and value. Strengthen your natural skills and talents. This will give you back the energy that the person who bullies is trying to take away.

8. Reprogram your brain. Every night, picture yourself strong, confident, and standing up to the person who's bullying you. See yourself triumphing by being confident and assertive.

Lesson 99: If You've Bullied Others

self-control · personal responsibility · respect · compassion · fairness

Lesson 99 is a lesson to conduct with all students, focused on helping kids who have bullied or who are bullying recognize that they can change.

Students will

- review the three roles involved in bullying
- assess themselves to see if they've been bullying others
- learn ways to help themselves stop if they've been bullying someone

Materials

- chart paper and marker
- handouts: "Are You Bullying Anyone?" (page 233); "Help Yourself Stop Bullying: What to Do If You've Bullied Others" (pages 234–235)

Preparation. On chart paper, write:

"Three Roles in Bullying

- *the person who bullies*
- *the person who is bullied*
- *the bystanders"*

Introduction. Ask students: **What are the three *roles* in bullying?** Refer to the chart and go over each role. Ask students to define *bystander*. Emphasize that bystanders play an extremely important role. Bystanders can decide to help or to hurt. Often, bystanders remain silent, which doesn't help. If they start to laugh, do something to encourage the bullying, or join in themselves, they become part of the bullying. Say: **But bystanders can transform themselves into upstanders. How?**

Let students know that people may experience all three roles at some point in their lives. Briefly share your own examples of roles you've played. Be honest—this helps students be honest, too. Ask which roles students have experienced. Discuss briefly.

Note: Students may be reticent to disclose that they have bullied others. Don't push or put anyone on the spot.

Discussion. Refer again to the terms you wrote on chart paper and say: **Some people know they bully. Others bully without realizing it, or get drawn in without really meaning or wanting to.** Pass out the "Are You Bullying Anyone?" handout and say: **This is a quiz you can take home and fill out to figure out if you are bullying anyone.** Briefly review the items on the handout together; ask if students have any questions.

Tell students that if they have bullied someone else or are doing it now, today's lesson will help them stop.

Pass out "Help Yourself Stop Bullying: What to Do If You've Bullied Others" and ask for a volunteer to read the opening paragraph. Ask students how bullying hurts the person who is doing it. Discuss.

One by one, ask for volunteers to read the individual steps to stop bullying. Discuss each step briefly, making sure students understand. Invite ideas for ways to own the problem, promise to stop, make amends, give yourself credit, and be part of a solution to the wider problem of bullying. Help kids identify appropriate adults to talk to also.

Activity. Ask for a volunteer to role-play the part of a student who has been bullying. Have another volunteer play the role of a trusted friend or adult. Have them play out the conversation that takes place when the child who bullies decides to do the things on the "What to Do If You've Bullied Others" handout.

Afterward, have the class give feedback. Ask: **How did it go? What else could the student have said or asked? Is this something you could do in real life?**

Note: Although recent research indicates that some kids bully strictly because of the desire for power, research also shows that kids sometimes bully because they're depressed or carrying around intense feelings of anger. They may be, or have been, the targets of bullying or abuse themselves. They may also be dealing with family issues like divorce, unemployment, mental health problems, serious illness, domestic violence, or substance abuse. Any time a child is at risk in these ways or seems motivated by cruelty, contempt, or anger, it's essential to take steps to help that child. Reach out to your school nurse, counselor, or psychologist for interventions and follow-up.

Wrap-Up. Reiterate to students that we all make mistakes, and that many people have bullied someone at one time or another. Every day is an opportunity to do better.

Let students know they can write you a note or come to you confidentially at any time to discuss these issues.

Acknowledge students for their honesty, respectful listening, and openness. See if students want to acknowledge others in the class.

Follow-Up. Be sure to check in with students in a day or two about what was discussed in this lesson. Follow up with any students who ask for help or appear to need it.

Extensions. Allow separate times for additional students to role-play ways to ask for help from an adult and to apologize and make amends.

Also allow a time for small-group discussions about ways to stop the problem of bullying in the school.

As a class, take the "No Bullying Pledge":

- I will not take part in any actions that purposely hurt another person.
- I will join with friends to stand up for kids who are being picked on.

Are You Bullying Anyone?

Some people know they bully—others bully without realizing it. To find out if you do things that could be considered bullying, take this quick self-test. Be honest and check off any statements that apply.

REGULARLY or OFTEN . . .

_____ I try to make someone else feel really bad or embarrassed.

_____ I make fun of someone in a mean or humiliating way.

_____ I take part in lots of mean name-calling.

_____ I leave people out on purpose and make them feel bad about it afterward.

_____ I purposely cause physical pain to another person.

_____ I threaten people.

_____ I try to make someone feel like she or he isn't as good as I am.

_____ I send mean emails, IMs, and texts, or I post mean things on social networking sites about another person.

_____ I spread mean rumors about others.

_____ I try to get other people to do any of these things.

Need Help?

If you need help to stop bullying, talk to an adult you trust.

Think About It

What can you do to be part of the solution to bullying?

_____

_____

_____

Help Yourself Stop Bullying

What to Do If You've Bullied Others

When you bully, it hurts *you* as well as the person you're picking on. Kids who bully can form long-term negative habits: habits of meanness, trouble managing anger, difficulty getting along with others, broken relationships. But you don't have to go down that road. Here are six important things you can do to break the habit of bullying:

1. **Own the problem.** It takes a lot of courage to admit to yourself that you've done something wrong, but only by doing so can you change. If you've bullied and you're willing to be honest and face up to it, you're taking a BIG first step.

2. **Tell a trusted adult.** Telling an adult can help you feel better about yourself again. He or she can help you figure out how to stop bullying. You might say, "I've been really mean to someone. I feel bad about it and I want to stop, but I'm not sure how."

What adult can you talk to? It can be a parent, teacher, guidance counselor, nurse, social worker, principal, or a youth leader at an after-school program or at your place of worship. If you have big problems on your mind and feel bad inside, an adult can help you deal with these issues, too.

If you can't figure out who can help and need to talk to someone right now, call the Boys Town National Hotline: 1-800-448-3000. (Even though it says "Boys Town," the hotline is for everyone, girls and boys.) You can call anytime, day or night. A trained professional will be there to talk to you and your call will be confidential. Don't hang up if there's a little wait time. A real person who cares will be there.

Help Yourself Stop Bullying (continued)

3. **Make a promise to yourself to stop bullying now.** Write it down and put it in a safe place. You might want to share your promise with the adult you spoke to.

4. **Make amends.** This means apologizing to the person you've hurt, then doing something to make up for the pain you've caused. For example, you can start including the person in games, or telling your friends that you've gotten to know the person better and you're sorry you were mean. Or invite the person to your home or offer to help with a homework assignment or a sport.

5. **Give yourself credit for the steps you're taking to stop bullying.** It takes a lot of courage to own up to bullying and change. It's a big deal for the kid you've bullied and for yourself. You can use your journal to write down the steps you're taking and give yourself credit for taking them.

6. **Be an upstander to help stop bullying in your school.** Think of ways you can do this. Talk to your teacher and other kids about ending bullying in your school. Stick up for kids who are being picked on and get your friends to do it, too. Be part of the solution.

Remember, bullying will only stop when enough kids make the decision to stop it. Congratulate yourself if you decide to become one of them.

Lesson 100: Strengthen Yourself from the Inside Out

| self-respect · compassion · kindness · self-acceptance · personal responsibility |

Lesson 100 helps kids build internal strength and courage in the face of bullying and supports healthy self-esteem for all students. This lesson is a follow-up to Lesson 98.

Students will

- create lists of their own talents and competencies
- write notes of affirmation to classmates
- reflect on other ways they can strengthen themselves from the inside out to protect themselves from bullying

Materials

- "8 Keys to Putting on Your Anti-Bullying Armor" chart from Lesson 98 (see page 228)
- handout: "8 Keys to Putting on Your Anti-Bullying Armor" (page 230)
- writing paper and pencils or pens for each student
- student journals

Introduction. Look together at the chart and the handout, briefly reviewing the first six keys.

Activity. Direct students' attention to the seventh key and have a student read aloud the text from the handout.

Have students pair up. Pass out paper and have them write the following heading: "Talents I Have and Things I'm Good At."

In pairs, have students discuss and list everything each of them is good at, including things such as helping, caring, being a true friend, being funny, and being kind. Encourage them to list at least ten things. Model ways kids can encourage each other to come up with more ideas. For example, a partner can ask, "What else are you good at?" or say, "I've noticed that you're good at _____." Allow five minutes or less for this activity; circulate and give coaching as needed.

When the lists are complete, have students exchange papers with their partners. On the back of their partner's sheet, have them each write a paragraph of affirmation about the partner, elaborating on all the positive qualities they have noticed or discussed. You can model this ahead of time or read aloud the following example:

Dear Alex,

I think you're a really cool person. You're funny and nice. I would have been scared moving here and being the new kid in the class, but you handled it really well. I know you're good at math, building things, and running. It's cool the way you can explain a math problem

to people when they don't get it. It's been really nice getting to know you.

Mark

After students are done writing, have them exchange papers again, read the note from their partner, and then put their paper with the note into their journals. Then have them turn to a clean page and write the following heading: "I Did It." Tell them to take a minute or two to write at least three things they accomplished today. An accomplishment can be as simple as "I handed in my homework on time."

Discussion. Gather students back in a circle and ask: **How can the lists and paragraphs you wrote today help you strengthen yourself from the inside out?** Discuss. Make sure students understand that focusing on their strengths and accomplishments will help them gain confidence and remember their own worth and value. Ask: **How can this help you be more bully-proof? How can it help you find the courage to be an upstander or to stop bullying?**

Ask students what else makes them feel confident and happy. Discuss and have students write down other strengthening activities they can do. Say: **For example, if you like to draw, do it as often as you can.**

Wrap-Up. Tell students to add to their "Talents I Have and Things I'm Good At" and "I Did It" lists every single day, noting all their capabilities and accomplishments, large and small.

Let students know that these lists are an ongoing way to strengthen good feelings about themselves. Remind them to go back to their lists and the affirmation their partner wrote about them whenever they need to build their confidence or courage "muscles."

Lesson 101: Reprogram Your Brain

courage · self-respect · compassion

Lesson 101 has students engage in an envisioning exercise that builds confidence in the face of bullying and supports healthy self-esteem. This lesson is a follow-up to Lesson 98.

Students will
- reflect on the words of a real student who was bullied and still maintained a sense of confidence and pride
- further protect themselves from bullying by envisioning their most "confident selves"
- understand that regularly envisioning their confident selves can strengthen them from the inside out

Materials
- "8 Keys to Putting on Your Anti-Bullying Armor" chart from Lesson 98 (see page 228)
- handout: "8 Keys to Putting on Your Anti-Bullying Armor" (page 230)

Introduction. Tell students that it's possible to be bullied and still manage to keep an attitude of confidence inside oneself. Read aloud the following story, reported by a fifth-grade girl, to illustrate this:

"I get bullied because of my lisp. This boy used to call me 'tongue-talker.' Every time I saw him, he made fun of me. It made me want to cry, but I didn't. Even though I felt mad, sad, and stressed, I figured out that when people bully you, you shouldn't listen to them or believe what they say. At all times, be yourself and believe in yourself."

Discussion. Ask: What did this student learn from the experience of being bullied? What were some of the feelings the student had at first? What does she know that helps her cope confidently? Discuss briefly.

Tell students that the dignity and confidence this girl expressed are possible for everyone, and the exercise you're going to take them through right now will help build it.

Activity. Look together at the chart and handout, briefly reviewing the first seven keys. Then direct students' attention to the eighth key and have a student read aloud the text from the handout.

Lead students in three rounds of slow, deep abdominal breathing. Ask why this kind of breathing is so important to do. (It calms the body and mind and helps us focus.)

Have students close their eyes. Read the following in a slow, calm, soothing voice:

Take another slow, deep breath, all the way down. Hold the breath inside yourself for a few seconds. (Pause.) Now let it out very slowly. Continue breathing slowly and deeply. Imagine that your mind is a blank movie screen. If any thoughts come up as I'm speaking, put them on a cloud, and let the cloud float the thoughts away. Then bring your mind back to the blank movie screen.

Project onto the screen of your mind an image of yourself. See yourself looking wonderful! You are happy, confident, strong, and proud. See yourself standing tall and smiling. You're filled with confidence and happiness. (Pause.)

Picture yourself feeling completely respected and cared for. Let those good feelings go directly into your heart and mind. Take another slow, deep breath as you bring feelings of self-care, confidence, and respect deeper inside yourself.

Now, if there's anyone who has ever hurt you, past or present, see yourself confidently walking over to that person. You are fully in charge. Tell that person whatever you need to say. Say it with strength, confidence, and respect. (Pause.)

Now see yourself walking away with your head held high. You are filled with pride and confidence. You will always have the power to be an upstander for yourself, because you know just what to do, and you deserve respect.

Pause a moment; then have students open their eyes. Ask how the envisioning was for them. Discuss. If any students had difficulty envisioning, or

if negative thoughts intruded, remind them that the more they practice this the easier it becomes—the more they focus on the image of themselves that they envision today, the more calm and confident they will feel. It's like learning any other new skill.

Wrap-Up. End by telling students to practice this process every night before going to sleep. Doing so can reprogram their brains, helping them feel proud, confident, and empowered under any challenging circumstance. Remind students that this can help them deal with all aspects of bullying.

Follow-Up. Have students draw pictures of their most confident self, and write a statement of affirmation expressing their confidence and pride. Have them write in present tense. (For example: "I am happy and filled with confidence," or "I know exactly how to handle any challenge that comes my way.")

Lesson 102: Projects to Prevent Bullying

self-respect · courage · compassion · personal responsibility · cooperation

Lesson 102 provides students with sound advice from a teen who learned how to handle being bullied and to rise above it. They will also work on anti-bullying projects.

Students will
- be reminded of ways to hold onto their sense of self-worth if they are bullied
- learn some emotionally healthy ways to deal with the impact of being bullied
- begin projects that reinforce ways to "shake off" bullying

Materials
- handout: "'Shake It Off': Tips from Quinn on Getting Past Being Bullied" (page 240)
- chart paper and marker
- paper, markers, crayons, chart paper, and pencils for each of six groups

Preparation. Write the following six ideas from the handout on six large strips of chart paper:

- *"Shake it off. Remember that nothing can diminish you."*

- *"No one can take away from you who you really are."*

- *"Talk to a trusted adult to let your feelings out and get help."*

- *"Let the bad stuff go. Don't keep replaying it in your mind."*

- *"Focus your mind on things you're good at and people who care about you."*

- *"Remember that at any given time there are probably more people who care about you than don't."*

Introduction and Discussion. Ask: How can bullying make people feel? Entertain responses. Remind students that everyone has worth and value, even if bullying causes them to temporarily forget that they do. Reassure them that the bad feelings will likely pass if they do the things they're learning to deal with bullying and to protect themselves.

If the bad feelings linger, it's critical to talk to a trusted adult.

Ask: **What are some things you've learned that can help you remember your worth and value?** Discuss ideas from handouts and activities you've covered in the "Dealing with Bullying" section, including students' "Talents I Have and Things I'm Good At" lists (Lesson 100), adults they've identified who can help them, and the "confident self" envisioning process (Lesson 101).

Pass out a handout to each student. Tell students they'll be reading ideas from Quinn today. Say: **Quinn is a teenager who was bullied in elementary and middle school. At first, he started feeling really lonely and wondered if there was something wrong with him. But then Quinn got help from an adult and started to remember his own worth and build his own confidence.** Ask for a volunteer to read aloud Quinn's words. Make sure students know what *diminish* means (to make someone feel less than they are). Ask students what the following words from Quinn mean to them personally: "Remember that nothing can diminish you. No one can take away from you who you really are." Say: **If you ever feel temporarily diminished by bullying, that's your signal to do the things you've learned to help yourself—including some of Quinn's ideas.**

Discuss students' responses to this and to the rest of Quinn's advice. Then ask: **What did Quinn learn from his experience?** Discuss, making the point that after deciding to confide in a trusted adult, Quinn learned to strengthen himself from the inside out and started feeling better about himself.

Activity. Divide students into six groups. Pass one sentence strip to each group. Ask each group to discuss the words on their sentence strip, then choose one of the following activities to do together based on the words:

1. Make a group poster or collage using the words. Illustrate and decorate it.

2. Create a poem, rap, or song about the words on their sentence strip or the entire story.

3. Create a web with the words of their sentence strip in the middle, and four examples using pictures or words radiating out from the web's center.

Circulate as students work in groups making sure everyone understands the task. Compliment groups for positives you observe.

Wrap-Up. Acknowledge students for their hard work and for any positives you observed in the way they worked together and ask if they would like to acknowledge each other.

Follow-Up. Set aside time for students to complete projects and share them with the class. Have each group explain what they did and what they learned from working on this together. Display all projects in the room or hall.

Encourage students to complete the questions on the handout and keep it in their journals as another resource to help them when they need confidence and support.

"Shake It Off"

Tips from Quinn on Getting Past Being Bullied

Quinn is a teenager who was bullied in elementary and middle school. Based on what he learned through these experiences, Quinn has this to say to kids who are being bullied:

"Shake it off. Remember that nothing can diminish you. No one can take away from you who you really are. If a part of you feels sad, admit it to yourself and feel what you feel, *but don't try to do it alone.* Make sure you talk to a trusted adult so you can let the feelings out and get help. Then focus your mind on things you're good at and people who care about you. Do healthy things to help yourself shake off the bad stuff and see the good again. Don't keep replaying it in your mind. And remember that at any given time there are probably more people who care about you than don't."

Think About It

1. Do you have bad feelings you need to let go of relating to bullying or any other problem? Write about them on the back of this sheet or in your journal.

2. Who are two trusted adults you can talk to if you need help?

    _____   _____

3. If you can't see either adult in person, try using phone or email. Is there anyone else you can reach out to? If you can't figure out who can help and need to talk to someone right now, call the Boys Town National Hotline: 1-800-448-3000. (Even though it says "Boys Town," the hotline is for everyone, girls and boys.) You can call anytime, day or night. Don't hang up if there's a little wait time. A real person who cares will be there.

4. Quinn reminds kids who feel sad to focus on things they're good at and people who care about them. What are five things you're good at?

    _____

    _____

5. Name three people who care about you a lot.

    _____   _____   _____

6. What can you do to help yourself feel better when you're feeling down?

    _____

    _____

Lesson 103: Fostering Compassion—"I Know What It's Like"

compassion · kindness · courage · respect · personal responsibility

Lesson 103 fosters in students a deeper level of kindness and compassion and encourages them to be upstanders for those who are bullied and left out.

Students will

- reflect on a story from a real student who learned greater compassion from her experience of being bullied
- reflect on the importance of having compassion and acting in compassionate ways
- examine their level of willingness to be an upstander and reach out to kids who are bullied and excluded

Materials

- chart paper and marker
- handout: "Rena's Story: 'I Know What It's Like'" (page 242)

Preparation. On chart paper, write the following: *"Compassion: Understanding the feelings of others and feeling what they feel in your own heart."*

Introduction. Ask a student to read the definition of compassion. Make sure everyone understands the meaning. Ask: **How does being an upstander show compassion?** Tell students that expressing compassion through our actions is one of the highest forms of kindness.

Activity and Discussion. Pass out the handout and introduce the story on the handout by saying: **A girl named Rena was bullied throughout her years in elementary school. Now she's in high school. Rena understands what it's like to be bullied. Because of this, she has become a very compassionate person who likes to reach out to people. Rena is an example of someone who is a true upstander.**

Have a student read aloud Rena's story from the handout. Then ask: **What did Rena learn from her experience of being bullied? Why is it important to have compassion for others? Why is it so important to act in compassionate ways?**

Discuss. Then ask: **What did Rena discover about people by reaching out?** (Everyone has something interesting about them. Everyone will respond to kindness.)

Ask students if they've ever reached out to someone who's been left out. Ask: **What did you gain from that experience?**

Ask students if they've been an upstander in other ways for someone else. If so, have them describe what it was like.

Ask if anyone has had someone be an upstander for them. Discuss.

Ask why it's important to be an upstander, even if you feel nervous about doing it.

Wrap-Up. Ask your students to notice at lunchtime or on the playground if anyone is being teased or left out. Encourage them to be upstanders for that person. Encourage them to notice how willing they are to do this, and what might stand in their way.

Rena's Story
"I Know What It's Like"

I was bullied for a long time, so I know what it's like. That's why I always help kids who are left out.

There are some kids no one will sit with at lunch. I know how lonely it can be to sit by yourself and I know how it feels to be picked on, left out, and bullied. So I decided that I would be the one to sit with kids who are excluded. I've learned a lot from doing it, and it's actually become fun.

I've discovered that anyone will respond to kindness. Once you take the time to get to know someone, you see that everyone has something interesting. If you take an interest, it makes them happy and they open up more. Then they start to take an interest in you. I've become friendly with some of the kids I've sat with who were alone. Soon you end up with a whole table of friends you never knew before. Even if they're all people who don't necessarily fit in with the popular group, you fit in with each other. Sometimes kids who don't "fit in" are actually some of the nicest people.

Think About It

Is there anyone you know who is left out? Would you ever consider reaching out to that person with kindness the way Rena did? What might give you the courage to do it? What might stand in your way?

_____

_____

_____

_____

_____

_____

_____

_____

Lesson 104: The Courage to Be an Upstander

courage · personal responsibility · compassion · kindness

Lesson 104 helps students build their courage and confidence so they can be upstanders for kids who are bullied.

Students will

- reflect on why it takes courage to be an upstander for someone who is bullied
- learn specific steps for building their courage and think of other ways to do this as well
- role-play being upstanders for someone who's being bullied

Materials

- chart paper and marker
- handout: "What Real Kids Have to Say About Being an Upstander When Someone Is Bullied" (page 245)

Preparation. On chart paper, copy the following, leaving blank spaces so students can suggest additional entries:

Build Your Courage to Be an Upstander Against Bullying

1. *Practice the Dignity Stance. It will help you stand tall to help others.*
2. *Use deep breathing to keep your cool.*
3. *Rehearse what you're going to say or do.*
4. *Ask someone to partner up with you. Have a friend join you to support someone who's being bullied.*
5.
6.
7.

Introduction. Tell students that today they'll be learning more ways to build their courage "muscles" so they can be upstanders for kids who are bullied. Ask: **What are you already doing to help when someone is being bullied, teased, or picked on?** Discuss.

Ask: **Why does it take courage to be an upstander? What stops you from helping someone who's being bullied?** Discuss, emphasizing that each time someone stands up against bullying, this helps put an end to it. Ask: **What are some things you've learned that can help you gain the courage to be an upstander for kids who are bullied?** Discuss and review strategies that have been introduced.

Discussion. Pass out copies of "What Real Kids Have to Say About Being an Upstander When Someone Is Bullied." Ask for four volunteers to read aloud the quotes from kids who've been upstanders. Ask for students' responses.

Then direct students' attention to "Build Your Courage to Be an Upstander Against Bullying" on the handout and chart. Go through the four steps with students, discussing each one and answering questions. For the fourth step, help students recognize how partnering with another person can give them courage by not having to face the situation alone.

Then ask: **What else would give you the courage to be an upstander if you see someone who's being bullied?** Write suggestions on the board. Discuss, then ask students which two they find the most helpful. Add these to the chart. If there are more than two, include them as well.

Activity. Ask for four volunteers to role-play an example of kids being upstanders in a bullying situation. Do not have students act out the bullying itself, as this can reinforce negative behaviors. Read aloud the following scenario, or another bullying scenario you think students will relate to, and have them act out how upstanders can help.

Note: Confronting a bullying situation alone can be daunting. For this reason, many experts believe that it's preferable for kids to be upstanders in partnership. However, if no one else is around to buddy up with, it's helpful for kids to know how to do it alone. For this reason, you will want to vary the role playing so students can practice being upstanders alone and with others.

Ahmed sees Tommy being bullied by Stewart on the playground. He decides to be an upstander for Tommy. Ahmed stands tall, breathes deep, and thinks of what he's going to do to help. Then he stands even taller and walks over. He says something kind to Tommy and asks him to hang out with him on another part of the playground.

After the role play, ask the volunteer who played Tommy: **How did it feel when Ahmed came over to help you?** Ask the volunteer who played Ahmed: **How did it feel to be an upstander for Tommy? Was it easy or hard to do? Can you picture yourself doing this in real life? Why or why not?** Discuss as a group.

Ask for one new volunteer to join the others and play the part of a student named Clara. Replay the scene, this time having Ahmed ask Clara to partner up with him to be an upstander for Tommy. After the role play, ask the student who played Ahmed: **How did it feel this time to be an upstander? Was it easier to do with Clara helping?**

Also ask students: **What could have happened if no one had stepped in to help Tommy?** Discuss, making sure to address students' questions or concerns about being upstanders.

Wrap-Up. Remind students that each time they practice being an upstander for kids who are bullied, they will strengthen their courage muscle and help stop bullying from happening at their school. Say: **The more upstanders we have, the closer we get to making ourselves and our school free of bullying.**

Follow-Up. Conduct Lessons 105, Stand Up to Bullying, and 106, More Practice for Being an Upstander, which provide more opportunities for students to role-play being upstanders.

What Real Kids Have to Say About
Being an Upstander When Someone Is Bullied

In a national survey of more than 2,100 students in grades 3–6, kids wrote about finding the courage to be an upstander for someone who is being bullied. Here are some things they wrote:

> "It's hard when you see someone being bullied for something they can't help. If you're scared to help them, do it anyway. You have the right to stand up."
>
> "I tell the person who is bullying to quit it. Then I take the person who was being bullied to another place, away from the person doing the bullying."
>
> "I tell the person bullying to stop, and try to comfort the person who was being bullied."
>
> "I help kids who are bullied by staying with them. I've learned that kids who bully don't go after people if they have at least one friend."

Build Your Courage to Be an Upstander Against Bullying

1. Practice the Dignity Stance. It will help you stand tall to help others.

2. Use deep breathing to keep your cool.

3. Rehearse what you're going to say or do.

4. Ask someone to partner up with you. Have a friend join you to support someone who's being bullied.

5. _____

6. _____

7. _____

Lesson 105: Stand Up to Bullying

compassion · courage · personal responsibility · kindness · respect

Lesson 105 has students practice being upstanders by role-playing helping kids who are bullied. This lesson is a follow-up to Lesson 104.

Students will

- review the steps to being an upstander for someone who is bullied
- reflect on their willingness to be upstanders and anything that might stand in the way
- role-play situations where students are being bullied and upstanders offer support
- envision a scenario where they serve as an upstander for someone in need of help

Materials

- "Build Your Courage to Be an Upstander Against Bullying" chart from Lesson 104 (see page 243)
- *optional handout:* "What Real Kids Have to Say About Being an Upstander When Someone Is Bullied" (students' copies from Lesson 104; see page 245)

Introduction and Discussion. Referring to the chart, review ideas about being an upstander when someone is bullied. Ask students: **Since we last talked about this, has anyone helped someone who was being picked on or included someone who was left out? How did it feel to help?** Discuss. If no one helped out, ask what stopped them from doing so.

Activity. Ask for volunteers to role-play supporting kids who are being bullied in the following scenarios, or others students suggest. Suggest that they use ideas from the class chart. Read each scenario aloud. Have students role-play only what they do to support the person being bullied, not the bullying itself. After each role play, briefly discuss how it went, what worked, what was difficult, and why.

- Every day when Gabe, a second grader, is outside on the playground, one of the older kids pushes him down and takes his money. You decide to be an upstander for Gabe. What can you do to support him and help him know that someone cares?

- Audra is in a special class, but comes to your class for social studies. That's when Ronnie and Ali pick on her and call her mean names. You decide to ask someone to help you be an upstander for her. What can you do to support Audra?

- On the bus, Nick and Marco always pull Zoey's hair and knock her down. You and your friends decide to be upstanders for Zoey. How will you support her?

After all the role plays, ask the upstanders: **How did it feel to stand up for someone who was being bullied? What helped you do it? What was hard about doing it? Can you picture yourself doing it in real life?** Then ask all students: **What would make it easier to be an upstander?** Tell students that people who become upstanders often get the courage to do so by focusing on helping somebody rather than on the fear they might be feeling. They become stronger people with greater self-respect as a result. Discuss.

Wrap-Up. Close the lesson with a brief visualization exercise. Have students close their eyes and take three slow, deep abdominal breaths. Then read the following aloud to them:

Imagine yourself seeing someone who is being picked on. You feel really bad for that person. You decide you're going to support that person. Think of what you can do. See yourself as strong, brave, and confident. (Pause.) Now picture yourself walking over and doing what you just envisioned. Picture yourself walking away with the person who was being picked on. Picture the person thanking you. Imagine yourself filled with a deep sense of pride and inner strength.

Now open your eyes and know that you have the power to do this in real life, either alone or with a partner. Picture other kids learning from your example.

Follow-Up. Encourage students to practice being upstanders this week. Remind them they don't have to do this alone.

Extension. Give students several days to write anonymous essays about their experiences with bullying—as someone who was bullied, as someone who bullied, or as a bystander. Share these essays with your principal. With students' permission, post the essays around your school to build awareness.

Lesson 106: More Practice for Being an Upstander

compassion · respect · courage · personal responsibility

Lesson 106 gives students practice being an upstander for kids who are bullied. This lesson is a follow-up to Lesson 104.

Students will

- review the steps to being an upstander for someone who is bullied
- discuss roadblocks to being an upstander and ways to overcome them
- role-play being upstanders for someone who's being bullied

Materials

- "Build Your Courage to Be an Upstander Against Bullying" chart from Lesson 104 (see page 243)
- *optional handout:* "What Real Kids Have to Say About Being an Upstander When Someone Is Bullied" (students' copies from Lesson 104; see page 245)

Introduction and Discussion. Start by leading students in a round of deep breathing. Tell them that during this lesson they will be practicing being upstanders. In real life, deep breathing will help them get mentally prepared to intervene.

Ask: **Why is it important to be an upstander? How does it help other people? How does it help you? How does it help our school?** Discuss. Emphasize that being an upstander not only helps the person being bullied. It demonstrates to bystanders and the person who's bullying that someone cares enough—and is *brave* enough—to stand up and offer support to a person who needs it.

Help students see that being upstanders will strengthen their courage muscle, give them more confidence, and make them feel proud of themselves.

Do a quick review of the chart and ask: **Since we last talked about this, has anyone been an upstander for someone who was bullied? How did it go?**

Ask if anyone observed bullying, but held back from helping. Discuss the reasons students hold back from being upstanders. Ask the class: **What can help you find the courage to be an upstander when it seems hard to do?** Let students know that the more they practice being upstanders, the easier it will get.

Activity. Have students role-play being upstanders in the following bullying situation. Read the scenario aloud, and have students role-play only the supportive actions:

Every day at recess, Raj calls Andy a loser and other mean things, and he makes mean remarks about Andy's family. Andy tries to ignore him, but Raj keeps doing this every day. Van and Jason always see this happening, and they feel really bad for Andy, but they're afraid that if they step in Raj will pick on them, too. One day, they decide Raj's abuse has to stop and that they are going to be upstanders for Andy.

Ask for volunteers to play the parts of Van and Jason as they discuss how they'll be upstanders for Andy. Before the role play begins, talk the upstanders through the Dignity Stance and remind them to take deep breaths and think about the words they want to speak and the actions they want to take. Have them rehearse what they will say and do.

Afterward, debrief with the class about how it went, what worked, what didn't work, and what made it easy or hard to be an upstander.

If time permits, ask students for other situations to role-play (remind them not to use real names when bringing up incidents), or suggest some you think would be good for your group. Invite different volunteers to role-play being upstanders in each scenario. Briefly discuss.

Wrap-Up. Ask: **Can you see yourself being an upstander in real life when you face situations like the ones we talked about today? Briefly discuss.**

Let students know you will continue to check in with them about how they're doing as upstanders in real life. Remind them they can talk with you about any questions or concerns they have in doing this.

Follow-Up. Encourage students to share with their families what they're learning about being upstanders, and how they're preparing to do this in real life.

Extensions. Have students create upstander role plays to enact for a class of younger students, at a school assembly, or for a school podcast.

Invite students to write "I Was an Upstander" essays; collect the essays in a class book or display them at a parent conference or open house event.

Lesson 107: Bullied on the Playground

compassion · courage · respect · personal responsibility

Lesson 107 has students role-play being upstanders for someone who is being physically bullied; they will also reflect on things they could have done if they were the person who was bullied.

Students will

- consider what they can do if they're being physically bullied
- learn how upstanders can help if they see someone being physically bullied
- role-play a situation in which upstanders support a student who is being physically bullied

Materials

- handouts: "Jon's Story: 'No One Would Help Me'" (page 249); "Keep Yourself Safe from Physical Harm" (page 250)
- charts: "Dignity Stance" from Lesson 68 (see page 162); "8 Keys to Putting on Your Anti-Bullying Armor" from Lesson 98 (see page 230); "Build Your Courage to Be an Upstander Against Bullying" chart from Lesson 104 (see page 243)

Introduction. Say: **Today we're going to look at a bullying situation that happened to a boy we'll call Jon. After you hear his story, you'll get a chance to role-play ways Jon's friends could have been upstanders for him.**

Discussion. Distribute the handout and ask for a volunteer to read aloud Jon's story. Ask: **What did Jon do that finally ended the bullying?** (He talked to his dad and he talked to the parents of the kid who was bullying him.) Point out to students that Jon had to go for help to more than one grown-up. Emphasize the importance of continuing to look for adult help when it's needed.

Ask: **What might Jon have done before that to put a stop to the bullying?** (Go back to the teacher immediately after the kid beat him up, tell his dad sooner, go to the principal.)

Then ask: **What about Jon's friends? How could they have helped?** Have students pair up for a minute or two and talk about things the friends could have done to help him when they saw him being bullied on the playground. Address kids' real fears about being retaliated against if they intervene. Let them know that the more upstanders there are, the less likely retaliation will occur.

Afterward, discuss what students came up with. Refer to the "Steps You Can Take to Be an Upstander Against Bullying" and "Dignity Stance" charts.

Remind students that upstanders should never put themselves in physical danger. Tell students that if they see someone being physically harmed, they can do three things:

1. Shout out, "Leave him alone!" or "Leave her alone!" Sometimes that can be enough to get the person to stop.

2. Beckon for the student who's being harmed to come with them, then run fast together, preferably to a place where other people are. There's power in numbers.

3. *Always* let an adult know what happened as quickly as possible. Harming someone physically is against the school rules and against the law.

Activity. Ask for volunteers to play the roles of Jon, the kid who bullied him, and upstanders who decide to help him out.

After the role play, discuss how it went, what worked, what didn't work, and other options the friends or Jon might have used.

Have another set of students role-play the same scene, this time having a single student be the upstander on his or her own. Discuss. If time permits, do additional role plays using new ideas from the discussions.

Wrap-Up. Ask: **What have you learned from Jon's story and from our role play?** Remind students that they have the right to protect themselves against bullying. Emphasize that each time they serve as upstanders, they help put an end to bullying.

Distribute the "Keep Yourself Safe from Physical Harm" handout. Go over the information on the handout.

Follow-Up. Review the "Keep Yourself Safe from Physical Harm" handout with students. Cover in detail any questions they have.

Jon's Story
"No One Would Help Me"

One day I was at recess just playing tag. It was a normal day until this kid pushed me over. Then I kept ending up on the ground because he kept tripping me. I didn't know how to stop him, so he kept doing it. Two of my friends were there, but they went over to the other side of the playground. I think they wanted to get away from him. He tripped me each time we played tag from May 3 to May 11. No one would help me. Finally I told the teacher.

The next week he beat me up at recess and told me not to ever tell on him again. I went home with a black eye and lied to my mom and told her I got hit by a football. The boy kept bullying me until July because we lived really close to each other. Finally I told my dad. He talked to this kid's parents, and the kid finally stopped bullying me.

Think About It

What could Jon have done to get more help sooner? What could his friends have done to help?

_____

_____

_____

_____

_____

_____

_____

_____

_____

Keep Yourself Safe from Physical Harm

If you're in danger of being physically harmed, you need to keep yourself safe. Here are ways to gain control and exit a dangerous situation:

- Stand up straight, look the person in the eye, and say in a firm, clear voice, "Leave me alone!" Then walk (or run) away quickly and calmly.

- Shout "Cut it out!" as loudly as you can, and get yourself away.

- Join a group of people nearby so you're not alone.

- If you're in real danger—for example, if you're facing a gang of kids who are about to harm you—run as fast as you can to a safe place, then seek the aid of an adult.

Lesson 108: Bullied by Friends

compassion · courage · respect · personal responsibility

Lesson 108 has students reflect on what can be done if they or someone they know is bullied by a friend.

Students will
- discuss in cooperative groups what kids can do if they're being bullied by a friend
- consider actions students can take when someone is bullying a friend
- understand that if someone is mistreating them, the person is not being a true friend

Materials
- chart paper and marker for each group of four students
- handout: "Bullied by Friends: Stories from Real Kids" (page 252)

Introduction. Distribute the handout and ask for volunteers to read aloud each of the stories. Invite brief responses.

Discussion. Ask students: **Why would a person bully a friend? Is someone who does this really a friend?**

Ask: **Have you ever been bullied by a friend, or known someone who was?** Discuss, reminding students not to mention real names.

Ask: **What if you have a friend who bullies someone and you want to help? What can you say to your friend? What if your friend bullies you? What can you do?** Discuss briefly. These ideas will continue to be in focus during the activity and final discussion.

Activity. Put students into groups of four. Have each group choose a Leader, a Recorder, an Announcer, and an Encourager. Say: **Each group's goal is to brainstorm four possible things people can do if they or someone they know is bullied by a friend.** Explain that the role of the Leader is to keep the group focused on the task. The Encourager's job is to affirm people for sharing ideas and to encourage everyone to take part. Recorders should write down the ideas. Everyone in the group can contribute their ideas. At the end of the discussion time, the Announcers will share their groups' ideas with the class.

After five or ten minutes, have students reconvene in a large circle. Have Announcers share with the class what their group has come up with. Ask students to comment on each group's ideas. Discuss these and provide coaching and feedback as appropriate. Also ask about the role upstanders could play to help in such a situation. Be sure to share all of the following with students:

- If the person is bullying you, you can rehearse some assertive words you can say to that person. For example, "This bullying has to stop. I deserve to be treated with respect." Then use the Dignity Stance and speak to the person directly.
- If the person is bullying someone you know, be an upstander for the person being bullied. Do this on your own or with another friend.
- If the bullying doesn't stop, quit hanging out with the person. Find some new friends who treat you and others with respect.
- Talk to a trusted adult who can help get the bullying to stop. An adult can also help the person being bullied.
- If you are bullying a friend, get help from a trusted adult.

Wrap-Up. Remind students that they have the right to be safe. If they are ever in a situation where someone is harming them, it's important to go for help if nothing else has worked.

Note: Bullying between friends may occasionally be precipitated by a conflict. While mediation is rarely useful when dealing with bullying, you may want to try to mediate to get to the root of the conflict in cases where there was a real friendship that went sour. But it's extremely important to be mindful of any feelings of intimidation the child who was bullied might have. If you sense that the child is afraid to speak up in front of the friend who bullied him or her, do not try to mediate; instead, speak to each child separately. Remember that all acts of bullying need to have a consequence, regardless of whether you mediate.

Bullied by Friends

Stories from Real Kids

In a national survey of more than 2,100 students in grades 3–6, kids wrote about being bullied. Here are stories from a fourth-grade girl and boy:

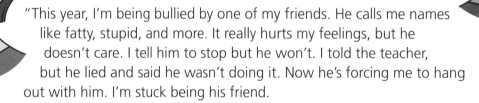

"At the beginning of the school year, when my friend got stressed she would hit me. She would hit me on the back, my arms, or my stomach. I told her to stop but she kept doing it. One day after class she picked up her textbook and whacked me across the back. She always says she's sorry, but she keeps on doing it. She calls me weak because I tell her it hurts. But, if I accidentally hit her with my pen, she calls me a name and starts crying.

"The problem still isn't solved, because she keeps doing it. My arms are sore from her hitting me. I can't tell her I don't want to be friends anymore. I'm afraid she'll hurt me more."

"This year, I'm being bullied by one of my friends. He calls me names like fatty, stupid, and more. It really hurts my feelings, but he doesn't care. I tell him to stop but he won't. I told the teacher, but he lied and said he wasn't doing it. Now he's forcing me to hang out with him. I'm stuck being his friend.

"I try to get other people to be my friend, but they're all *his* friends, so I'm stuck with him. He's still bullying me, and I don't know what to do."

Think About It

How can these kids get help? What would *you* do in their situation?

_____

_____

_____

Lesson 109: Listening to Your Gut

courage · compassion · kindness · respect · personal responsibility

Lesson 109 has students consider ways to stay safe and prevent situations where physical bullying by a group can occur.

Students will
- understand possible precursors of a physical attack
- reflect on ways to avert such an attack
- learn how to listen to their gut instincts when it comes to dangerous or threatening situations

Materials
- chart paper and marker

Introduction. Ask students if they've ever had a "gut feeling" about something. Share your own experience of having a negative gut feeling that guided you to take care of yourself. Say: **It's important to listen to our gut feelings. They can help us keep ourselves safe.**

Ask: **In terms of being bullied, what have you learned about keeping yourself safe?** (Stay around other people, seek help if you're being threatened.) **Also in terms of bullying, have you ever had a gut feeling that someone was planning to physically hurt you?**

Activity and Discussion. Write *"Listening to Your Gut"* at the top of the chart paper. Say: **There are often signals ahead of time that physical bullying might happen. What might those signals be?** Write students' ideas on the chart paper. Signals might include threats, aggressive put-downs, attempts at humiliation, and rumors that kids might be planning something. Discuss, guiding students also to understand that when there's impending danger, people often can sense that something's wrong on a gut level.

Ask: **If someone is getting threats or hearing lots of mean put-downs, and feels like a bullying situation is getting worse or is going to get worse, what can the person do?** (Let an adult know what's going on, make sure not to be alone.) **If you get a bad feeling in the pit of your stomach each time you see a kid or a group of kids, what should you do?** (Listen to your gut, don't ignore the bad feeling, stick with other people, talk to an adult, avoid secluded or unmonitored areas.)

Wrap-Up. Acknowledge students for the very important work they are doing in learning how to prevent and address bullying. Encourage them to continue to bring any questions to you.

Lesson 110: "Gay, Nerd, Freak"

compassion · acceptance · personal responsibility · kindness · respect

Lesson 110 impresses upon students painful consequences of name-calling and put-downs.

Students will

- understand that the term *gay* is not to be used as a put-down
- discuss other terms that are not to be used as put-downs
- recognize that cruel name-calling can lead to deep emotional pain
- role-play being upstanders for themselves and others in a bullying situation where a child has been the object of pejorative name-calling and put-downs

Materials

- handout: "'Everybody Decided I Was Gay': A Story from a Real Kid" (page 255)
- student journals

Introduction. Tell students that sometimes bullying can be so upsetting that some kids get extremely depressed as the result of it. Say: **This is what happened with the boy who wrote the story you are about to hear.** Pause to see if anyone wants to comment or respond.

Discussion. Distribute the handout and ask for a volunteer to read aloud the story.

Have students respond with three minutes of automatic writing. Give them the following prompt: **"What came into my mind as I listened to the story was . . . "**

After students have had time to write, ask how the boy in the story felt. Ask: **What names was he called? Why did that hurt so much?**

Ask what else the boy could have done to address the bullying. (Go back to the teacher; go to the principal, counselor, or nurse; tell his parents what was going on.)

Students sometimes also use words like *gay* in a way that's not meant to put down a particular person, as when they say "That's so gay." Stress that the word *gay* should never be used as a put-down or to mean *anything* negative. Ask why this is so. Make sure students understand that this is disrespectful to people who are gay as well as to those who aren't.

Ask: **What about calling someone a *nerd* because he or she is smart—isn't that disrespectful, too? What are some great things about being smart? Why would people put someone down for being smart?**

Ask: **What about *freak*? Why is that disrespectful?** As appropriate within your group, discuss other names or insults that are issues in your classroom or that students are concerned about, including racial or sexual slurs and cruel labels for those with disabilities.

Activity. Refer once again to the handout and ask: **What would it be like if no student ever had to be made to feel the way this boy did? How can you be a part of making this happen?** Put students in pairs and have them brainstorm ways they can be upstanders if they see anyone treated like the boy was in the story.

After a few minutes, have students do one or two role plays of standing up for someone in a similar situation.

Wrap-Up. Remind students that one of the most important things they can do if they or others are bullied is *not* to remain silent. Emphasize the need for all people to decide not to use cruel language and to speak out when they hear others using it.

Affirm students for their courage, kindness, and honesty during the lesson; encourage them to acknowledge each other, too.

Follow-Up. Check in with students to see if they have questions or want to talk about ideas that were discussed in the lesson.

"Everybody Decided I Was Gay"

A Story from a Real Kid

In a national survey of more than 2,100 students in grades 3–6, kids wrote about being bullied. Here is a story from a fifth-grade boy:

"It started at lunch when everybody decided I was gay. So that's what they started calling me, and I'm not. They also called me freak because I don't buy lunch, and a nerd because I get straight A's. About a month ago this kid calls me a nerd and other names. So I go tell my mom. The next day his best friend hits me in the face because I told on his friend. Then I got mad and I wanted to hit him back, but I didn't. Now it's the end of the school year. It's like every day without crying is an accomplishment. Even some of my friends have turned on me."

Think About It

This boy is so sad, hurt, and lonely that he cries all the time. What got him this upset? Why do kids call people names like "gay" and "nerd"? What can be done to make kids stop this kind of name-calling? How can this boy get help?

_____

_____

_____

_____

_____

_____

_____

_____

_____

Lesson 111: Cyberbullying

personal responsibility · compassion · kindness

Lesson 111 highlights the impact of cyberbullying and cautions students against using electronic media to harm another person in any way.

Students will
- learn what constitutes cyberbullying and reflect on its impact
- learn what to do if they are ever cyberbullied
- gain a deeper sense of responsibility regarding cyberbullying
- be encouraged to be upstanders if they know cyberbullying is taking place

Materials
- chart paper and marker
- handout: "Cyberbullying: Stories from Real Kids" (page 257)

Preparation. On chart paper, write the following: *Cyberbullying—Using a cell phone, computer, or any other form of electronic technology to purposely harm another person. Cyberbullying happens online: through email, instant messages, text messages, podcasts, blogs, chat rooms, apps, social media, and more.*

Introduction. Ask students: **What is cyberbullying?** Show the definition and go over it with students, elaborating as needed. Ask if students can share any examples of cyberbullying from the news, TV shows, videos, books, or stories they've heard. Discuss. Share an example that you're aware of.

Ask: **Why is cyberbullying so harmful?** Discuss.

Discussion and Activity. Pass out the handout. Have a student read the first story. Ask: **In what way was Amanda cyberbullied? What could she have done to help herself?** Discuss, guiding students to understand that it's important to do two things: save any available evidence and immediately get help from a trusted adult.

Ask: **What if Amanda did something mean in the first place? Would it be okay for her friends to cyberbully her then?** Remind students that cyberbullying, like any other form of bullying, is never justified and is always wrong.

Read or have a student read Jay's story. Ask: **How was Jay cyberbullied? What could he have done to help himself?** Discuss, reiterating that it's very important to save available evidence and to show it to a trusted adult.

Let students know that even if cyberbullying happens after school hours, if it affects kids when they're at school, it needs to be reported. Schools have rules against bullying, and those rules apply to cyberbullying as well.

Ask for volunteers to role-play one of the scenarios from the handout. Before beginning the role play, ask the class to coach the student who was bullied on how she or he could handle it. Ask: **What can _____ say to people who are involved? Who can she or he approach for help?** Have the volunteer playing the role of the student who was cyberbullied incorporate these suggestions into the role play.

Wrap Up. Ask students what they can do if someone they know is cyberbullying someone else. Remind them of the importance of being an upstander. Ask how else they can be upstanders when it comes to cyberbullying.

Follow-Up. Check in with students to make sure they remember the two things to do if they experience or know about cyberbullying.

Extension. Refer students to the StopBullying.gov website. Have them click on "Cyberbullying" to find some facts they didn't know before. They can also click on the kids' page (stopbullying.gov/kids) and read up on bullying and what they can do about it.

Cyberbullying
Stories from Real Kids

Amanda's Story

"I had an argument with these girls who used to be my friends. That night they messaged each other saying all these mean things about me. Someone printed one of the messages and brought it to school. She started passing it around to other people, making it sound like everything was my fault. I was so upset. But I didn't know what to do."

Jay's Story

"One day I woke up late and couldn't find any clean clothes. I threw on a dirty sweatshirt and some old jeans that were too short. There wasn't time to comb my hair, and I didn't realize there was jelly on my face from a donut I ate on the way to school. I looked like a mess. When I got to school some kids started laughing at me and saying mean things. I didn't know it right then, but one of them took a picture of me with his cell phone. Then he and his friends set up a website where they posted the picture. They called the website 'Jay's a Loser.' The next day all the kids were talking about it and laughing at me. It was horrible. I wanted to hide."

Think About It

Have you ever used a computer or cell phone to hurt someone or get even? If so, you're cyberbullying.

Why is it wrong to cyberbully?

_____

_____

What can you do if cyberbullying happens to you?

_____

_____

What can you do if someone you know is about to cyberbully someone else?

_____

_____

Lesson 112: Picture a School Without Bullying

personal responsibility · respect · collaboration · courage · compassion

Lesson 112 guides students to imagine and brainstorm ways your school can prevent, reduce, and eliminate bullying. If you wish, use it to lay the groundwork for Lesson 113.

Students will
- take part in an envisioning exercise that lets them imagine their school completely free of bullying
- brainstorm concrete actions your school can take

Materials
- chart paper and marker
- student journals
- *optional:* mural or poster paper, markers, and other art materials

Introduction. Say: Imagine putting an end to bullying in our school. Imagine all of us helping make this happen. Tell students that today they'll have a chance to think of what this might be like and ways they could help make that happen.

Activity and Discussion. Start by doing an envisioning activity to help students picture an end to bullying in the school. Say: **As we do this activity, I'm going to ask you to let go of the voice that says "It's not possible" and allow your mind to be completely open. Don't judge any ideas that come up, and let your mind be free to think of creative ideas to stop bullying.**

Have students sit comfortably in chairs or on the floor. Have them close their eyes or cover them and look down. Lead your kids in taking two or three slow, deep abdominal breaths. Then read aloud the following:

Take another slow, deep breath. Picture yourself capable of doing anything you set your mind to. Picture everyone in our class capable, kind, and working together on putting an end to bullying. (Pause.)

Imagine that you've all come up with an excellent plan to end bullying in our school. This is a plan that really works. Picture our principal thanking you. Picture the principal, teachers, students, and others putting the plan into action throughout our entire school. (Pause.)

Now picture our school becoming a place where all people are respected and accepted for exactly who they are. (Pause.) **Picture all kids treating each other with respect in the halls, in the lunchroom, on the bus, on the playground—everywhere. Picture all kinds of kids learning and playing together in peace. Everyone feels safe here, and no one, no matter how different they may seem, is left out or put down.** (Pause.)

What are *your* **ideas for ending bullying in our school? I'm going to give you a minute or two to let your ideas come into your mind. Don't stop or judge any ideas that come up. Just let your mind go free.**

After a minute or two have students open their eyes and write in their journals the ideas they came up with. Caution them not to judge their ideas. Next, have students get into pairs and share their ideas with their partners.

Wrap-Up. Bring students back to the circle and ask them to share a few ideas. Tell students that during the next lesson, they will share in more detail. Ask them to keep thinking of ideas and to note them in their journals.

Follow-Up. Be sure to follow up with Lesson 113, in which students can create a concrete list of ideas to present to the school administration.

Extension. Have students make posters or a mural depicting the school without bullying.

Lesson 113: Ways to End Bullying in Our School

personal responsibility · respect · collaboration · courage · compassion

Lesson 113 guides students to come up with concrete actions they and the school can take to reduce bullying in the school.

Students will
- come up with a cohesive list of actions their school can take to put an end to bullying
- prepare to present their ideas to the principal or other administrators

Materials
- chart paper and marker
- student journals

Preparation. On chart paper, write the "No Bullying Pledge":

- *I will not take part in any actions that purposely hurt another person.*
- *I will join with friends to stand up for kids who are being picked on.*

If you conducted Lesson 112, remind students to bring their journals with ideas they brainstormed about stopping bullying at school.

Introduction. Tell students that today they'll have a chance to think of things people in the school might do to reduce and prevent bullying, and to perhaps someday eliminate it completely. Ask: **What are some things you think would help us do this?**

Briefly discuss a few responses. If the idea surfaces that it's impossible to get rid of bullying, let students know that other schools have succeeded in drastically reducing bullying, and reducing bullying is the first step toward stopping it completely. Stress that every person can help make this happen.

Have students partner up and discuss ideas that could help eliminate bullying at school. (If you conducted Lesson 112, pair students up with partners from that activity.)

Discussion and Activity. After a couple of minutes, have students convene in the large circle. Ask them to share their ideas. Remind students not to judge each other's suggestions. List all the ideas on a chart entitled "Put a Stop to Bullying."

Next, go through the list with your students, and together choose five to ten ideas your class would

like to present to the principal. Help your students choose practical, doable activities that are low-cost and can be done schoolwide. Share the ideas from the list on page 260 to give them an idea of what other schools have done.

Wrap-Up. Display the "No Bullying Pledge." Recite it together, as a class.

(Alternatively, you and your students may want to create your own "No Bullying Pledge.")

Note: If any students hesitate or object to the pledge, see them after the lesson to hear what their considerations are. Encourage them to give the words of the pledge a chance, and let them know that they're an important part of helping reduce and prevent bullying.

Follow-Up. Invite the principal (or other appropriate administrator) into your room to hear your class's ideas for preventing and reducing bullying schoolwide. See which ideas she or he would like to see implemented. Follow through with the administrator and other school personnel to help bring students' ideas to fruition.

Choose a committee of students in your class to work on spreading the word schoolwide. Consider starting with a "Put a Stop to Bullying" poster contest. Your campaign might include a "No Bullying Pledge" and other ideas students come up with.

Extensions. Have your students work in small groups to start implementing ideas. Have them visit other classes to get more students involved.

PART TWO
Dealing with Bullying

Put a Stop to Bullying

This is a compilation of ideas from schools that have formed bullying prevention and anti-bullying committees. Many of these committees are comprised of student and teacher representatives from each grade, the school counselor, and the principal:

- Quote of the Week read on intercom; responses from students to be posted on a "Respect Board" in the hallway
- "Stop Bullying" convocation at the start of the school year
- Each homeroom creates a poster and slogan to go along with a monthly character education/anti-bullying theme; these are posted throughout school
- "No Bullying" pledge posted in all classrooms
- Notes to parents about the school's bullying prevention program
- Back-to-school night based on a motivational student-led activity with an anti-bullying message that focuses on respect
- Student-made respect posters and artwork in the showcase
- "Respect" message posted on a sign in front of the school
- Certificates for acts of respect, caring, and "upstander" behaviors
- Reward system for positive behavior
- Several assemblies throughout year on bullying prevention with students presenting skits and role plays

Accepting Differences

Much of the bullying that takes place among students is based on perceived differences. Research has shown that biases are a key source, whether these biases are based on ethnicity, gender, religion, race, or sexual orientation. This section gets to the core of the issue, emphasizing that people are all the same inside even though different on the outside. Through the following lessons, students can see that we are all a part of the same human family, one in which every person deserves to be treated with respect.

Many lessons from Fostering Kindness, Compassion, and Empathy (pages 51–81) and Addressing Name-Calling and Teasing (pages 189–216) introduce concepts that are relevant here, so it's suggested that you conduct some of those prior to introducing these. Also familiarize yourself with Lesson 68 (The Dignity Stance).

Be sure to have these charts displayed: "Respectful Listening" (introduced in Lesson 2), "The Win/Win Guidelines for Working Out Conflicts" and "Stop, Breathe, Chill" (Lessons 8 and 9), "No More Hurtful Words" (Lesson 22), and "Dignity Stance" (Lesson 68).

Lesson 114: Step into the Circle

acceptance · respect · compassion · kindness

Lesson 114 focuses students on their similarities and helps them see their connections to one another.

Students will

- discover ways they are like each other, even if they appear to be different
- gain in their understanding that all human beings have things in common
- consider what our world would be like if people were more accepting of differences

Materials

- chart paper and marker
- globe (see page 7)
- *optional:* student journals

Introduction and Activity. Tell students they're going to be playing a game called "Step into the Circle."*

Have them stand in a circle. Say: **Step into the circle if you have a heart that beats inside you.**

Of course, the whole class will step into the circle. Say: **Look around. Is this something we all have in common?**

Have students return to the exterior circle. Say: **Let's see what else people in our class have in common.** One at a time, read the statements below (or similar ones you come up with) and have students step into the circle every time one applies to them. After students step in, say: **Look around and see who you have this in common with.** Then have them step back to the exterior circle with the rest of the class.

Step into the circle if . . .

- your favorite color is red (blue, green, purple, etc.).
- your favorite subject is science (geography, English, Spanish, math, etc.).
- you like soccer (baseball, gymnastics, dancing, skateboarding, etc.).
- you like to draw.
- you hate homework.
- you enjoy reading.
- you enjoy playing video games.
- you care about your family.
- you like pizza.
- you like peppers.
- you like ice cream.
- you feel bad when someone calls you a name.
- you care about having a get-along classroom.
- you wish there was no bullying in our school.

Discussion. Afterward, ask students: **Were you surprised by any ways you're like some of your classmates? What surprised you? Were the same people always inside the circle, or were there different things that different people had in common?** Discuss responses briefly.

Then ask: **Did you notice you have things in common with people who look different from you on the outside?** (Examples: a boy and girl might both like soccer; a tall person and short person might both have red as their favorite color; a black person and white person might both feel bad when someone calls them a name; people of different nationalities might like video games or might dislike homework.)

Have students pair up. Give them two to three minutes to brainstorm at least five things all people have in common. Have them start by thinking about basic human needs.

Afterward, have students share what they came up with. Record their ideas on a chart entitled "Ways We Are All Alike."

Wrap-Up. End by asking students what our world would be like if people were more in touch with ways they are alike, rather than focusing on differences.

Hold up or point to the globe. Say: **We're all part of the human family. Each time we choose to accept the ways we're different and focus on ways we're alike, we help create a kinder, more peaceful world.**

Follow-Up. Encourage students to write in their journals about something they learned when they stepped into the circle. This might be a likeness they were surprised to share with someone, a difference that surprised them, or ideas that came to them about things students in the classroom or people in the world have in common.

---

* Many thanks to school counselor Paula Eisen for sharing the idea of "Step into the Circle."

Lesson 115: This Is Who I Am

respect · acceptance · compassion · kindness

Lesson 115 helps students see the commonalities they have with others.

Students will
- identify in writing things they feel and care about
- share what they've written with a partner and look for things they share in common
- practice good listening and respectful interactions with their partner

Materials
- handout: "This Is Who I Am" (page 264)

Introduction and Activity. Tell students that today they're going to take a few minutes to think about some things that are important to them. Distribute the handout and give students a few minutes to individually complete as much of it as possible.

Discussion. Have students bring their handouts to the circle. Tell them they will be pairing up to share their "This Is Who I Am" sheets with a partner. Ask: **As you share, how can you show your partner respect?** Be sure the discussion includes being good listeners, refraining from put-downs or negative body language, using reflective listening, and giving full attention.

Tell students that after one partner finishes sharing what he or she wrote on the handout, the other partner will then do two things:

1. Give a sincere compliment (for example, "You said drawing makes you happy. That drawing you did last week is really cool").

2. Tell the person things you realized you have in common as you listened (for example, "I'm scared of snakes, too. I didn't know you were").

Give students about ten minutes to share. Let them know that if they didn't finish filling out the handout, they can still talk about the ideas on it. Circulate as they do so, making sure everyone is on track.

After partners have shared, have the class reconvene in a large circle. Ask students what they learned about each other through this activity.

Wrap-Up. Affirm students on acceptance, respect, and good listening you observed.

Follow-Up. Allow time for students to finish filling in their handouts, including drawing pictures of themselves. Encourage them to write in their journals about what they learned about each other through this experience, what new insights or ideas occurred to them, and what they learned about themselves.

This Is Who I Am

_____ makes me happy.

_____ makes me sad.

_____ makes me laugh out loud.

_____ makes me mad.

_____ makes me feel frightened.

_____ makes me feel stressed.

Something I really need is: _____.

I really wish: _____.

What interests me most in life is: _____

These people are especially important to me: _____

_____

Something I care about more than anything else is: _____

_____

My greatest hope for the world is: _____

My name is: _____

On the back of this page or on a separate sheet of paper, draw a picture of yourself.

Lesson 116: Different and Alike Interviews

acceptance · compassion · kindness · respect

Lesson 116 helps students look at the likenesses and differences they share with classmates and see that some differences can be dynamic and interesting.

Students will
- interview each other to find out likenesses and differences
- see the positives in having certain differences
- be better able to accept and appreciate the differences in each other

Materials
- handout: "Different and Alike Interview Questions" (page 266)

Introduction. Pair students with partners who are different in some way (gender, size, race, personality, interests, etc.). Have partners stand together in the large circle. Ask a few partners: **How are you different from each other?** Tell students that partners are now going to have a chance to learn more about ways they are different and alike.

Activity and Discussion. Pass out the "Different and Alike Interview Questions." Have students write their partner's name on their sheet. Then have them spend a few minutes interviewing each other, noting the answers to the questions on their sheets.

When students finish, have them reconvene in the circle. Ask students: **What did you learn about your partner? What are some ways you're alike? What do you have in common? What differences did you discover?**

After several students share ideas, ask: **Who learned something surprising or interesting about their partner? What did you learn? Why did that surprise or interest you?** Continue the discussion, emphasizing what's interesting and valuable about

differences among people as well as the many commonalities students share.

Ask the group: **Why is it important to be aware of the ways we are all alike?** (It helps us understand each other better and realize we're not alone; it helps us see that even if someone seems different on the outside, we still may have things in common.) **What if everyone were exactly like everyone else? What's good about the fact that we're all different in some ways, too? Why is it important to appreciate the ways we're different?** (We each have unique things to contribute to the class and the world; we learn from each other; without differences the world would be pretty boring.)

Wrap-Up. Remind students that all human beings have similarities, no matter how different they may appear to be. Encourage them to be open to getting along with and getting to know people who seem different than they are. Affirm students for things they did in today's lesson to accept and appreciate differences in each other.

Different and Alike Interview Questions

Talk About It

Find someone who is different from you in some way. Talk about the following questions together to discover what you do and don't have in common:

What do you care most about in the world? _____

Who do you care most about in the world? _____

What makes you happy? _____

What makes you angry? _____

What makes you sad? _____

What makes you most proud? _____

What is one special thing about you that many people don't know? _____

_____

If you could change the world in one way, how would you change it? _____

_____

If you could have three wishes granted, what would they be? _____

_____

Think About It

After you have both talked about all the questions, answer the following:

What are three things you both have in common? List them.

_____

_____

What's one way you and your partner are different from each other? What's interesting about this difference?

_____

_____

Lesson 117: Differences Can Separate Us, Part 1

acceptance · respect · personal responsibility · compassion

Lesson 117 explores the ways differences can be a source of separation.

Students will
- reflect on ways all human beings are alike
- identify and reflect on the differences that separate us
- recall a time they were perceived as different and how they were affected by this

Materials
- handouts: "What Real Kids Have to Say About Differences" (page 268); "Many Kinds of Differences" (page 269)
- chart paper and marker
- student journals
- *optional: In the Year of the Boar and Jackie Robinson* by Bette Bao Lord

Preparation. On chart paper, copy the web of differences depicted on the handout.

Introduction. Ask: **What are some of the ways all human beings are alike?** (We all need food, clothing, shelter, love; we all have a heart that beats and a brain that thinks; we all have feelings; we all need respect.)

Say: **Even though all human beings have so many things in common, what are some of the ways we might be different on the outside?** (Students might suggest size, gender, race, color, etc.) List a few on the board.

Discussion. Distribute the "Many Kinds of Differences" handout and direct students' attention to the chart you copied. Discuss the differences, and see if students suggest others to add.

Ask: **How can these differences separate us?** Discuss, bringing out the fact that people often judge each other negatively based on differences.

Distribute the "What Real Kids Have to Say About Differences" handout and ask for volunteers to read the statements from real kids. Then ask: **Do any of these sound familiar?** Say: **At one time or another just about all of us have had the experience of being seen as different in some way.** Ask students to think of a time they were treated negatively because they were seen as different. Ask for one or two volunteers to share. Share your own story.

After several responses, ask: **Why do people sometimes mistreat or make fun of people they see as different from themselves?** Discuss.

Activity. Have students take their journals to a place in the room where they feel comfortable writing, and have them do three to four minutes of automatic writing on the topic of what it's like to be treated negatively because of a perceived difference. Tell them to be sure to include what they learned from the experience.

Afterward, give students time to reread what they wrote. See if anyone would like to share.

Wrap-Up. Tell students: **Even though it can really hurt to be treated badly because you're seen as different in some way, sometimes the experience of being hurt can make us more compassionate (caring and understanding) toward other people.**

Follow-Up. Ask students to observe how they treat others throughout the rest of the day. Are they treating someone negatively because they see the person as different? Tell them to take home their "Many Kinds of Differences" handouts and their journals so they can write about this before the next lesson.

Plan to follow up with Lesson 118 as soon as you are able.

Extension. Read and discuss *In the Year of the Boar and Jackie Robinson* by Bette Bao Lord. In this book, ten-year-old Shirley Temple Wong arrives from China and struggles to be accepted until she discovers Jackie Robinson and is inspired by how he overcame tremendous odds.

What Real Kids Have to Say About
Differences

In a national survey of more than 2,100 students in grades 3–6, kids wrote about differences. Here are some things they said:

> "I get mad when people make fun of my culture and my name."
>
> "A bunch of kids pick on a guy on my bus because he's kind of overweight."
>
> "There's this kid with only one leg. Some kids are nice to her face, and then they make fun of her when she's not around. Why are people so mean?"
>
> "It makes me mad when people tease or insult kids about their race or religion."
>
> "I don't like it when someone gets teased because they're not American."
>
> "I get angry when I see people teasing others because they are different."
>
> "Why can't people just accept the fact that every living person on the face of the earth is different in their own way?"
>
> "I want people to learn that it's okay to be different."

What do YOU think about differences?

Why do people sometimes act mean or make fun of people who are different from them?

_____

_____

_____

_____

_____

_____

Many Kinds of Differences

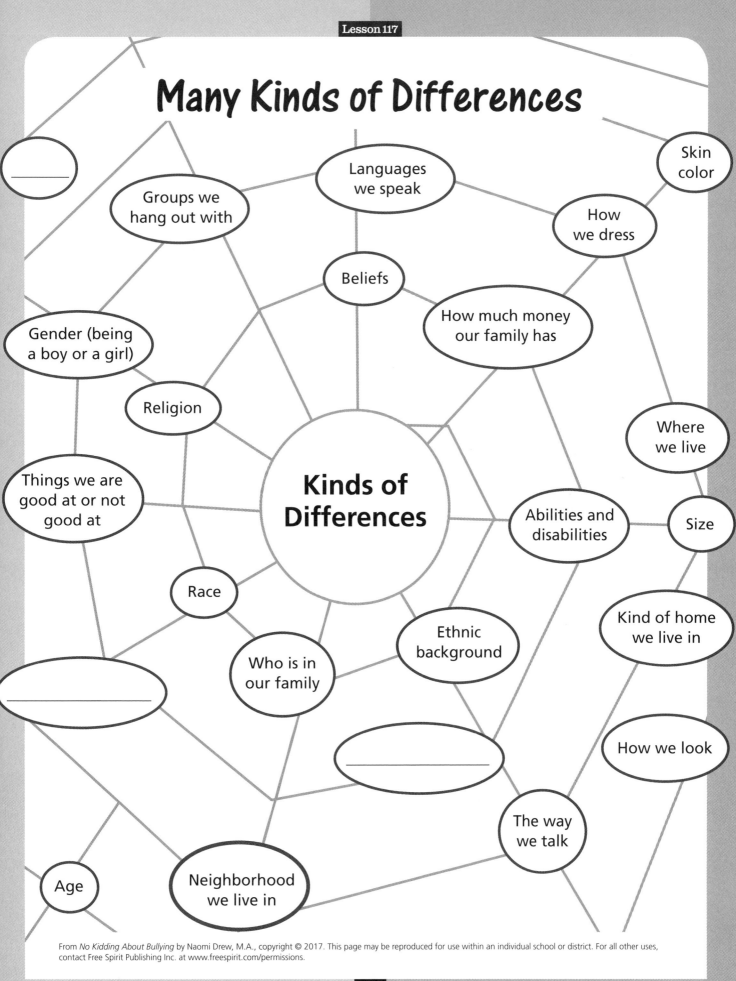

Skin color

Groups we hang out with

Languages we speak

How we dress

Beliefs

How much money our family has

Gender (being a boy or a girl)

Religion

Where we live

Kinds of Differences

Things we are good at or not good at

Abilities and disabilities

Size

Race

Kind of home we live in

Who is in our family

Ethnic background

How we look

The way we talk

Age

Neighborhood we live in

Lesson 118: Differences Can Separate Us, Part 2

acceptance · tolerance · respect · compassion · kindness · personal responsibility

Lesson 118 has students reflect upon the way they allow differences to create separations in their lives.

Students will

- understand the meaning of *prejudice* and *bias*
- examine their own prejudices
- understand that prejudice and bias are harmful
- reflect on how people can let go of prejudice

Materials

- chart with differences from Lesson 117
- handout: "Many Kinds of Differences" from Lesson 117 (page 269)
- poster or drawing paper and markers
- *optional:* student journals, *The Christmas Menorahs* by Janice Cohn

Preparation. On chart paper, write: *"Prejudice: A strong feeling of unfair dislike toward a person or group because they seem different in some way."*

Introduction and Discussion. Display the differences chart from Lesson 117 and ask students what they've learned about themselves so far when it comes to differences. Do they tend to be accepting or not accepting? Do they feel like the different one sometimes? If so, how does that make them feel? Are they becoming more compassionate toward people they see as different? Discuss.

Tell students that even the most open-minded people are not always open to every kind of difference. Display the definition of *prejudice* and go over it with students. Connect the idea of prejudice to the differences on the chart, such as race, color, gender, religion, size, and so forth. You might also add that another word for *prejudice* is *bias*: people can have a *prejudice* or *bias*, and they can feel or be *prejudiced* or *biased*. Say: **We all have certain prejudices, and that doesn't mean we're bad people. But it does mean that we need to open ourselves a little more to the difference we have a bias about. Each time we recognize a prejudice inside ourselves is an opportunity to open our minds some more.**

Ask: **Why is it important to let go of prejudices?** (Prejudices separate people; keep them from really knowing each other; stop them from becoming friends; lead to conflict, hatred, and war.) Also ask: **What leads to prejudice? Is it hard or easy to let go of prejudice? Why or why not? If it's hard, what could help make it easier?** (Recognizing prejudice inside ourselves and being willing to let go of it, getting to know people who we see as different, learning about their lives and cultures, opening our hearts and minds.)

Note: If someone brings up the issue of prejudice in the family, tell students that as we learn deeper levels of acceptance, we set an example for people in our families.

Activity. Remind students about the journaling you asked them to do after the last lesson. Ask: **Are there any attitudes about differences you have that you would like to change? Are there people and groups you are not as open and friendly to because of a prejudice? Is there a prejudice you would like to let go of?** Have students pair up and talk about this for a few minutes.

Reconvene in the circle and ask students why it's important to have an open heart and an open mind when it comes to differences. Discuss.

Distribute drawing materials and have students work individually or with a partner to create posters entitled: "Don't Let Differences Separate Us."

Wrap-Up. Affirm students for their willingness to look at their own prejudices and try to change them. Encourage students to continue writing in their journals about their attitudes toward differences.

Follow-Up. Plan time for students to finish their posters. When they are completed, display them in the classroom or the halls.

Extensions. Have students be on the lookout for examples of prejudice and bias on the internet, on TV, in movies, in magazines, and in other aspects of public life. Have a discussion where students share examples they've found and consider ways they can learn more about themselves from what they observe. Also discuss how they can speak out against prejudice. The Teaching Tolerance website (tolerance.org) has excellent information on this.

Read and discuss *The Christmas Menorahs* by Janice Cohn, the true account of how the entire community of Billings, Montana, united to combat prejudice.

Lesson 119: Prejudice, Bias, and Stereotypes

acceptance · tolerance · respect · compassion · kindness · personal responsibility

Lesson 119 sensitizes students to the impact of prejudice, bias, and stereotyping.

Students will

- reflect on the meaning of *prejudice, bias,* and *stereotype*
- understand that any form of prejudice or stereotyping is wrong
- reflect on the impact of prejudice and stereotyping on two real kids

Materials

- chart paper and marker
- globe (see page 7)
- *optional: The Watsons Go to Birmingham—1963* by Christopher Paul Curtis

Preparation. On a sheet of chart paper, write the following:

"Prejudice: A strong feeling of unfair dislike toward a person or group because they seem different in some way.

Stereotype: An oversimplified and inaccurate judgment about a whole group of people based on prejudice."

Introduction. Invite one boy to come to the center of the circle. Ask him if he likes peanut butter. Depending on his answer, say: **Then I guess all the boys in the class must (like/not like) peanut butter because you're a boy and you like/don't like peanut butter. Aren't all boys the same?** Let the class respond to your comment. Discuss.

Invite one girl to come to the center of the circle. Ask if she is good at math. Depending on her answer, say: **Then I guess all girls (are/are not) good at math because you're a girl and all girls are the same, right?** Have students respond again.

Ask: **Is it a good idea to assume something about a whole group based on one person? Why or why not?** Display the definitions of *prejudice* and *stereotype* and go over these with students. Connect the idea of prejudice to things like gender, race, color, religion, size, and so forth. Help students understand that when we make blanket assumptions, we are stereotyping and showing prejudice or bias.

Activity and Discussion. Read aloud the following real-life story from a student named Khaled (not his real name):*

My family is from Iran so people call me a terrorist. The other day when we were playing baseball, a kid on the other team said, "Oh, you're probably happy about 9/11." I was crushed. How could he say that to me? How could he think something like that? I'm just as upset about 9/11 as everyone else in this country. I have an uncle who died in the World Trade Center. Why do people behave this way?

Ask: **How were people stereotyping Khaled? What bias were they showing toward him?**

Ask: **If you were Khaled, how would you feel about what people were saying about you?** Discuss. Ask if they have ever had a similar experience.

Then ask: **Why was it unfair for people to treat Khaled this way?** Discuss.

Share another story, this one from a fifth-grade girl called Jasmine (not her real name):

Once when I was just sitting around, this boy came up to me and said, "You look funny. What are you?" I replied to him that I was Dominican and Spanish. He told me, "You can't be Spanish, because you don't have long hair." I just walked away, because I knew he was being ignorant.

---

* Quotes and stories attributed to real students and teachers come from author interviews and from responses to the Survey About Conflicts conducted by the author and publisher. See pages 1 and 282–284 for further information.

The next day, he started talking about the color of my skin, saying I was dark chocolate. He said mean things about my family and made up a horrible song about us. Then he got all his friends to do these things every day. It got uncomfortable to be at school. When my friends stood up for me, this boy and his friends threw things at us.

I went to an adult even though it was hard. I needed someone. That person was my mom. I know I can count on my family to be there for me.

Ask students what they thought as they heard this story. Ask: **How were people stereotyping Jasmine? What bias were they showing toward her?**

Let students know that acts of prejudice can happen toward anyone, regardless of race or religion. They can be focused on many different groups of people. Ask the girls in the class if people ever assume particular things about them just because they're girls. Ask the boys the same question. Ask how it makes them feel when people assume things about them without knowing who they really are.

Tell students: **Any act of prejudice is unacceptable, even if someone says "I didn't mean it" or "It was only a joke."** Discuss.

Wrap-Up. Ask students what Jasmine did to help herself. Emphasize that talking to a parent or another trusted adult is an important thing to do if they are ever treated the way Khaled or Jasmine were.

Hold or point to the globe and ask children to imagine what a world without prejudice might be like. Encourage them to talk about this with their families and friends and to write about it in their journals.

Follow-Up. Conduct Lesson 121, in which students come up with ways to respond to prejudice and stereotyping.

Extension. Read and discuss *The Watsons Go to Birmingham—1963* by Christopher Paul Curtis, which tells the story of an African-American family at the start of the civil rights movement from the perspective of a fourth-grade boy.

Lesson 120: Combating Hate

compassion • respect • courage • personal responsibility

Lesson 120 helps students understand that words have power and that hateful words or actions are never okay.

Students will

- understand that words or actions that attack someone's race, religion, ethnicity, disability, sexual orientation, or gender identity are harmful and never acceptable
- gain a deeper understanding of the impact of prejudice and hatred
- know how to respond if someone is the target of hateful words or actions

Materials

- large piece of paper (big enough to trace a student's outline), marker, scissors
- chart paper
- a roll of masking tape
- student journals
- *optional handout:* "Thanh's Story: 'A Horrible Year'" (page 275)

Preparation. Prior to this lesson, trace the body of a student on a large piece of paper and cut it out. Hang it in the front of the room so that it's at eye level with your students when they are standing.

On chart paper, write the following:

"Prejudice: An unfair opinion or feeling about a person or group that's not based on truth or knowledge. Prejudice is often based on race, religion, country of origin, gender, sexual orientation, or disability.

Hate speech: Words that attack or insult someone's race, religion, country of origin, sexual orientation, gender, or disability."

Introduction. Have a volunteer read the definition of prejudice. Say: **I'd like you to recall a time when someone was put down or harmed because of his or her skin color, nationality, gender, or religion.** These recollections can be from kids' lives (in which case, advise them not to use real names), books, movies, or news stories. You can share a story of your own if you are comfortable doing so. Ask: **How do you feel when you witness or experience prejudice? Why is it unkind to behave this way? Why is it unfair?** Discuss.

Discussion and Activity. Ask: Why is prejudice wrong? Discuss. Say: **Today we're going to talk about the impact of prejudice, especially when it is expressed as hate speech.**

Have a second volunteer read the definition of hate speech. Ask: **How is hate speech harmful to people? To our community?** Discuss. Emphasize that hateful actions or words are never justified.

Then direct students' attention to the paper cutout, letting them know that it represents all of them. Ask them to silently think of an unkind word that is used against others, or has been used against them personally, for their religion, race, country of origin, gender, sexual orientation, or perceived disability. Say: **Keep this word in your mind, but don't say it out loud. I'm going to ask you, one at a time, to come up and face this cutout while thinking of your word. As you do, I want you to make a small rip in the cutout using your hands.** Demonstrate.

After students do this, have them return to their seats and look at the cutout with its many rips. Say: **This is what hateful words and actions can do to people.** Have the class sit in silence for about thirty seconds, eyes on the cutout, to let this idea sink in.

Now have students stand, stretch, and sit back down. Ask them to think of kind words they might say to someone who's experienced prejudice or hatred. One at a time, have each student approach the cutout. Hand each of them a piece of masking tape, and ask them to say the kind word or phrase aloud while taping up a rip.

When they've returned to their seats, have students look at the cutout again. Guide them to understand that even though the kind words put this "person" back together, scars will always remain. Ask: **How do hateful words and actions harm us and our communities? If you see someone expressing hatred or prejudice, what can you do?** Accept responses. Say: **If the person expressing prejudice is a family member or a close friend, you could try saying how uncomfortable you feel when you hear this kind of talk and that you don't think it's right.** Additionally, emphasize to students the importance of being upstanders in the face of prejudice. They can support someone being targeted by saying something kind, offering to walk the person to class or to sit with him or her, checking in with the person later, or helping the person tell an adult what happened. Say: **Hateful words and actions should** *never* **be ignored.**

Wrap-Up. Have students do three minutes of automatic writing in their journals about their thoughts on today's discussion and activity.

Follow-Up. As time permits in the week following this lesson, give students five minutes to pair up and discuss the insights they gleaned from the lesson. Afterward, discuss these ideas with the large group. Ask how students might respond differently to prejudice as a result of what they've learned. If you like, distribute and discuss "Thanh's Story: 'A Horrible Year.'"

Thanh's Story
"A Horrible Year"

I had just moved to this country from Asia (leaving my awesome friends and the relatives I loved). I became a new student in my school and couldn't speak English very well. I was in ESL (special classes for learning English as a second language) for two years. I thought kids would be nice to me, but I was wrong. Every day, these boys made fun of my religion, my culture, my language, my accent, and everything else. I felt so bad I wanted to go back to my country. I endured this situation for a whole year. After the horrible year passed, I asked my mom to ask the board of education to let me repeat my grade, because I didn't want to be with those same people the next year. I won't ever forget that first, awful year.

Think About It

How do you feel about the way Thanh was treated?

_____

_____

_____

If the kids who mistreated this boy said they were just kidding, would it change the way you feel? Why or why not?

_____

_____

_____

What if you were Thanh? Imagine being him. Imagine coming to a new country where everything is unfamiliar and having to endure what he went through. What would that be like?

_____

_____

_____

Lesson 121: Be Part of the Solution

acceptance · tolerance · compassion · respect · personal responsibility

Lesson 121 focuses on responding to prejudiced remarks and standing up against prejudice. This lesson is a follow-up to Lessons 119 and 120.

Students will
- learn ways to respond to words of prejudice
- role-play being an upstander in response to prejudice
- understand that each person needs to be part of the solution to prejudice

Materials
- chart paper and marker
- definitions of *prejudice* and *stereotype* from Lesson 119 (see page 271)
- globe (see page 7)
- *optional handout:* "You Belong" (see digital content)

Introduction and Discussion. Say: **Sometimes people who don't know better might speak words of prejudice. Sometimes they'll make jokes about another race, religion, or group of people. If that happens, what do you think you can do?**

Discuss, noting students' ideas on chart paper. Be sure to include the following in your discussion:

- Don't join in if people are making jokes about or stereotyping people of a particular race, religion, gender, etc.

- Speak up. If you don't, people might think you agree.

After brief discussion, focus attention on the importance of speaking up respectfully. Relate this to the idea of being an upstander, rather than a bystander, in a bullying situation. People can be upstanders for themselves and others when it comes to prejudice and stereotyping, too.

At the top of a new sheet of chart paper, write *"Responding to Prejudiced Remarks."* Ask: **What are some things you could say if you hear a prejudiced remark, or if someone directs one at you?** Invite students' ideas about what to say, and note ideas for respectful responses on the chart. Include a range of suggestions. Here are a few to get you started:

- "I'm uncomfortable hearing that."

- "That's not funny."

- "Please don't make remarks like that."

- "People who are _____ (specific race, religion, nationality, etc.) are human beings and deserve respect."

- "All people deserve to be respected."

- "That comment wasn't right."

- "That's not cool."

Activity. Have students role-play using the previous comments and those they come up with themselves. Have them use the Dignity Stance and keep their body language neutral. Allow time for several students to practice different statements in pairs or with the larger group.

Wrap-Up. Remind students that each time they stand up against prejudice they are part of the solution to it. Point to the globe and tell students that standing up against prejudice makes the world better for all people.

Extensions. Have a brainstorming session to come up with ideas for making your school a place where all people feel safe, respected, and accepted. Follow up with something you can implement schoolwide, such as a poster, essay-writing, or video campaign.

Stress that we share this earth together, and we all belong to the human race. Give your students copies of the poem "You Belong" (from the digital content). After reading it together, have them create their own poems based on the feelings the poem elicits for them. Students can share their poems with the class and school.

Lesson 122: Differences Writing Activities

personal responsibility · compassion · acceptance · kindness

Lesson 122 gives students writing projects to help reflect on their own personal responsibility, acceptance, and compassion toward others.

Students will
- write thoughtfully and critically about accepting differences or speaking up in response to prejudice
- work independently and in pairs
- recognize their role in building a classroom climate of acceptance

Materials
- differences chart from Lesson 117 (see page 267)
- definitions of *prejudice* and *stereotype* from Lesson 119 (see page 271)
- handout: "Writing About Accepting Differences" (page 278)
- *optional:* art, print, or technology resources for making a class book

Note: This lesson introduces one or more writing activities on topics related to accepting differences. Before conducting it, determine how you want to approach the assignment with students. Review the seven assignments on the handout and decide if you want to assign one topic only, assign several topics one at a time, or give students a choice of topics. Also consider whether you want students to write one- or two-page essays or if you want to offer the option of other genres (such as poetry, a short story, dialogue, or a letter). Plan how much time students should have in and out of class to complete the assignment.

Preparation. If you want to distribute the handout to students, make copies. If you are assigning a single topic, write the topic on the board or chart paper.

Introduction and Discussion. Display the charts and review with students ideas you have discussed about commonalities, differences, and prejudice. Ask students: **What's prejudice? What's bias? What does it mean to stereotype? What have you learned about your own prejudices? About how it feels to be stereotyped?** Share something you have learned as well.

Activity. Explain the assignment and time frame and ask if students have any questions. Then have students partner up and talk briefly about the assignment—what they can write about, how they'll get started, who they might want to talk to for ideas, and so forth.

After just a few minutes, have students find places to write independently for the remainder of the lesson.

Wrap-Up. Reconvene in the circle and affirm students for the work they are doing to understand and accept differences among their classmates and others.

Follow-Up. Continue to allow time for students to finish their writing projects.

Extension. When the projects are completed, put together a class book or a Web page where students may share their writing if they wish.

Writing About Accepting Differences

1. Write about a time you left someone out because you saw that person as different. How do you think he or she felt? What did you learn from this experience?

- -

2. Write about a character in a story, movie, or video who was left out because he or she was seen as different. What happened? How did the person feel? What lessons can be learned from this story or experience?

- -

3. Do you believe kids in our school accept people they consider to be different? Write about this. Give examples without using names.

- -

4. How can we help kids accept people they see as different? What are some possible solutions? Talk to friends and family members to get their thoughts.

- -

5. How would our world be different if people accepted each other they see as different? Write about this. What suggestions do you have for promoting acceptance? Talk to friends and family members to get their thoughts.

- -

6. What is prejudice? Look it up in the dictionary. Ask people you know what this word means to them. How does prejudice hurt all of us? What can you do to be part of the solution to prejudice?

- -

7. Who are some people who have fought prejudice? Write about one of them. What did this person do? What can you do to fight prejudice?

- -

Four Review Lessons You Can Use at Any Time

Here are four activities you can use to review content in this book. Insert them anywhere to help your students remember, digest, and reflect upon what they've been learning. Be sure to question your students about how they are applying what they have learned in real-life situations.

Lesson 123: Ball-Throw Review

Purpose

To review key concepts and strategies

Materials

- soft ball suitable for being thrown in the classroom
- list of questions you have prepared based on what you've recently taught in *No Kidding About Bullying*

Procedure

Have students form a circle, standing or seated. Throw the ball to a student and ask one of the questions you have prepared. If the student answers correctly, he can throw the ball to another student who will get to answer the next question. If he answers incorrectly, he throws the ball back to you, and you choose the next student.

Encourage students to throw the ball to people who have not been chosen yet. After your questions have been answered, have students come up with their own questions and continue throwing the ball to each other to answer them.

Lesson 124: Brainstorming Web

Purpose

To have students create webs in which they brainstorm the key things they remember from content covered

Materials

- large piece of chart paper for each group of three
- marker for each student

Procedure

Place students in groups of three. Give each group a large sheet of chart paper and a marker. Instruct students to create a web on their chart paper including every key point they can remember from a given topic area you have covered. The center of the web should name whatever topic you want to review: "Getting Along," "Working Out Conflicts," "Being an Upstander," and so forth.

Give students about ten minutes to work on their webs. When they are finished, have each group share their web with the rest of the class, talking about concepts they have included. Every so often ask, "How are you applying this in real life?"

Lesson 125: Note Card Review/Reflect

Purpose
To help students recall the information they have learned and air questions and comments

Materials
- 3" x 5" note card and pencil for each student
- box, bowl, or bag to put the cards in

Procedure
Have students name strategies and concepts they have learned so far through lessons in this book. List these on the board.

Pass out note cards. Ask students to write down any questions or comments they have about anything they've learned thus far. Encourage them to ask the hard questions they're grappling with or to express comments they've been holding back, like, "Deep breathing is silly. I don't like to do it" or, "What if I tell an adult and then the kid hurts me more?" Once the questions and comments have been written, have students put the note cards in the container.

Have a student come to the container, close her eyes, and randomly choose a question. Have another student read the question/comment aloud. Ask for responses from the class before you give yours. Sometimes kids will have already successfully dealt with challenges they are struggling with. If you get a question or comment you're not sure how to respond to, email me at Naomi@LearningPeace.com and I will do my best to answer it.

Encourage students to use their journals to list questions that come up as they're applying what they've learned. Every couple of weeks, gather together for five to ten minutes and go over these questions.

Lesson 126: TV Show Review

Purpose
To help students recall, in a fun and creative way, a wide range of ideas and strategies they have learned

Materials
- large piece of chart paper and marker for each group of four
- tape
- pretend microphone
- stickers or other small rewards

Procedure
Place students in groups of four. Have each group choose a recorder who is able to write quickly and an announcer who will come to the "mic" to share the group's ideas with the class in an animated way.

Give each group chart paper and markers. Instruct students to brainstorm everything they remember learning thus far (or in the section you have just covered). Ask them to see how many ideas they can list in five minutes. Say, "1, 2, 3, GO!" and have groups begin brainstorming. After five minutes, ask each group to hang up their chart on the wall. The announcer holds the "microphone" and animatedly shares what the group has brainstormed. The group that has brainstormed the largest list of legitimate items gets a sticker or other fun, simple reward.

No Kidding About Bullying
Pre- and Post-Test

	Never	Sometimes	Usually	Always
Kids in my class are kind to each other even when no one's looking.	❏	❏	❏	❏
I am kind to other kids even when no one's looking.	❏	❏	❏	❏
Kids in my class get into lots of conflicts.	❏	❏	❏	❏
I get into lots of conflicts.	❏	❏	❏	❏
I know how to work out conflicts peacefully.	❏	❏	❏	❏
I wish I could handle conflicts better.	❏	❏	❏	❏
Kids in my class are mean to each other.	❏	❏	❏	❏
There are times I am mean to other kids.	❏	❏	❏	❏
Kids in my class know how to manage their anger.	❏	❏	❏	❏
I know how to manage my anger.	❏	❏	❏	❏
Kids in my class care about the feelings of others.	❏	❏	❏	❏
Kids in my class bully when no one's looking.	❏	❏	❏	❏
I get bullied.	❏	❏	❏	❏
I bully others.	❏	❏	❏	❏
I know what to do if someone bullies me.	❏	❏	❏	❏
I know how to help if someone bullies a friend.	❏	❏	❏	❏
Kids in my class get along with each other.	❏	❏	❏	❏
I feel emotionally and physically safe with my classmates, anywhere in and around school.	❏	❏	❏	❏

Survey About Conflicts

conflict: an argument, fight, or disagreement

About YOU

_____ I am a boy.   _____ I am a girl.   My age: _____   My grade: _____

About CONFLICTS

1. How often do you see conflicts happen in your school or other places? (check one)

____ never   ____ sometimes   ____ often   ____ every day   ____ all the time

2. How often do YOU get into conflicts? (check one)

____ never   ____ sometimes   ____ often   ____ every day   ____ all the time

3. Check whatever things below start conflicts for YOU _or_ OTHER KIDS. Use the lines to add things that aren't listed here.

____ being teased or made fun of   ____ rumors and gossip

____ being blamed for something   ____ threats

____ being picked on for being different   ____ mean notes or text messages

____ being left out   ____ _____

____ someone being unfair   ____ _____

____ name-calling   ____ _____

____ cheating at games   ____ _____

Survey About Conflicts (continued)

4. What do you usually do to deal with conflicts you get into?

_____

_____

_____

5. On a scale of 1–10, how mean do you think kids are to each other?
(circle a number)

1	2	3	4	5	6	7	8	9	10

not mean at all ➔ ➔ ➔ ➔ ➔ ➔ ➔ ➔ ➔ ➔ ➔ very mean

6. How do you keep yourself out of physical fights?

_____

_____

Would you like to learn more about how to do this? ____ yes ____ no

Why or why not? _____

7. How often does bullying happen in your school or other places?

____ never ____ sometimes ____ often ____ every day ____ all the time

8. Do you ever step in and help kids who are being bullied?

____ yes ____ no

If so, how do you try to help? _____

_____

Survey About Conflicts (continued)

9. What do people do that makes you really mad? _____

_____

10. What do you do when someone gets you mad? _____

_____

11. What stresses you out? _____

_____

Very IMPORTANT Question

12. What would you most like to learn about conflict, anger, bullying, or getting

along with other kids? _____

_____

Optional: Tell YOUR Story

Tell about a conflict you were in. In at least 2 to 3 paragraphs, describe what happened. Did it get solved? If so, how? You can use the back of the paper if you need more room.

_____

_____

_____

_____

_____

Thank you for completing the Survey About Conflicts.

References and Resources

Books for Kids

Blubber by Judy Blume. Fifth grader Linda is teased and bullied by her peers for being overweight. Jill is drawn into the bullying because she wants to be accepted. This book is a powerful lens on the impact of bullying, the need to be an upstander, and the need for compassion and acceptance.

The Christmas Menorahs: How a Town Fought Hate by Janice Cohn. When a rock is thrown through the window of a house containing a menorah, the people of Billings, Montana, take a stand against bigotry and all put menorahs in their windows. This story is a powerful example of what upstanders can do. It teaches personal responsibility, compassion, and acceptance.

Circle of Gold by Candy Dawson Boyd. After her father dies, Mattie Benson tries to bring her family back together with the help of a beautiful golden pin. Her story teaches integrity, conscience, problem solving, and conflict resolution. This book is a Coretta Scott King Award winner.

Crash by Jerry Spinelli. Crash has bullied his neighbors and classmates his whole life. When his grandfather has a stroke, Crash finds that friends and family have a new meaning for him. This book highlights issues such as accepting differences, compassion, bullying, and the ability to change.

Dear Mom, You're Ruining My Life by Jean Van Leeuwen. Sam is eleven and she's completely mortified by everything her mother does. Through Sam's story, readers learn to face issues of anger, problem solving, accepting differences, and dealing with peer pressure.

Eagle Song by Joseph Bruchac. Danny Bigtree is teased and bullied when his family moves from a Mohawk reservation to Brooklyn. With the help of a legendary Iroquois peacemaker, Danny explores how he can transform anger, bullying, and adversity into friendship.

Ethan, Suspended by Pamela Ehrenberg. As one of the only white kids in school, Ethan finds himself to be a racial minority in an almost entirely African-American and Latino junior high. Lessons about prejudice, acceptance, and understanding are explored.

Fourth Grade Weirdo by Martha Freeman. Dexter is different, and through his humorous story, readers learn that, "Even if everybody thinks you're weird, you've gotta pay attention to the handsome guy inside." This book addresses put-downs, gossip, being different, and having feelings.

Gaffer Samson's Luck by Jill Paton Walsh. James has to move to a strange new place. He wants to be accepted by the kids there but ends up making friends with an old man next door. This book helps readers examine issues of exclusion, accepting differences, problem solving, anger, and avoiding physical fights.

In the Year of the Boar and Jackie Robinson by Bette Bao Lord. Ten-year-old Shirley Temple Wong struggles to fit in when she moves to the United States from her home in China. She learns to overcome her own obstacles through her discovery of the courageous actions of Jackie Robinson, the first African-American Major League baseball player. This story addresses issues of exclusion, prejudice, and accepting differences.

The Janitor's Boy by Andrew Clements. Jake is embarrassed by his janitor father. His embarrassment causes him to lash out at his father until he learns some important lessons about acceptance and compassion.

Joshua T. Bates Takes Charge by Susan Shreve. Joshua is supposed to be helping a new student who becomes the target of bullying. This book helps address issues of conscience, peer pressure, personal responsibility, and avoiding physical fights.

Junebug by Alice Mead. When Junebug turns ten, he is confronted with the prospect of joining a gang. This book helps highlight issues such as keeping out of a fight, dealing with peer pressure, and making the right choice.

Just Kidding by Trudy Ludwig. D.J.'s friend Vince has a habit of teasing D.J. and then saying, "Just kidding," as if it will make everything okay. D.J. is afraid that if he protests, his friends will think he can't take a joke.

Losers, Inc. by Claudia Mills. Ethan can't compete with his older brother's perfect GPA, so he and his friend decide to start a Loser's Club. Ethan starts to reevaluate his quest for super-loser status when he meets a teacher he is determined to impress. This book helps kids look at bullying, compassion, and taking responsibility for one's actions.

The Misfits by James Howe. Overweight seventh grader Bobby Goodspeed and his five friends are all put down for being different. They form their own group and start a No Name-Calling Movement in their school. Teaches acceptance, compassion, kindness, and personal responsibility.

Mr. Peabody's Apples by Madonna. Based on a 300-year-old tale, this picture book is a good teaching tool about the devastating impact of gossip. It fosters personal responsibility, compassion, kindness, and conscience.

My Secret Bully by Trudy Ludwig. When Monica's friend Katie begins to call her names and humiliate her in front of other kids at school, she feels betrayed and isolated. But with help from her mother, Monica gains the confidence to stand up to bullying that comes from someone she thought was a friend.

One City, Two Brothers by Chris Smith. Based on a folktale told by both Jewish and Arabic people, this picture book shows how the spirit of brotherhood can survive amid differences. It highlights compassion, kindness, acceptance, and altruism.

The Revealers by Doug Wilhelm. At Parkland Middle School, three seventh graders decide to share their personal bullying stories online. Their forum, the "Revealer," allows other kids who are bullied to connect and share their stories. This book attests to the transformative power of speaking out.

Save Me a Seat by Sarah Weeks and Gita Varadarajan. Ravi, who recently moved from India, and Joe, whose best friend just moved away, are fifth graders at the same school. They each struggle in their own way to adapt to their new situations, and both are bullied by fellow fifth grader Dillon Samreen. In response, Ravi and Joe team up to try to take control of their lives.

Shiloh by Phyllis Reynolds Naylor. This Newbery Award–winning novel tells the story of eleven-year-old Marty, who finds an abused dog and faces powerful ethical questions as a result. This story offers an excellent way to examine issues of conscience, compassion, and personal responsibility.

Sixth Grade Secrets by Louis Sachar. This humorous book shows what happens when Laura and her friends start a secret club with secret messages and secret codes. This book helps readers look at gossiping, exclusion, fairness, conflict, and dealing with peer pressure.

Slump by Dave Jarzyna. When longtime pal Annie orders him to shape up, Mitchie starts to think seriously about his bullying ways. This book fosters discussions about the impact of put-downs, taking responsibility for one's actions, and making positive and negative choices.

Sparks Fly Upward by Carol Matas. Rebecca has to confront prejudices inside and outside her family when a fire forces her to live with a Ukrainian foster family. Rebecca eventually bonds with Sophie, the daughter of her foster family. Through her travels, Rebecca learns courage, acceptance, and compassion.

Speak Up and Get Along! by Scott Cooper. This book presents twenty-one assertiveness strategies kids can learn and use to express themselves, build relationships, end arguments and fights, halt bullying, and beat unhappy feelings. Includes examples and dialogue kids can practice and try.

Stand Up for Yourself & Your Friends: Dealing with Bullies & Bossiness and Finding a Better Way by American Girl. This book gives girls the tools they need to recognize and handle bullying and make the world a safer, happier place for everyone. It presents quizzes, advice from other girls, and practical tips.

Surviving Brick Johnson by Laurie Myers. Alex is certain he will be bullied when Brick, the big new kid at school, sees Alex imitating him. But Alex has a lot more to learn about Brick than what he sees on the surface. Through the boys' relationship, readers examine issues of bullying, dealing with fear, accepting differences, and challenging one's perceptions.

Through My Eyes by Ruby Bridges. Bridges's moving memoir takes readers back to 1960, when she was escorted by federal marshals to be the first black child to attend an all-white school in New Orleans. This book speaks to the need for compassion, acceptance, and understanding.

Trouble Talk by Trudy Ludwig. Maya's new friend Bailey begins to talk too much, is hurting people's feelings, and is spreading harmful rumors. Maya realizes Bailey is not the friend she needs and discovers the harmful consequences of "trouble talk."

The Watsons Go to Birmingham—1963 by Christopher Paul Curtis. This winner of the Newbery Honor and the Coretta Scott King Honor Awards tells the story of an African-American family at the start of the civil rights movement. Told by fourth grader Kenny, this book shows the results of prejudice and helps readers examine such issues as acceptance, compassion, and the need for kindness.

Organizations, Programs, and Websites

Bullying UK
bullying.co.uk
This award-winning anti-bullying charity is full of valuable resources for parents, schools, and kids and teens.

Bully Police USA
bullypolice.org
This site lists and evaluates U.S. bullying legislation state by state. Learn how each state's bullying laws are graded and pick up best practices from states and schools that are highly ranked.

Collaborative for Academic, Social, and Emotional Learning (CASEL)
casel.org
CASEL advances the research, policy, and practice of social-emotional learning. This site maintains an annotated guide to evidence-based social-emotional learning programs for kids in preschool through high school.

The Cyberbullying Research Center
cyberbullying.org
This site includes research, stories, cases, fact sheets, tips and strategies, and current news headlines on cyberbullying, plus downloadable materials for educators and parents to use and distribute.

KidsHealth
kidshealth.org
The award-winning KidsHealth website helps teachers, parents, and kids deal with bullying and other issues.

National Crime Prevention Council: Programs
ncpc.org/programs
This site provides a quick set of facts on a variety of initiatives and campaigns dedicated to improving safety and reducing crime.

Olweus Bullying Prevention Program
violencepreventionworks.org
This comprehensive program is designed to reduce and prevent bullying schoolwide. The program materials provide thorough instructions to help teachers and school administrators mediate and control bullying in every school classroom and corner.

PREVNet
prevnet.ca
This comprehensive site outlines Canadian laws on bullying by province and territory, along with resources and fact sheets for teens, parents, and educators, plus up-to-date news on bullying in Canada.

Responsive Classroom
responsiveclassroom.org
The Responsive Classroom approach follows seven guiding principles on how to incorporate social-emotional skills in schoolwide practice. Informed by independent research and teacher expertise, this site has much to offer toward the creation and maintenance of a safe school.

Second Step Program
cfchildren.org/second-step
Organized by the Committee for Children, this classroom-based social skills program can be used in preschools through

junior high schools. The program uses group discussion, modeling, coaching, and practice to teach empathy, impulse control, problem solving, and emotional management. Second Step also offers a Bullying Prevention Unit, a research-based anti-violence curriculum that helps elementary students recognize, respond to, and report instances of bullying.

StopBullying.gov
stopbullying.gov
This site provides information from various U.S. government agencies on what bullying is, what cyberbullying is, who is at risk, and how you can prevent and respond to bullying.

Teaching Tolerance
tolerance.org
This anti-violence website includes teaching materials for every grade level on a large variety of issues related to promoting justice and equality. Type "bullying" into their search engine to find anti-bullying games, surveys, tips, and songs.

Hotlines

Boys Town National Hotline: 1-800-448-3000. This number is for boys and girls even though the message says Boys Town national hotline. It's free, confidential, and available 24–7. Be patient. Sometimes there's a short wait. Available in Spanish.

IMAlive: 1-800-442-HOPE (4673). This 24-hour national suicide hotline is confidential and available in Spanish. You can also visit the website at hopeline.com.

National Runaway Safeline: 1-800-RUNAWAY (786-2929). This 24-hour, toll-free hotline offers counsel and safe housing alternatives to kids at risk of running away and their families. The organization also has a website at 1800runaway.org.

National Suicide Prevention Lifeline: Call 1-800-273-TALK (8255) anytime, 24–7, to talk to someone who can help. Available in Spanish and for people who are deaf or hard of hearing.

PsychCentral: Telephone, Hotlines and Help Lines: psychcentral.com/lib/telephone-hotlines-and-help-lines. This site maintains a current list of toll-free hotlines and help lines.

The Trevor Project Lifeline: 1-866-488-7386. This organization for lesbian, gay, bisexual, transgender, and questioning young people offers a free and confidential helpline 24 hours a day. For more information, visit thetrevorproject.org.

Your Life Your Voice: Visit yourlifeyourvoice.org to chat online or email someone for support. Or text "Voice" to 20121 to access a free and confidential textline.

Books for Educators

Bluestein, Jane. *The Win-Win Classroom: A Fresh and Positive Look at Classroom Management.* Thousand Oaks, CA: Corwin, 2008.

Coloroso, Barbara. *The Bully, the Bullied, and the Not-So-Innocent Bystander: From Preschool to High School and Beyond: Breaking the Cycle of Violence and Creating More Deeply Caring Communities.* New York: HarperCollins, 2015.

Davis, Stan, and Charisse L. Nixon. *Youth Voice Project: Student Insights into Bullying and Peer Mistreatment.* Champaign, IL: Research Press, 2013.

Davis, Stan, and Julia Davis. *Empowering Bystanders in Bullying Prevention.* Champaign, IL: Research Press, 2007.

Elias, Maurice J., and Harriett Arnold (editors). *The Educator's Guide to Emotional Intelligence and Academic Achievement: Social-Emotional Learning in the Classroom.* Thousand Oaks, CA: Corwin, 2006.

Goldman, Carrie. *Bullied: What Every Parent, Teacher and Kid Needs to Know About Ending the Cycle of Fear.* New York: HarperCollins, 2012.

Goleman, Daniel. *Social Intelligence: The New Science of Human Relationships.* New York: Bantam, 2006.

Jones, Tricia S., and Randy Compton (editors). *Kids Working It Out: Stories and Strategies for Making Peace in Our Schools.* San Francisco: Jossey-Bass, 2003.

Kim, Bob, and Judy Logan. *Let's Get Real Curriculum Guide: Lessons & Activities to Address Name-Calling and Bullying.* San Francisco: GroundSparks, 2004.

Krznaric, Roman. *Empathy: Why It Matters, and How to Get It.* New York: Perigee, 2014.

Olweus, Dan, Susan Limber, and Sharon Mihalic. *Blueprints for Violence Prevention, Book Nine: Bullying Prevention Program.* Boulder, CO: Center for the Study and Prevention of Violence, 1999.

Swearer, Susan M., Dorothy L. Espelage, and Scott A. Napolitano. *Bullying Prevention and Intervention: Realistic Strategies for Schools.* New York: Guilford, 2009.

Index

A

Abuse, mandatory reporting, 13
Acceptance. *See* Tolerance and acceptance
Accountability, of students, 11
Active listening, Digital Content
Administrators. *See* School administrators
Adults
    getting help from, 118, 183, 227
    talking to about bullying, 228–229
Affirming and acknowledging positive
    behavior
    put-ups, 71, 72
    self-affirmation, 211–214, 215, 236–237
    student-to-student affirmations, 13
    teachers' roles, 10–13
Aggressiveness, compared to assertiveness,
    155, 197–198
Agreements, classroom, 10–11, 20–22
American Journal of Public Health, 3
American Psychological Association, 3
Anger management
    angry reactions, 87–89
    appropriate responses, 103–105,
        107–108, 109–111
    awareness of triggers, 84–86
    Breath Out/Breathe In strategy, 106
    chilling out, 38–39, 94–96, 100–101, 102
    conflict habits, 123–125, 126
    detaching from teasing, 206–207
    getting help, 118
    group conflicts, 175–177
    making changes, 109–111
    mean words, responses to, 199
    physical fights, avoiding, 112–113,
        163–164, 175–177, 183–186
    Picture the Cake, Blow Out the Candles,
        100
    review, 107–108
    role plays, 117–118
    Stop, Breathe, Chill strategy, 7, 11, 38–39,
        94–96
    talking someone down, 175–177
    temper tamers, 112–113
    10-minute time crunchers, 102, 116, 118
    Think-Alouds, 116, 180
    unhooking from mean words, 201–204,
        205
    See also Self-control
Anger triggers
    student awareness of, 84–86
    teacher anticipation of, 14
Apologies
    conflicts with friends, 172–173
    eliciting from students, 10
Assertiveness
    bullying prevention, 226–227, 228–230
    confronting someone who hurt you, 180
    Dignity Stance, 160–162
    learning about, 155–156
    responses to mean words, 197–198, 199
Assessments
    listening skills self-test, 27
    pre- and post-test, 281
Automatic writing technique, 8

B

Ball-throw review, 279
Basement or Balcony? activities, 147–151,
    152, 153–154
Bias. *See* Prejudice and bias; Tolerance
Blaming, 43–45, 134–137, 138–140
Blubber (Blume), 70, 285
Blume, Judy, 70, 285
Body language/facial expressions
    Dignity Stance, 160–162, 196
    disrespectful, 158–159
    mean gestures, 200
    neutrality of, 155
    practicing I-messages, 41
    of teachers, 11
Books
    creating, Digital Content
    for educators, 287
    for kids, 285–286
Boys Town hotline, 234, 240, 287
Brainstorming solutions, 46, 174
Brainstorming web review activity, 279
Breathing
    Breath Out/Breathe In, 106
    deep breathing, 8–9, 28–29
    Picture the Cake, Blow Out the Candles,
        100
Bruchac, Joseph, 176, 285
Bullying
    bias-based, 1–2, 3, 273–275
    consequences for, 2–3, 219–222,
        Digital Content
    definition of, 2
    cyberbullying, 2, 12, 175–177, 256–257
    defining and understanding, 219–222,
        223–225
    do's and don'ts, 219, 222, Digital
        Content
    between friends, 251–252
    hate crimes, 1, 273–275
    hate speech, 1, 273–275
    helping kids who bully, 231–235
    intolerance for, 12
    keeping safe, 250, 253
    No Bullying Pledge, 232, 259
    of LGBTQ students, 2–3, 14
    physical bullying, 250, 253
    playground bullying, 248–250
    prevention strategies, 11–12, 15,
        238–240
    response protocols, Digital Content
    responsibility for, 134
    roles in the bullying cycle, 219, 221
    schoolwide prevention programs, 12,
        258, 259–260
    statistics, 1–3
    strategies for dealing with, 225, 226–227,
        228–230
    suggestions for helping children,
        Digital Content
    teacher's role, 218
    teasing compared to, 193, 195
    upstanders, 241–242, 243–245, 246, 247
    "What If?" questions about getting help,
        227
    See also Mean words and name-calling

"Bullying in U.S. Schools" (report), 2
Bullying victims. *See* Kids who are bullied
Bystanders, 4, 219

C

Calming strategies
    Breath Out/Breathe In, 106
    chilling out, 38–39, 94–96, 100–101, 102
    deep breathing, 8–9, 28–29
    Dignity Stance, 160–162
    getting help with anger, 118
    peaceful place visualization, 92–93
    Peace Shield, 114–115
    Peace Table/Peace Place, 9, 35–37
    personal calming statements, 97–99
    Picture the Cake, Blow Out the Candles,
        100
    responses to mean words, 199
    Stop, Breathe, Chill, 7, 11, 38–39, 94–96
    Think-Alouds, 116, 180
    unhooking from mean words, 201–204,
        205
Casals, Pablo, 78
Cell phones. *See* Cyberbullying
Centers for Disease Control and Prevention,
    3
Charts, using, 7–8
Chilling out, 10, 38–39, 94–96, 100–101,
    102
Christakis, Nicholas A., 5
Christmas Menorahs (Cohn), 271, 285
Circle seating, 7
Clemente, Roberto, 216
Cohn, Janice, 271, 285
Collaboration. *See* Cooperation/
    collaboration
Compassion. *See* Kindness and compassion
Complimenting students. *See* Affirming and
    acknowledging positive behavior
Compromise
    assertiveness, 155–156
    Basement or Balcony? strategy, 147–151,
        152, 153–154
    brainstorming solutions, 174
    conflict solver interviews, 156, 157
    conflicts with friends, 172–173
    I-messages and reflective listening,
        168–169
    10-minute time cruncher, 146
    willingness to resolve conflict, 141–142,
        143–144, 145, 167–168
Confidence building. *See* Courage
Confidentiality
    emphasizing to students, 13
    Leave It at the Door exercise, 9, 33–34
    in mediating conflict resolution, 187
Conflict
    concept of, 35
    survey about, 282–284
Conflict resolution
    anger management role play, 117–118
    assertiveness, 155–156
    Basement or Balcony?, 147–151, 152,
        153–154
    brainstorming solutions, 46, 174
    compromise, 146

To download the reproducible forms and other digital content for this book, visit **freespirit.com/nkab-forms**. Use the password **upstander**.

About the Author

Photography by Barbara L. Peterson
for portfolio b.

Naomi Drew, M.A., is the award-winning author of eight books. She is recognized around the world for her work in conflict resolution, peacemaking, and anti-bullying. Her work has been instrumental in introducing the skills of peacemaking into public education and has been recognized by educational leaders throughout the world. United Nations staffer Michiko Kuroda praised her work saying, "Naomi Drew has adapted the techniques of negotiation to the needs of children." She has been called a "master teacher and pathfinder in our culture." Her work has been featured in magazines and newspapers, and on radio and national TV, including NBC, *The New York Times*, *Time* Magazine, and *Parents* Magazine. She has also served as a peaceful parenting expert for *Classroom Close-up*, an Emmy-winning public television show.

Naomi is a dynamic speaker who has inspired audiences far and wide. She has served as a consultant to school districts, parent groups, and civic organizations and headed up the New Jersey State Bar Foundation's Conflict Resolution Advisory Panel for nine years, training K–12 trainers to develop more harmonious schools. Her work is rooted in a deep desire to create a more peaceful future for all people, her own two sons being the genesis of this desire. Imprinted on her brain are Gandhi's words: "If we are to reach real peace in the world . . . we shall have to begin with children."

Other Great Resources from Free Spirit

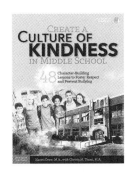

Create a Culture of Kindness in Middle School
48 Character-Building Lessons to Foster Respect and Prevent Bullying
by Naomi Drew, M.A., with Christa M. Tinari, M.A.

For middle school educators.
272 pp.; paperback; 8½" x 11"
Digital content includes customizable student handouts from the book.

The Kids' Guide to Working Out Conflicts
How to Keep Cool, Stay Safe, and Get Along
by Naomi Drew, M.A.

For ages 10–15.
160 pp.; paperback; illust.; 7" x 9"

A Leader's Guide to The Kids' Guide to Working Out Conflicts
by Naomi Drew, M.A.

For grades 5–9.
128 pp.; paperback; 8½" x 11"

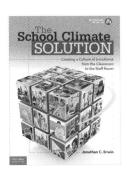

The School Climate Solution
Creating a Culture of Excellence from the Classroom to the Staff Room
by Jonathan C. Erwin

For administrators, teachers, counselors of grades K–12.
200 pp.; paperback; 8½" x 11"
Digital content includes customizable forms from the book.

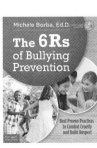

The 6Rs of Bullying Prevention
Best Proven Practices to Combat Cruelty and Build Respect
by Michele Borba, Ed.D.

For administrators, teachers, counselors, youth leaders, bullying prevention teams, parents of children in grades K–8.
288 pp.; paperback; 7¼" x 9¼"
Digital content includes customizable forms from the book and a PDF presentation for use in professional development.

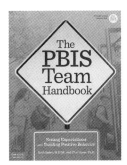

The PBIS Team Handbook
Setting Expectations and Building Positive Behavior
by Beth Baker, M.S.Ed., and Char Ryan, Ph.D.

For K–12 PBIS coaches and team members, including special educators, teachers, and other school staff members.
208 pp.; paperback; 8½" x 11"
Digital content includes PDF presentation and customizable forms.
Free downloadable PLC/Book Study Guide available at freespirit.com/PLC

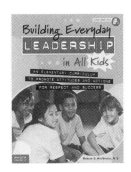

Building Everyday Leadership in All Kids
An Elementary Curriculum to Promote Attitudes and Actions for Respect and Success
by Mariam G. MacGregor, M.S.

For teachers, grades K–6.
176 pp.; paperback; 8½" x 11"
Digital content includes customizable reproducible forms.

Bully Free Classroom®
Elementary School Poster Set
4 posters; high gloss; 13⅜" x 19"

Join the Free Spirit Advisory Board

Teachers, Administrators, Librarians, Counselors, Youth Workers, and Social Workers
Help us create the resources you need to support the kids you serve.

In order to make our books and other products even more beneficial for children and teens, the Free Spirit Advisory Board provides valuable feedback on content, art, title concepts, and more. You can help us identify what educators need to help kids think for themselves, succeed in school and life, and make a difference in the world. Apply today! For more information, go to **www.freespirit.com/Advisory-Boards.**

What Do You Stand For? For Kids
A Guide to Building Character
by Barbara A. Lewis

For ages 8–12.

176 pp.; paperback; illust.; 7¼" x 9"

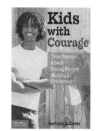

Kids with Courage
True Stories About Young People
Making a Difference
by Barbara A. Lewis

For ages 11 & up.

184 pp.; paperback; B&W photos; 6" x 9"

Bullying Is a Pain in the Brain
(Revised & Updated Edition)
by Trevor Romain, illustrated by Steve Mark

For ages 8–13.

112 pp.; paperback; color illust.; 5⅛" x 7"

Speak Up and Get Along!
Learn the Mighty Might, Thought Chop, and More Tools to Make Friends, Stop Teasing, and Feel Good About Yourself
by Scott Cooper

For ages 8–12.

128 pp.; paperback; two-color; illust.; 6" x 9"

Stand Up to Bullying!
Upstanders to the Rescue!
by Phyllis Kaufman Goodstein and Elizabeth Verdick

For ages 8–13.

128 pp.; paperback; color illust.; 5⅛" x 7"

Stick Up for Yourself!
Every Kid's Guide to Personal Power and Positive Self-Esteem
by Gershen Kaufman, Ph.D., Lev Raphael, Ph.D., and Pamela Espeland

For ages 8–12.

128 pp.; paperback; illust.; 6" x 9"
See freespirit.com for information on
A Teacher's Guide to Stick Up for Yourself!
eBook.

Real Kids, Real Stories, Real Character
Choices That Matter Around the World
by Garth Sundem

For ages 9–13.

168 pp.; paperback; two-color; 5¼" x 7½"
Free Leader's Guide available at
freespirit.com/leader

For pricing information, to place an order, or to request a free catalog, contact:

Free Spirit Publishing Inc. • 6325 Sandburg Road, Suite 100 • Minneapolis, MN 55427-3674
toll-free 800.735.7323 • local 612.338.2068 • fax 612.337.5050
help4kids@freespirit.com • www.freespirit.com